HOLIDAY
ROUNDUP

Other books by Frances Cavanah

THE BUSTERS
WE CAME TO AMERICA
MEET THE PRESIDENTS
(in collaboration with
Elizabeth L. Crandall)

Revised Edition

HOLIDAY

Illustrated by
Elsie McCorkell

ROUNDUP

Selected by
FRANCES CAVANAH and
LUCILE PANNELL

MACRAE SMITH COMPANY · Philadelphia

Library of Congress Catalog Card Number 68-18811
Manufactured in the United States of America

Book design by William E. Lickfield

6810

Acknowledgments

For permission to reprint material copyrighted or otherwise controlled, our thanks are gratefully extended to the following:

ABINGDON-COKESBURY PRESS—for "The Birthday Orchard," condensed from *Appleseed Farm*, by Emily Taft Douglas, and used by permission of the publishers.

AMERICAN NATIONAL RED CROSS—for "Vasil Discovers America," by Leslie G. Cameron, originally published in American Junior Red Cross News and reprinted by permission of American National Red Cross and Miss Leslie G. Cameron; for "Saint Valentine," which originally appeared in the *Toronto Globe* and was published in American Junior Red Cross News, February, 1944, and reprinted in the Canadian Red Cross Junior.

BLOCH PUBLISHING COMPANY—for "Simon and the High Holy Days" and "The Most Precious Thing," from *The Story of Jewish Holidays and Customs*, by Dorothy F. Zeligs, copyright, 1942, and used by permission of the publishers, Bloch Publishing Company.

JOSEPH COTTLER—for "The Grand Old Man of Labor," condensed from *Champions of Democracy*, published by Little, Brown & Company, copyright by Joseph Cottler. All rights reserved.

COWARD-McCANN, INC.—for "He Believed in the Western Country," a selection reprinted by permission of Coward McCann, Inc. from *The Cabin Faced West* by Jean Fritz. Copyright © 1958 by Jean Fritz.

CROWN PUBLISHERS—for "The Midnight Rider, Paul Revere," from *Cavalcade of America* by Carl Carmer. © 1956 by Lothrop, Lee & Shepard Co. Inc. Used by permission of Crown Publishers, Inc.

DOUBLEDAY & COMPANY, INC.—for "The Christmas Spider," a selection from *Up the Hill*, by Marguerite de Angeli. Copyright 1942 by Marguerite de Angeli. Reprinted by permission of Doubleday & Company, Inc.

DOUTY, ESTER M.—for "The U.N.'s Marian Anderson." All rights reserved.

A. FLANAGAN COMPANY—for "The Jack-o'-Lantern Witch," from *Boys and Girls of Colonial Days*, by Carolyn Sherwin Bailey, and used by permission of the publishers, A. Flanagan Company.

GINN AND COMPANY and the author—for "They Heard a Horseman Singing," condensed from *Never Surrender*, by Brassil Fitzgerald, copyright by Ginn and Company, 1943. "The Creation of Man" is taken from *In the Reign of Coyote* (folklore from the Pacific Coast) published by Ginn and Company in 1905.

HARCOURT, BRACE AND COMPANY, INC.—for "And So He Grew," condensed from *Abe Lincoln Grows Up,* by Carl Sandburg, copyright, 1926, 1928, by Harcourt, Brace and Company, Inc.; "Mama and the Graduation Present," condensed from *Mama's Bank Account,* by Kathryn Forbes, copyright, 1943, by Harcourt, Brace and Company, Inc.; "Soldier of the Revolution," by Dorothy Canfield Fisher, copyright, 1949, by Harcourt, Brace and Company, Inc. These selections are used by permission of the publishers, Harcourt, Brace and Company, Inc.

HARPER & ROW, PUBLISHERS—for adapted selection from *The Tomahawk Family* by Natalie Savage Carlson. Copyright © 1960 by Natalie Savage Carlson. Used with permission of Harper & Row, Publisher. For permission to reprint "Sailing West to Find the East," from *Christopher Columbus* by Ruth Cromer Weir (Group I of The Real People Series, edited by Frances Cavanah).

HOUGHTON MIFFLIN COMPANY—for "The Smithy," from *Good Stories for Great Holidays,* by Frances Jenkins Olcott, and used by permission of the publishers, Houghton Mifflin Company.

GRACE HUMPHREY—for "The Pilgrims' Thanksgiving" (originally published as "The First Thanksgiving") condensed from *Stories of the World's Holidays,* published by Milton Bradley Company, copyright by Grace Humphrey. All rights reserved.

JACK AND JILL, Curtis Publishing Company, and the authors—for "The Valentine Box" by Maud Hart Lovelace, and "Why the Old Man Planted Trees" by Dan Murdoch.

KTAV PUBLISHING COMPANY, INC.—for "Passover, the Jewish Festival of Freedom" from *A Pictorial Treasury of Jewish Holidays and Customs* by Morris Epstein.

THE JEWISH PUBLICATION SOCIETY OF AMERICA—for "Hanukkah at Valley Forge," condensed from *Hanukkah,* by Emily Solis-Cohen, Jr., and used by permission of the publishers, The Jewish Publication Society of America.

J. B. LIPPINCOTT COMPANY—for "The Birthday of a Nation," a condensation of *The Birthday of a Nation* by Frances Rogers and Alice Beard. Copyright, 1945, by Frances Rogers and Alice Beard. Published by J. B. Lippincott Company.

LITTLE, BROWN AND COMPANY—for "The Twelve Months" from *Favorite Fairy Tales Told in Czechoslovakia.* Copyrighted © 1966 by Virginia Haviland.

LOTHROP, LEE AND SHEPARD CO., INC.—for "My Mother is the Most Beautiful Woman in the World," condensed from *My Mother is the Most Beautiful Woman in the World—A Russian Folktale,* retold by Becky Reyher, copyright, 1945, by Becky Reyher and Ruth Gannett, and used by permission of the publishers, Lothrop, Lee and Shepard Co., Inc.

MACRAE SMITH COMPANY—for "The Giant Ghost," from *Heigh-ho for Halloween* by Elizabeth Hough Sechrist copyright, 1948; for "Dwight Eisenhower, Hero" and "Jack Kennedy, Navy Veteran" from *Meet the Presidents* by Frances Cavanah and Elizabeth L. Crandall, copyright, 1962.

HUBERT J. MERWIN—for "Paul Revere Rides Again" by Jack Bechdolt, from *Story Parade*, September, 1951.

THOMAS NELSON & SONS—for selection, "Danny Kaye, UNICEF Ambassador," from *The Danny Kaye Story* by Kurt Singer, copyright, 1958. Published by Thomas Nelson & Sons.

L. C. PAGE & COMPANY—for "Christmas in the Street of Memories," reprinted from *Beacon Hill Children,* by Elizabeth Rhodes Jackson, and used by permission of the publishers, L. C. Page & Company.

MARGARET PHELPS—for "The Silver City," condensed from *Pico and the Silver Mountain,* published by Macrae Smith Company, copyright by Margaret Phelps. All rights reserved.

RAND McNALLY & COMPANY—for "Following the New Year Across the United States," from *Happy New Year Round the World* by Lois S. Johnson. Copyright 1966 by Rand McNally & Company. Acknowledgment also is made to Rand McNally & Company, and to the authors, for the following stories published in CHILD LIFE: "The Emigrant Fairy" by Jean Muir (1939); "Pinney's Easter Hunt" by Lavinia R. Davis (1940); "The Thanksgiving Stranger" by Ruth Gipson Plowhead, originally published under the title *Polly Prence's Thanksgiving* (1929); "Ring in the New" by Cornelia Meigs, originally published under the title "Ringing in the New Year" (1939); "Don Pedro's Christmas" by Eric P. Kelly (1939).

JOHN SCHAFFNER—for *Papa Was a Riot* by A. J. Ciulla. Copyright © 1952, by *Every Woman's Magazine, Inc.* Reprinted by permission of John Schaffner, Literary Agent.

CHARLES SCRIBNER'S SONS—for "The Festival of Lights," reprinted from *Augustus Caesar's World,* by Genevieve Foster, copyright, 1947, by Genevieve Foster, and used by permission of the publishers, Charles Scribner's Sons.

STORY PARADE, INC.—for "Horace the Happy Ghost" by Elizabeth Ireland, copyright 1951 by *Story Parade, Inc.,* reprinted by permission. For "Saint Patrick and the Last Snake," by Lavinia R. Davis, copyright, 1940, and used by permission of the publishers, *Story Parade, Inc.,* and the author.

TABER, GLADYS—for "Father's Day." All rights reserved.

THE VIKING PRESS, INC.—for "The Star-Spangled Banner Girl" from *Children of the Handicrafts* by Carolyn Sherwin Bailey. Copyright 1935 by Carolyn Sherwin Bailey, © 1963 by Rebecca Davies Ryan. Reprinted by permission of The Viking Press, Inc. For "Easter Eggs," condensed from *The Good Master,* by Kate Seredy, copyright, 1935, by Kate Seredy and used by permission of The Viking Press, Inc.

Thanks are also due to Miss Muriel Fuller, editor and agent, for her helpful suggestions on this revised edition, and to Mrs. Barbara Hewitt Williams, who helped to prepare the manuscript for the printer.

Contents

Contents

HOLIDAY ROUNDUP

New Year's Day

(January 1)

New Year's is undoubtedly the most widely celebrated of all holidays, but not everybody celebrates it on the same date. Among the ancient Greeks, Romans, and Persians the new year was supposed to begin when winter gave place to the beauty of spring, and in Iran (the modern name for Persia) New Year's Day is still observed on March 21. The ancient Hebrews began their year in the autumn with Rosh Hashana.

Most Americans and other peoples of the western world celebrate New Year's on the first of January. This month was named for Janus, the old Roman god with two faces—one looking back toward the past, the other looking forward to the future, and that is the special significance of the New Year holiday. It is a time for remembering what we have done or left undone, and—more important—it is a time for beginning again, which is why many of us make New Year resolutions. We like to recall a stanza from Tennyson's famous poem:

Ring out the old, ring in the
*   new.*
Ring happy bells across the
*   snow.*
The year is going, let it go.
Ring out the false, ring in
*   the true.*

An old English custom was to leave all the doors of a house open, so that it would be easy for the Old Year to leave and for the New Year to come in. Most of us like to stay up until midnight on New Year's Eve to enjoy the

magic moment when one year gives place to another.

Some people take part in solemn watchnight services at church. Others like to go to gay parties. When the ringing of bells and the blowing of whistles announce that the new year has come, friends shake hands or kiss one another and join in singing *We'll take a cup of kindness yet for auld lang syne!*

We call out "Happy New Year!" to our friends, in the hope that the months ahead will bring them good fortune and much joy.

The Twelve Months

Retold by

VIRGINIA HAVILAND

There was once a widow who had a daughter named Holena. In the cottage with them lived Holena's stepsister, Marushka. Now Marushka was so pretty and good that the other two disliked her and made her do all the hard work. She had to sweep the rooms, cook, wash, sew, spin and weave, and she had to bring in the hay from the meadow and milk the cow. Holena, who was not pretty, did nothing but dress up in her best clothes and amuse herself with one thing after another.

But Marushka never complained. Patiently she bore the scoldings and bad tempers of the mother and daughter. Holena's ugliness increased, while Marushka became even lovelier to look at. This made the other two more tyrannical and grumpy than ever. At length they determined to get rid of her, for they knew that Holena would have no suitors while Marushka was there to be seen.

One day in the middle of winter Holena said she wanted some violets. "Listen!" she cried to Marushka. "You must go up on the mountain and find me some violets. And they must be fresh and sweet-scented. Do you hear?"

"But whoever heard of violets blooming in the snow!" cried Marushka.

"You wretched creature! Do you dare to disobey me? Not another word! Off with you, and don't come back without the violets!"

The stepmother added her threats, and the two pushed Marushka out of the cottage and shut the door behind her.

Marushka, weeping, made her way to the mountain. The snow lay deep and there was no trace of any other human being. For a long time she wandered hither and thither, and lost herself in the woods. She became hungry and she shivered with cold and was almost ready to give up when she saw a light in the distance. She climbed toward it, until she had reached the very top of the mountain.

Upon the highest peak she found a large fire burning and twelve

4

men in long white robes sitting around it. Three had white hair, three were not quite so old, three were young and handsome, and the rest still younger. These were the twelve months of the year, and they sat silently looking at the fire, each one on a block of stone. The great January was placed higher than the others. He was older than they, and his hair and beard were white as snow. In his hand he held a wand.

At first Marushka was afraid, but after a while her courage returned. Drawing near, she said, "Good men, may I warm myself at your fire? I am chilled by the winter cold."

The great January raised his head and asked, "What brings you here, my child? What do you seek?"

"I am looking for violets," replied Marushka.

"This is not the season for violets. Do you not see the snow everywhere?"

"Yes," was Marushka's reply, "but my stepmother and my stepsister have ordered me to bring them violets from your mountain. If I return without them, they will kill me. I pray you, good sirs, to tell me where to find them."

The great January arose and went over to one of the youngest of the months. Placing his wand in that month's hand, he said, "Brother March, do you take the highest place."

March obeyed, at the same time waving his wand over the fire. Immediately the flames rose toward the sky. The snow began to melt, the trees and shrubs to bud. The grass became green and between the blades peeped the pale primrose. It was spring, and the meadows turned blue with violets.

"Gather them quickly, Marushka," said March.

Joyfully, Marushka hastened to pick the flowers, and soon had a large bouquet. She thanked the months and hastened home. Holena and her mother were amazed at the sight of the flowers and at their fragrance, which filled the house.

"Where did you pick them?" asked Holena.

"Under the trees on the mountain," replied Marushka.

Holena took the flowers, but without thanking Marushka for the trouble she had taken to get them.

The next day Holena called to Marushka again and said, "I long to taste strawberries. Run and fetch me some from the mountain, and see to it that they are sweet and ripe."

"But whoever heard of strawberries ripening in the snow?" said Marushka.

"Hold your tongue! Go after the strawberries and don't come back without them."

Holena's mother also ordered Marushka to gather the berries. They pushed her out of the house and bolted the door behind her.

Unhappily, Marushka made her way to the mountain again and climbed until she came to the fire around which sat the twelve months.

"Good men, may I warm myself at your fire? The winter wind chills me."

The great January raised his head and asked, "Why do you come here? What do you seek?"

"I am looking for strawberries," she replied.

"But we are in the midst of winter. Strawberries do not grow in the snow."

"I know," said Marushka sadly, "but my stepmother and stepsister have ordered me to bring them strawberries. I dare not return without them. Pray, good sirs, tell me where to find them."

The great January arose and went over to the month opposite him, and putting his wand into that month's hand, said, "Brother June, do you take the highest place."

June obeyed, and as he waved his wand over the fire, the flames leaped toward the sky. Instantly the snow melted, the earth became green with grass and the trees with leaves. Birds began to sing and flowers blossomed in the forest. It was summer, and in the sunny glades star-shaped blooms changed into ripe red strawberries.

"Gather them quickly," said June.

Joyfully, Marushka thanked the months, and when she had filled her apron, ran happily home. The strawberries greatly surprised Holena and her mother. "Wherever did you find them?" asked Holena, crossly.

"Up on the mountain," replied Marushka.

Holena gave a few to her mother and ate the rest herself. Not even one did she offer to Marushka. But on the third day she had tired of strawberries and fancied having some fresh red apples.

"Run, Marushka," she demanded, "and fetch me fresh red apples from the mountain."

"Apples in winter!" exclaimed Marushka. "Why, the trees have neither leaves nor fruit on them now."

"You idle girl! Go this minute, and don't come back unless you bring the apples."

As before, the widow added her commands and threats. The two seized Marushka roughly and turned her out of the house.

Poor Marushka went weeping through deep snow up the mountain till she came again to the fire around which sat the twelve months.

"Good men, may I warm myself at your fire?"

The great January raised his head and asked, "Why come you here? What do you seek?"

"I come to look for red apples," replied Marushka.

"But this is winter and not the season for apples," answered January.

"I know. But my stepmother and her daughter have ordered me to fetch them red apples from the mountain, and I dare not return without them. Pray, good sirs, tell me where to find them."

The great January arose and went to one of the elderly months, to whom he handed his wand. "Brother September, do you take the highest place."

September moved to the highest seat, which January had occupied. He waved the wand over the fire and a flare of red flames made the snow disappear. The trees leafed out, then brightened with autumn colors. A frosty wind began to scatter the leaves through the forest.

Marushka looked about and spied an apple tree on which hung ripe red fruit. She ran and shook the tree. One apple fell and then another. "That is enough," said September. "Now hurry home."

Marushka thanked the months and went down the mountain joyfully.

At home Holena and her mother marveled at the fruit. "Where did you gather these apples?" Holena asked.

"On the mountaintop," answered Marushka.

"Why did you not bring more?" said Holena fretfully. "You must have eaten them on your way back, you wicked girl."

"No, I have not even tasted them," declared Marushka. "I shook the tree twice. One apple fell each time. I was not allowed to shake it again, but was told to return home."

Holena would not believe her, and spoke so harshly that Marushka wept bitterly and took refuge in the kitchen.

Holena and her mother ate the apples. Never before had they tasted such delicious fruit. When they had finished the two apples, they both longed for more.

"Mother," said Holena, "give me my cloak and I will go fetch more apples. I will not send Marushka because the good-for-nothing wretch would eat them on her way. I will find the tree, and no matter who cries 'Stop!' I shall not leave until I have shaken all the apples from the tree."

Holena's mother brought a warm cloak and hood and helped her daughter put them on. Then Holena took the road to the mountain while her mother stood at the window and watched her disappear in the distance.

Snow covered everything and not a footprint was to be seen anywhere, but Holena pushed on until she reached a mountaintop. There were the flaming fire and the twelve months seated about it. At first Holena was frightened and she hesitated to go nearer. But then she went close and warmed her hands, without asking permission. The great January inquired severely, "What has brought you here? What do you seek?"

"I need not tell you," replied Holena. "What business is it of yours?"

January frowned and waved his wand over his head. Instantly the sky filled with clouds, snow began to fall, and the fire and the twelve months disappeared. Holena found herself alone in a wild storm. Although she tried to make her way home, she only wandered vainly hither and thither through the white forest.

Meanwhile, Holena's mother looked from the cottage window for her return. The hours passed slowly and she became alarmed. "Can it be that the apples have charmed her away from home?" she wondered. Finally, she put on her own hood and cloak and set out to search for her daughter. But the snow continued to blow in great drifts, covering everything. The icy north wind whistled through the mountain forests. No voice answered her cry. Neither mother nor daughter ever returned home.

Marushka lived on in the little cottage, and it and the field and cow became hers. In time an honest young farmer came to share them with her, and they were contented and happy as long as they lived.

Ring In the New!

CORNELIA MEIGS

Julia Stone was singing to herself as she walked down Franklin Street in the little New Hampshire village. Above her she could just barely make out the tall spire of the church against the gray sky with the cloud of falling snow wrapping it all around. How wonderful to have it snow again the day before New Year's, so that, as Judy thought, everything will look fresh and clean and special for the New Year.

For Judy it was going to be a very special New Year, indeed. Her mother had said that when she was eleven, she could sit up until midnight to see the old year out. Nancy Hyde, her best friend, had been told the same thing by her mother. This year they were both eleven, and she was going to spend the night at Nancy's house. They would sit up together to watch the New Year in!

Just as Judy opened the front door of her own house, the telephone rang. Her parents had gone to see some friends in the next town.

"Judy, can you hear me? We'll have to spend the night with our friends. The road through Lyme Hollow will be drifted so deep we ought not to try it when it is getting dark. Anna will see that you have your supper and get safely over to Nancy's. But I'm worried about one thing. You know your father and I always go on the last day of the year to see Mr. Townly and take him a load of firewood. Simon Hammonds was to bring it this afternoon. But the snow——"

The telephone sputtered, and then gave no sound. The storm was interfering with it. Then suddenly it began to be clear again.

"Judy—Judy, are you still there? I'm afraid Simon can't get into town with his little truck. I know Mr. Townly will be out of wood because he expects ours. Ask Nancy's father if he won't send one of his trucks and see that Mr. Townly gets it somehow——"

Once more the telephone broke off. At last Central spoke. "I can't get the connection any more. The weight of the snow has brought down a wire or a pole somewhere."

Judy put down the receiver. Yes, of course, someone had to see that Mr. Townly got his wood. Mr. Townly was the pleasant old man who made the fires in the church and swept the Sunday-school rooms and always had such a kind word for every boy and girl in town. It was he who rang the bell in the tall spire of the church, rang it mornings and evenings, for Sunday services and for particular occasions. Mr. Townly was poor, and his little house at the end of the street could be very cold. Judy knew that on a winter night a low woodpile was a serious matter even in her own household.

In houses like Mr. Townly's there were no furnaces. In bitter weather someone often had to be up until morning to keep fires in stoves and fireplaces from going out. If you had nothing to burn, you could not just telephone a dealer down the street and have him bring a load of coal or wood. No, you had to send word to Mr. Hammonds, and he had to fetch it over three miles of humpy road—if his truck would run. In this snow it probably would not.

Judy turned and ran out of the house. She was breathless when she got to Nancy's house, three blocks beyond the church. Nancy ran to take her wet coat, but Judy could not stop except to get her breath. She explained about Mr. Townly's wood, but Nancy's father had driven out to the power plant and her mother was out and would not be back until evening.

But Nancy's cousin, Martha Hand, was sitting by the fire knitting. She went to college and was here for the Christmas vacation. Nancy's brother Tom had just come in, and was still in his big boots and heavy jacket. He had been shoveling snow at the kitchen door.

Cousin Martha put down her knitting to listen, and Tom stopped beating his snowy mittens against the fender. "That's bad," Tom said. "Of course, Hammonds can't get in with the wood. Poor old Mr. Townly!"

Everyone was fond of Mr. Townly. His father and his grandfather had rung the church bell before him. Every man, woman, and child in the town got up by him, started to school by him, went to church in the quiet of Sunday morning to his ringing. He, and those who had rung before him, had never missed a morning or a church service or a public festival. Everybody knew that Mr. Townly had to be taken care of. And now all the older people were out of reach and these younger ones must do it. But how?

"There's the big truck out in the barn," Tom said. "Father had it brought in last night from the plant. That could get out to the Hammonds' place, but who's to drive it? I know how, but I haven't got my license yet." Tom was fifteen, and the law would not let him drive for another year. Cousin Martha jumped.

"I could drive it. I drove a truck when I was visiting on the farm last summer. But how will we get the wood loaded if Mr. Hammonds isn't there?"

"Oh, we can get plenty of people, like Jim Stevens and Polly and the others. If there are enough of us we can get it on all right. We'll pick them up as we go down the street."

They were off in no time at all. Martha, in her bright ski suit, climbed to the high seat and shifted the big gears. The truck groaned and creaked and began to creep backward out of the shed. Martha backed it around neatly and came out onto the road. The drifts were getting deeper, but the truck went ploughing steadily along. They stopped at one house after another and explained the situation. Warmly clad boys and girls climbed aboard at each stop.

Three miles is a long way in the snow, but they got to Mr. Hammonds' house at last. He threw open the door when they chugged into his yard and came running out. "There now, I'm glad you came," he said. "I could never get into town myself with my small truck. I couldn't even get the wood loaded, for I'm trying to dig out a path to the stable and the sheep shed before the snow gets too much for me. The wood is piled back of the big barn. If each of you takes a stick at a time, you can get it loaded all right. It's lucky there are so many of you. But do you know how to take down a woodpile and load it in the truck? It has to be done right."

They all were sure that they could load the wood. Six of the boys and girls, Nancy and Judy among them, stood knee-deep in the snow and handed up the cut sticks, one at a time, to the other six in the truck. How they worked!

"We're all so plastered with snow, you'd think we had been having a snowball fight," Martha said. "Climb on and hold tight. There will be plenty of bumps going home."

It was dark as they rumbled back to town, with the long fingers of the headlights feeling out the way ahead. The windows of all the houses were bright behind the holly wreaths as they rolled down Franklin Street. "Now run home to your suppers," Martha said, "and come back when we take the wood to Mr. Townly. It will have to be unloaded and piled up in his shed to do him any good."

It was quite late before they were all together again. People kept sending word. "Don't go without Jane or Fred." "I have a package of cookies," or, "Mr. Smith's overcoat that he isn't wearing." Anna and Martha were sewing up a flannel jacket for Mrs. Townly. It was really as late as everybody's bedtime when they were ready to start out again. But it was New Year's Eve tonight, and nobody's bedtime really mattered.

Judy thought she had never seen Mr. Townly's house look so small or so cold as it did that night. There must be only one light and one fire in it, and two people sitting close together, wondering how they could get through that bitter night.

What fun it was to shout, when the door opened, "Hello, Mr. Townly; hello, Mrs. Townly," to see their surprised faces, to put wood on the fireplace, to feed the cold stove in the kitchen until it roared. While some of the company stayed outside with Tom to pile the wood up in the shed, the others ran back and forth carrying in the boxes and bundles that had been sent. Martha had brought a can of milk and some packages in a basket, and she opened them in the kitchen.

When all of them were gathered in the house at last, there was hot cocoa to hand around and there were plates piled up with cookies. They all sat down in front of the fire, most of them on the floor. Then Mr. Townly told them about when he was the age of Tom and went away to sea because the little New Hampshire town "seemed a sight too small for me."

He had had many adventures everywhere in the world. "But I

came back in the end," he said. "When my father could not ring the church bell any more, I came back, first to help him, and then to keep on ringing it after he was gone. My son will do the same thing. He's out West now, driving cattle on that big ranch in Montana that belongs to Tom's uncle. But he'll come home, too. There are some jobs that are for the young, and some for those who are growing older. This is a good town to come home to."

He looked at the big clock ticking on the wall. "Time's getting on. I can't be late ringing the church bell to bring the New Year in." He hurried into his worn old overcoat.

Tom had been out to look at the weather and came in stamping the snow off his boots. "The drifts are deep, Mr. Townly," he said. "We can't hope to drive the truck home tonight."

"Mr. Townly," asked Martha, "would it be so terrible if just this one year the bell didn't ring for New Year's Eve?"

"Why, such a thing has never happened," he answered. "Do you know that bell rang when the news came that the Declaration of Independence was signed in Philadelphia? It rang when George Washington was made President; it rang when Abraham Lincoln died; it rang for peace at the end of the last war. There's many who will listen for it. If they don't hear it, they will think bad luck has come to the town for certain. They'll begin the New Year with heavy hearts and no courage. Oh, it has to ring!"

In spite of all they could say, he started out. Amongst them, they managed to help him through the big drift at the gate, but when they got out into the road the way was even harder. He struggled on for a few yards, then stopped and swayed. He would have fallen if Tom had not caught him.

Somehow they got the old man back to his home and into a big chair before the fire. Anxiously, they clustered round, rubbing his hands, and helping Mrs. Townly cover him with warm blankets. No one noticed the time until Mr. Townly said, feebly, "The bell! It's nearly time to ring the bell."

The children looked at one another in dismay. It was a quarter of twelve!

"We'll ring it for you," Julia said. "We'll ring it on time."

The children seconded her eagerly. In a moment, warmly wrapped, they were out of the house and on their way. The snow had stopped falling, but it lay so deep and smooth everywhere that it was hard to know places and corners and fenceposts that marked the way. The clouds had broken and the stars were out, very small and high in the cold air. Silently, the children pushed and fought their way through the deep snow, the older ones helping the little ones.

As they came nearer to the middle of the town, they found that some of the walks had been cleared and they could make more haste. Out of a few houses came the sound of voices, where there were parties going on. Then even these sounds ended, for it was nearly midnight and everyone was listening for the bell. Judy could see the church spire, going up above them against the stars. They were on time, she thought happily.

Tom had Mr. Townly's lantern and watch and the big key. Inside, the church was very black and little warmer than was the clean, crisp air outdoors. The light of the lantern showed the narrow door and the steps going up, up into the dark. Tom went first, carrying the lantern. Martha came last with a tiny flashlight like a will-o'-the-wisp. They all climbed together, breathless from their struggle through the storm, their footsteps sounding hollow on the stairs.

It was within one moment of twelve o'clock. At last, they passed the little window that they had seen so often from far below. It was strange to look down on the long snowy street, with its small beautiful old houses under the sleeping roofs. Tom's voice sounded loud and echoing as he spoke from above.

"Here is the rope. Everybody take firm hold of the stair rail with one hand and a good grip on the rope with the other. When I say 'Three,' pull—pull together, one stroke for liberty, one for peace, one for George Washington, one for Abraham Lincoln, and all the rest for the New Year, one—two—three—!"

The bell sounded terrifying, the first stroke was so loud in their ears. By the second they were a little more used to it. By the third they were pulling all together, evenly and smoothly. "Clang, clang, clang. Good luck, everybody. Be brave for the New Year, because it is going to be a good one. Good cheer, good courage, peace on earth, good will toward men."

Judy was singing it to herself, although no one could hear her in the great sound of the bell, ringing so splendidly overhead to bring in the New Year.

Following the New Year
Across the United States

LOIS S. JOHNSON

Californians, and their neighbors along the West Coast of the United States, can, if they choose, celebrate the New Year's arrival for three continuous hours of merrymaking before the witching hour actually comes to them. By tuning in their television sets at nine o'clock on New Year's Eve, those living in the Pacific Time Zone can first watch the fun their cousins in New York City are having as they mill around Times Square, laughing, shouting, jostling, in a big, bright hip hip hooray to the new year.

From the first "blast off" on Times Square, the celebrations roll their merry way across the country as far as Hawaii and Alaska. New Year's Eve is the biggest and gayest party night of the whole year. Everyone seems bent on celebrating somehow—in a gay party at home, or in some brightly lighted night spot, hotel, or restaurant.

In many places over the country, there is a serious note to the observance, as churches conduct Watch Night services or hold midnight masses. It is at such services that Americans turn their thoughts to the real meaning of the events of the year just closing, and to the opportunities and responsibilities they face during the coming months.

Gala New Year's Eve celebrations were not always the custom in the early days of the country. In fact any special notice of the day was actually frowned upon by the Pilgrim Fathers in New England. So strict were they in their belief that any kind of New Year observance smacked of paganism that they even refused to call the month of January by that name. They felt it would be a sin to do so, since the name had come from the old Roman god Janus. Instead, they spoke of it as "The First Month" and permitted no notice to be taken of the new year. As one record of the time tells us of New Year: "We went to work betimes."

With the coming of other colonists, this situation changed.

The Dutch, who settled in New York, liked fun, especially on New Year. They brought with them from the old country the custom of holding Open House on New Year's Day. Callers were welcomed all day and into the evening. Punch and cake were usually served, and by the time all the eligible bachelors had called on all the eligible bachelor girls, they had really had their fill of good Dutch food and cheering drink.

When George Washington came to New York to be inaugurated as President of the new United States, he was introduced to the custom of Open House. He thought the idea a splendid one, and adopted it for his and Mrs. Washington's New Year receptions.

Later presidents continued the custom at the White House until January 1, 1934, when Open House was, with regret, given up by President Franklin Delano Roosevelt. He found that his affliction interfered with his standing in a receiving line to greet his callers. Since then, the custom of Open House has practically disappeared.

Other settlers also brought to the new country their favorite New Year customs from their homelands.

Moravians in Pennsylvania welcomed the new year with trombones and trumpets and held a love feast, as had been the custom in Austria and Germany.

Swedes brought to America their custom of eating baked ham on New Year for good luck. And the Swedish settlers in Philadelphia continued the old custom in their new homes of greeting the new year by marching, masked and in fancy costumes, making things merry as they paraded through the streets.

It was about the same time that English settlers introduced the old English custom of dressing in fantastic garb and going about during the holidays enacting pantomimes, or "silent" plays, featuring St. George and the Dragon and other characters. These actors were known as "mummers."

A combination of the Swedish and the English customs resulted in the beginning of the now-famous Mummers' Parade, which is held on New Year's Day in Philadelphia. Each year, the parade has become more elaborate, the costumes more gorgeous, the music of the bands more gay, and the antics of the mummers more amusing.

Across the country from Philadelphia and its wintry celebration, a far different kind of parade has been growing in popularity in the land of flowers and sunshine. This is of course the world-famous Tournament of Roses, a familiar sight to those who follow the parade on their TV sets. Held in Pasadena, California, this spectacle has become California's New Year greeting to the world.

Since its humble beginning in 1890, when horsedrawn buggies and surreys were decorated with fresh garden flowers, the floats in the parade have become fabulous in the lavish use of fresh flowers to depict storybook themes. As the Tournament has changed through the years, so have the sports events that follow in the afternoon. In the beginning, there was horseracing, then chariot racing. Since 1902 intercollegiate football games have been an increasing attraction. The great Rose Bowl of today, seating over 100,000, attracts football fans from many parts of the country.

So popular has the Rose Bowl become, that other communities have adopted the idea and have bowls of their own: Orange Bowl in Miami, Florida; Sugar Bowl in New Orleans, Louisiana; Cotton Bowl in Dallas, Texas; Gator Bowl in Jacksonville, Florida; Sun Bowl in El Paso, Texas.

A unique salute to the new year is the great fireworks display from the top of Pikes Peak in Colorado on New Year's Eve. The idea for such a display began in 1922 when five intrepid mountain climbers in Colorado Springs decided to hike to the top of Pikes Peak to watch the old year out and the new year in. On that first trip, they carried some two hundred pounds of fireworks through snowdrifts up the steep slopes to the summit. There at midnight the fireworks were lighted, and the sky above Pikes Peak burst into fountains of color that could be seen for miles.

Chinese citizens of San Francisco and New York celebrate in February at the time of the Chinese New Year. They stage an elaborate parade through the streets of Chinatown, in which appear a block-long Golden Dragon and many replicas of legendary Chinese fish, birds, and beasts. Besides, there are giants, some of which are fifteen feet tall, plus scores of elaborate floats and marching bands. Thousands of spectators thrill to this exhibition of Oriental splendor.

Early Indians of North America did not mark any particular day as New Year, but divided the year into seasons and lunar months. Notches were made on sticks by some tribes to record dates, but usually they depended upon their memories to keep track of time. Some of the buffalo-hunting Indians made pictures on buffalo skins to represent the changing seasons of the year.

Among the Cherokees, Creeks, and Choctaws, the New Year festival comes in August. It is called "The Fast." For two nights and one day, no food is eaten, and then the new crops are tasted first.

Hopi Indians hold a nine-day festival at the time of the summer solstice. They believe that on the fourth day of the festival the spirits of the dead return to the villages and join the living in the ceremonies.

Among the Navajos, the new year actually begins in October, the season when there is no thunder. October is also the time when the ceremonials associated with the summer season end. October is spoken of as *ghąąji*, meaning literally "back to back." Modern-day Navajos who celebrate New Year do so after the fashion of non-Indians on January 1.

Native Alaskans did not celebrate New Year until those living in the Aleutian Islands came under the influence of Christian missionaries. Today, Alaskan Indians, Eskimos, and their white neighbors are integrated in the schools, so that the customs practiced at New Year are usually the same for all of them—those familiar to most of us.

Early-day Hawaiians celebrated their New Year in November. On the first four days of the celebration, it was forbidden for anyone to go bathing in the ocean, or to do any fishing, or even to blow on conch shells. During this period of "Lent" the high priest, blindfolded, remained in seclusion. On the fifth day there was a brief recess. The priest's blindfold was removed, and the canoes were permitted to put out to sea for fishing. On the following day "Lent" was resumed for twenty more days. This custom was followed as a purification rite for the new year. Modern-day Hawaiians of course are very American and are proud to observe New Year in the American way.

And so the arrival of New Year is heralded across the United States in many ways. No matter how it is celebrated or at what hour, the underlying thought is the same, as fellow Americans across the country greet one another with a sincerely warm wish for "A happy new year!"

Abraham Lincoln's Birthday

(February 12)

The first formal celebration of this day took place in the House of Representatives in 1866, less than a year after Abraham Lincoln had been assassinated. Lincoln had given his last years to preserving the nation he loved as a united country, and his Emancipation Proclamation was one of a series of steps that led to

freedom for the slaves. Now more than a hundred years later, Americans are still quoting his Gettysburg Address, in which he resolved "that government of the people, by the people, for the people shall not perish from the earth." We also like to remember the man himself—his simple, homey ways, his joy in his children, and the experiences of his youth.

At the Lincoln Memorial in Washington, D.C., there is a constant stream of visitors from every state and from many countries abroad who climb the long flight of steps leading to the white marble temple. Beyond the white Doric columns is an immense seated figure of Abraham Lincoln, and there are few who do not feel a rush of emotion as they look up into the kindly, rugged face with the brooding eyes. Then they read the inscription on the marble behind the statue:

IN THIS TEMPLE
AS IN THE HEARTS OF
THE PEOPLE FOR WHOM
HE SAVED THE UNION
THE MEMORY OF
ABRAHAM LINCOLN
IS ENSHRINED FOREVER

The poet Carl Sandburg, who writes of Lincoln's boyhood in the following story, once talked with a flagman working on a railroad near the Sandburg home. This man had been present the night the President was killed. Sandburg once asked him if he could tell in a few words why Abraham Lincoln had been so greatly loved.

"He was humanity," was the reply.

And So He Grew

CARL SANDBURG

Little Abe and Sarah, living in the lonesome cabin on Little Pigeon Creek, Indiana, got a nice surprise one morning when four horses and a wagon came into their clearing, and their father jumped off, then Sarah Bush Lincoln, the new wife and mother, then John, Sarah, and Matilda Johnston, Sarah Bush's three children by her first husband. Next off the wagon came a feather mattress, feather pillows, a black walnut bureau, a large clothes-chest, a table, chairs, pots and skillets, knives, forks, spoons.

Abe ran his fingers over the slick wood of the bureau, pushed his fist into the feather pillows, sat in the new chairs, and wondered to himself, because this was the first time he had touched such fine things, such soft slick things.

"Here's your new mammy," his father told Abe, as the boy looked up at a strong, large-boned, rosy woman, with a kindly face and eyes, with a steady voice, steady ways. The cheekbones of her face stood out and she had a strong jawbone; she was warm and friendly for Abe's little hands to touch, right from the beginning. As one of her big hands held his head against her skirt, he felt like a cold chick warming under the soft feathers of a big wing. She took the cornhusks Abe had been sleeping on, piled them in the yard and said they would be good for a pigpen later on; and Abe sunk his head and bones that night in a feather pillow and a feather mattress.

Ten years pass with that cabin on Little Pigeon Creek for a home, and that farm and neighborhood the soil for growth. There the boy Abe grows to be the young man, Abraham Lincoln.

Ten years pass and the roots of a tree spread out finding water to carry up to branches and leaves that are in the sun; the trunk thickens, the forked limbs shine wider in the sun, they pray with their leaves in the rain and the whining wind; the tree arrives, the mystery of its coming, spreading, growing, a secret not even known to the tree itself; it stands with its arms stretched to the corners the four winds

22

come from, with its murmured testimony, "We are here, we arrived, our roots are in the earth of these years," and beyond that short declaration, it speaks nothing of the decrees, fates, accidents, destinies, that made it an apparition of its particular moment.

Abe Lincoln grows up. His father talks about the waste of time in "eddication"; it is enough "to larn readin', writin', cipherin' "; but the staunch, yearning stepmother, Sarah Bush Lincoln, comes between the boy and the father. And the father listens to the stepmother and lets her have her way.

When he was eleven years old, Abe's young body began to change. The juices and glands began to make a long, tall boy out of him. As the months and years went by, he noticed his lean wrists getting longer, his legs too, and he was now looking over the heads of other boys. Men said, "Land o' goshen, that boy air a-growin'!"

As he took on more length, they said he was shooting up into the air like green corn in the summer of a good corn-year. So he grew. When he reached seventeen years of age, and they measured him, he was six feet, nearly four inches high, from the bottoms of his moccasins to the top of his skull.

These were years he was handling the ax. Except in spring plowing-time and the fall fodder-pulling, he was handling the ax nearly all the time. The insides of his hands took on callus thick as leather. He cleared openings in the timber, cut logs and puncheons, split firewood, built pigpens.

He learned how to measure with his eye the half-circle swing of the ax so as to nick out the deepest possible chip from off a tree-trunk. The trick of swaying his body easily on the hips so as to throw the heaviest possible weight into the blow of the ax—he learned that.

On winter mornings he wiped the frost from the ax handle, sniffed sparkles of air into his lungs, and beat a steady cleaving of blows into a big tree till it fell—and he sat on the main log and ate his noon dinner of corn bread and fried salt pork—and joked with the gray squirrels that frisked and peeped at him from high forks of near-by walnut trees.

He learned how to make his ax flash and bite into a sugar-maple or a sycamore. The outside and the inside look of black walnut and black oak, hickory and jack oak, elm and white oak, sassafras, dogwood, grapevines, sumac—he came on their secrets. He could guess close to the time of the year, to the week of the month, by the way the leaves and branches of trees looked. He sniffed the seasons.

Often he worked alone in the timbers, all day long with only the sound of his own ax, or his own voice speaking to himself, or the crackling and swaying of branches in the wind, and the cries and whirs of animals, of brown and silver-gray squirrels, of partridges, hawks, crows, turkeys, sparrows, and the occasional wildcats.

The tricks and whimsies of the sky, how to read clear skies and cloudy weather, the creeping vines of ivy and wild grape, the recurrence of dogwood blossoms in spring, the ways of snow, rain, drizzle, sleet, the visitors of sky and weather coming and going hour by hour—he tried to read their secrets, he tried to be friendly with their mystery.

So he grew, to become hard, tough, wiry. The muscle on his bones and the cords, tendons, cross-weaves of fiber, and nerve centers, these became instruments to obey his wishes. He found with other men he could lift his own end of a log—and more, too. One of the neighbors said he was strong as three men. Another said, "He can sink an ax deeper into wood than any man I ever saw." And another, "If you heard him fellin' trees in a clearin', you would say there was three men at work by the way the trees fell."

He was more than a tough, long, rawboned boy. He amazed men with his man's lifting power. He put his shoulders under a new-built corncrib one day and walked away with it to where the farmer wanted it. Four men, ready with poles to put under it and carry it, didn't need their poles. He played the same trick with a chicken house; at the new, growing town of Gentryville near by, they said the chicken house weighed six hundred pounds, and only a big boy with a hard backbone could get under it and walk away with it.

A blacksmith shop, a grocery, and a store had started up on the crossroads of the Gentry farm. And one night after Abe had been helping thresh wheat on Dave Turnham's place, he went with Dennis Hanks, John Johnston, and some other boys to Gentryville where the farmhands sat around with John Baldwin, the blacksmith, and Jones, the storekeeper, and told stories, talked politics and religion and gossip. Going home late that night, they saw something in a mud puddle alongside the road. They stepped over to see whether it was a man or a hog. It was a man—drunk, snoring, sleeping off his drunk on a frosty night outdoors in a cold wind.

They shook him by the shoulders, doubled his knees to his stomach, but he went on sleeping, snoring. The cold wind was getting colder. The other boys said they were going home, and they went away leaving Abe alone with the snoring sleeper in the mud puddle. Abe stepped into the mud, reached arms around the man, slung him over his shoulders, carried him to Dennis Hanks' cabin, built a fire, rubbed him warm and left him sleeping off the whisky.

And the man afterward said Abe saved his life. He told John Hanks, "It was mighty clever of Abe to tote me to a warm fire that night."

So he grew, living in that Pigeon Creek cabin for a home, sleeping in the loft, climbing up at night to a bed just under the roof, where sometimes the snow and the rain drove through the cracks, eating sometimes at a table where the family had only one thing to eat—potatoes. His father spoke a blessing to the Lord for potatoes; the boy murmured, "Those are mighty poor blessings." And Abe made jokes once when company came and Sally Bush Lincoln brought out raw potatoes, gave the visitors a knife apiece, and they all peeled raw potatoes, and talked about the crops, politics, religion, gossip.

Days when they had only potatoes to eat didn't come often. Other days in the year they had "yaller-legged chicken" with gravy, and corn dodgers with shortening, and berries and honey. They tasted of bear meat, deer, coon, quail, grouse, prairie turkey, catfish, bass, perch.

Abe knew the sleep that comes after long hours of work outdoors, the feeling of simple food changing into blood and muscle as he worked in those young years clearing timberland for pasture and corn crops, cutting loose the brush, piling it and burning it, splitting rails, pulling the crosscut saw and the whipsaw, driving the shovel-plow, harrowing, planting, hoeing, pulling fodder, milking cows, churning butter, helping neighbors at house-raisings, log-rollings, corn-huskings.

He found he was fast, strong, and keen when he went against other boys in sports. On farms where he worked, he held his own at scuffling, knocking off hats, wrestling. The time came when around

Gentryville and Spencer County he was known as the best "rassler" of all, the champion. In jumping, foot-racing, throwing the maul, pitching the crowbar, he carried away the decisions against the lads of his own age always, and usually won against those older than himself.

He earned his board, clothes, and lodgings, sometimes working for a neighbor farmer. He watched his father, while helping make cabinets, coffins, cupboards, window frames, doors. Hammers, saws, pegs, cleats, he understood firsthand, also the scythe and the cradle for cutting hay and grain, the corn-cutter's knife, the leather piece to protect the hand while shucking corn, and the horse, the dog, the cow, the ox, the hog. He could skin and cure the hides of coon and deer. He lifted the slippery two-hundred-pound hog carcass, head down, holding the hind hocks up for others of the gang to hook, and swung the animal clear of the ground. He learned where to stick a hog in the under side of the neck so as to bleed it to death, how to split it in two, and carve out the chops, the parts for sausage grinding, for hams, for "cracklings."

Farmers called him to butcher for them at thirty-one cents a day, this when he was sixteen and seventeen years old. He could "knock a beef in the head," swing a maul and hit a cow between the eyes, skin the hide, halve and quarter it, carve out the tallow, the steaks, kidneys, liver.

And the hiding places of fresh spring water under the earth crust had to be in his thoughts; he helped at well-digging; the wells Tom Lincoln dug went dry one year after another; neighbors said Tom was always digging a well and had his land "honeycombed"; and the boy, Abe, ran the errands and held the tools for the well-digging.

When he was eighteen years old, he could take an ax at the end of the handle and hold it out in a straight horizontal line, easy and steady—he had strong shoulder muscles and steady wrists early in life. He walked thirty-four miles in one day just on an errand, to please himself, to hear a lawyer make a speech. He could tell his body to do almost impossible things, and the body obeyed.

Growing from boy to man, he was alone a good deal of the time. Days came often when he was by himself all the time except at breakfast and supper hours in the cabin home. In some years more of his time was spent in loneliness than in the company of other people.

It happened, too, that this loneliness he knew was not like that of people in cities who can look from a window on streets where faces pass and repass. It was the wilderness loneliness he became acquainted with, solved, filtered through body, eye, and brain, held communion with in his ears, in the temples of his forehead, in the works of his beating heart.

He lived with trees, with the bush wet with shining raindrops, with the burning bush of autumn, with the lone wild duck riding a north wind and crying down on a line north to south, the faces of open sky and weather, the ax which is an individual one-man instrument, these he had for companions, books, friends, talkers, chums of his endless changing soliloquies.

His moccasin feet in the wintertime knew the white spaces of snowdrifts piled in whimsical shapes against timber slopes or blown in levels across the fields of last year's cut cornstalks; in the summertime his bare feet toughened in the gravel of green streams while he laughed back to the chatter of bluejays in the red-haw trees or while he kept his eyes ready in the slough quack grass for the cow-snake, the rattler, the copperhead.

He rested between spells of work in the springtime when the upward push of the coming out of the new grass can be heard, and in autumn weeks when the rustle of a single falling leaf lets go a whisper that a listening ear can catch.

He found his life thrown in ways where there was a certain chance for a certain growth. And so he grew.

The Show in the White House Attic

JULIA TAFT BAYNE

> The United States was passing through a sad period when Abraham Lincoln became President, for the Civil War broke out soon after he took office. Though he bore heavy burdens, to his sons Willie and Tad he was just "Pa"—a man who comforted them when they were in trouble and who did not seem to mind when they got into mischief. Their playmates were the sons of Judge H. N. Taft, and it was the Taft boys' older sister, Julia, then sixteen, who later told the story of the good times they had in the White House.

Spring in Washington was never more beautiful than in April, 1861, when my two brothers and I crossed Lafayette Square on our way to the White House. At my mother's first meeting with Mrs. Lincoln, it had come out that they were about the ages of Willie and Tad Lincoln.

"Send them around tomorrow, please, Mrs. Taft," said Mrs. Lincoln. "Willie and Tad are so lonely, and everything is so strange here in Washington."

Thus began an intimacy between the Lincoln boys and my brothers. Horatio Nelson Taft, Jr., who was called Bud, was twelve, a year older than Willie. Thomas Lincoln (Tad) and Halsey Cook Taft (Holly) were eight. Willie was the most lovable boy I ever knew. Tad had a quick fiery temper but was very affectionate when he chose. I think there was hardly a day when the four boys were not together.

It was during the following May, as I remember, that Mrs. Lincoln went to New York to buy some furnishings for the White House. She sent a note to my mother asking that Bud and Holly be allowed to stay with Willie and Tad until she returned. Some days later Mr. Gideon Welles, Secretary of the Navy, told my father that Tad had bombarded the room where a Cabinet meeting was being held, with his toy cannon. President Lincoln had left the meeting to go out and comfort Holly Taft, who had pinched his fingers with some contrivance.

My father was greatly disgusted with these tidings, and I was instructed to go and see that "those young rascals don't tear down the White House." When I reached there, I noticed smiles on the faces of the sentry, doorkeeper, and messengers. I followed that peculiar smile upstairs and asked for the boys. "They are in the attic, miss," answered a servant, with that same grin on his face.

I ascended to the attic, and as I opened the door Tad rushed at me, shouting, "Come quick, Julie. We're having a circus. Willie can't get his dress on and Bud's bonnet won't fit."

The boys had two sheets pinned together for a curtain, behind which was a crowd of soldiers, sailors, gardeners, and servants. Anybody who had five cents could go up the back stairs and see the show.

Willie was struggling with a lilac silk dress of his mother's. Bud was wearing a white morning dress pinned around him in billowy folds. One of Mrs. Lincoln's bonnets was stuck sideways on his head.

"Boys," I said, highly scandalized by these proceedings, "does the President know about this?"

"Yep," said Tad. He began singing at the top of his voice "Old Abe Lincoln came out of the wilderness."

"Tad, Tad," I remonstrated, "don't sing that. Suppose the President hears you."

"Pa won't care," answered Tad. "I'm going to sing that song in the show."

I had had quite enough and made my escape from the attic. On the stairs I met Major John Hay, President Lincoln's secretary.

"Have those boys got the President's spectacles?" he asked angrily.

"I think they have," I answered. I had just seen them on Tad's nose.

As I went on, Tad rushed after me. "Julie, come back! Major Hay's taken Pa's spectacles away from us, and we have got to have 'em in the show. That old gentleman who is visiting at your house has two pairs. Make Holly go get 'em."

I disregarded this plea and went on. In the lower hall I met the President, who took my hand and said, "Well, here is Julie come to the circus. Having a great time up there, eh?"

"Yes sir," I said. "They are making a dreadful noise, and they have Mrs. Lincoln's things on, and they look horrid."

He threw back his head and laughed heartily. It was almost the only time I ever saw Mr. Lincoln laugh all over.

"Come, Julie," he said, "let's go up and see it. How much is it?"

"Five cents," I answered. "But, please, I don't want to go. They'll make me help them, and I don't want to. It's horrid of them to wear Mrs. Lincoln's clothes."

Eluding his hand, I went on downstairs. Later Bud told me that the President stayed through the show and seemed to enjoy the boys' jokes. I am glad to remember that hearty laugh of his.

President Lincoln liked to play with the boys whenever he had a little time from his duties. Once I heard a terrible racket in another room. Opening the door with the idea of bestowing some sisterly "don'ts" upon my young brothers, whose voices could be heard amid the din, I beheld the President lying on the floor. The four boys were trying to hold him down. Willie and Bud had hold of his hands; Holly and Tad sprawled over his feet and legs. The broad grin on Mr. Lincoln's face was evidence that he was enjoying himself hugely. As soon as the boys saw my face at the door, Tad called, "Julie, come quick and sit on his stomach." But this struck me too much like laying profane hands on the Lord's anointed, and I closed the door and went out.

You may infer that I was a conceited little prig. But I really don't think I was. I was dignified with the weight of sixteen years, remember, and many of the pranks of my young brothers and the Lincoln boys deeply shocked my sense of propriety.

I was not the only one thus impressed. I remember the rage of the head gardener, Major Watt, when Tad ate up all of the strawberries being forced for a state dinner. Willie brought the news. His mother said, "Now what made you do that, Tad? Major Watt hoped to have them for the state dinner."

I went out to view the plants. Watt was fuming and threatening to go to Madam.

"The Madam knows it. Willie told her," I said. Then, as he still seemed to be in a great rage, I added, "Tad is Madam's son, remember."

"The Madam's wildcat," snarled the head gardener.

In the fall of 1861, Mrs. Lincoln had a desk and blackboard put into one end of the State Dining Room and secured a tutor. She asked my brothers to study with her boys. I, too, was in and out of the White House every day. President Lincoln always appeared to me well dressed, and he never seemed awkward to me. My father was inclined to be critical in matters of etiquette, but he said he never saw Mr. Lincoln embarrassed in greeting foreigners of distinction.

"The President seemed anxious to make everyone comfortable and at his ease," said my father, "which is the essence of good breeding."

The weather that December was quite cold. Willie and Tad had been talking of winters in Illinois, of skating and sledding and snowballing. My brothers listened with round eyes. They had never known the delights of a real snowstorm. They possessed no mittens, no sled, no skates.

"Snow! Snow!" shouted Tad one morning, as some light flakes flew by the window. "That's what I like better'n anything. I hope it'll be over the fences."

To Tad's disappointment, the snowflakes grew more and more infrequent, and at last the sun shone out.

About noon that same day my cousin, Sam Andrus, a soldier in the Union army, and his colonel arrived at our house unexpectedly. As they wished to see the boys, I was sent to bring them home. I went at once to the White House. As I ran up to the sitting room, I almost collided with the tall form of the President, who was crossing the room on the way to the office. He had some papers in one hand, and with the other he stopped my flight.

"Here, here, flibbertigibbet," he said, using the pet name he often called me. "Where are you going in such a hurry?"

"I am looking for the boys."

"Have you looked in the attic, Julie?"

"I am going there now," I said, and left him watching my headlong progress toward the attic with that quizzical smile I remember so well.

In the attic was a large bin of visiting cards, which apparently had been lately disturbed. There was a nest hollowed out in the center, and the cards were scattered all around the floor. But the boys were not there, so I went home and reported.

After dinner, as the men were enjoying their cigars on the veranda, the four boys appeared. They were dragging a remarkable object which consisted of an old chair on barrel staves and the cover of a *Congressional Record* nailed to the broken seat. This, they proudly informed us, was a snow sled. But they hung back and seemed uneasy as they were presented to the colonel. Tad and Holly continually rubbed against the veranda railing.

When questioned by Mother, Tad said, "I s'pose it's the snowballs we've got down our backs."

"Snowballs," said Mother in surprise. "Where did you find any snow?"

"Up in our attic," said Tad. "Handfuls and handfuls and bushels and bushels."

Naturally we looked amazed. "Why, Mama Taft," Willie explained, "Tad's snow is cards. There are bushels in our attic in a big bin, and we throw them up and play it's snowing. There are all the cards all the people have left since General Washington."

"General Washington never lived in your house," said Bud. "The tutor said he didn't."

"Well, there's enough to make a snowstorm without his," said Willie. "Tad and Holly stuffed them down each other's backs like real snow, but the sharp corners stick into us."

Declaring that they couldn't stand it another minute, Holly and Tad went upstairs. The next morning, when I went into the boys' room, I saw in the middle of the card-strewn floor the name of Jenny Lind, the great singer. I picked up this card, and then another and another, and here are the names on some of the "snowflakes" from Tad Lincoln's snowstorm.

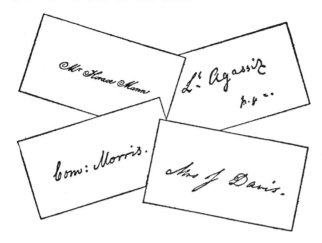

If there was any motto or slogan of the White House during the early years of the Lincolns' occupancy it was this: "Let the children have a good time." Often I have heard Mrs. Lincoln say this with a smile, as her two sons and my two brothers rushed through the room. And no less smiling and gracious was the tall, spare man who played with us and told us stories.

When the President came into the family sitting room and sat down to read, the boys would rush at him and demand a story. Tad perched precariously on the back of the big chair, Willie on one knee, Bud on the other, both leaning against him. Holly usually found a place on the arm of the chair, and often I would find myself swept into the group by the long arm which seemed to reach almost across the room.

I wish I could remember some of those stories. Usually they were melodramatic tales of hunters and settlers attacked by Indians. At the close of one favorite tale of frontiersmen chased by the Indians, the President would drawl impressively, "They galloped and they galloped, with the redskins close behind."

"But they got away, Pa, they got away," interrupted Tad.

"Oh, yes, they got away." Then, suddenly rising to his full height: "Now I must get away."

President Lincoln Reprieves a Turkey

NOAH BROOKS

After Willie Lincoln died, his younger brother, Tad, was the President's almost constant companion. Though often mischievous, Tad was also very tenderhearted. One day, when he saw a poorly dressed woman crying in the corridor, he bluntly asked her what was the matter. Her husband was in military prison, she explained, and she wanted to ask the President for help. Tad raced off to find his father and beg that the man be given a pardon, or reprieve. Some government officials complained that too many pardons were bad for military discipline, but if Abraham Lincoln could find an excuse for granting a pardon, he always did.

"Tad tells me I am doing right," he said, with his deep, sad smile, "and Tad's advice is usually pretty good."

The following account of some of Tad's adventures was given by Noah Brooks, a newspaper writer who knew the Lincoln family well.

A friend of the Lincoln family once sent a fine live turkey to the White House with the request that it should be served on the President's Christmas table. But Christmas was still several weeks off. In the meantime Tad won the confidence of the turkey, as he did the affection of every living thing with which he came in contact. Jack, as the fowl was called, was fed, petted, and taught to follow his young master.

One day, just before Christmas, 1863, while the President was meeting with his Cabinet, Tad burst into the room like a bombshell. He had just learned that the turkey was about to be killed, and he was crying with rage and indignation.

"But Jack was sent here to be eaten for this very Christmas," said the President.

"I can't help it," roared Tad between his sobs. "He's a good turkey, and I don't want him killed."

The President of the United States, pausing in the midst of important business, took a card and wrote on it an order of reprieve. The turkey's life was spared! Tad seized the precious bit of paper and fled to set his pet at liberty.

On another occasion Tad mounted guard at the foot of the public staircase and exacted toll of all who passed up. "Five cents for the benefit of the Sanitary Fund," he explained to the visitors.

He organized for himself, after the custom of the day, a Sanitary Fair (for the benefit of the soldiers). From a carpenter he secured a pair of trestles and a wide board, which he set up just within the portico of the White House. He had been saving his pocket money and bought out the entire stock of an old woman who sold apples, gingerbread, and candy near the Treasury building. Tad's enterprise was highly successful. But by evening both capital and profits had been spent, and the young speculator went penniless to bed.

Mr. Lincoln took great interest in everything that concerned his son. At night Tad would tell his father all that had taken place during the day. When he finally fell asleep, the weary President turned once more to his desk and worked far into the night. Then, shouldering the sleeping child, he made his way through silent corridors to Tad's bedroom.

One day Tad sauntered into the office of the Secretary of War, Edwin M. Stanton. Mr. Stanton, for the fun of the thing, commissioned him a lieutenant of the United States Volunteers. This elated the boy so much that he managed to get some muskets and began to drill the servants and gardeners. He also procured a suitable uniform and cut quite a military figure.

The President had intended to celebrate Tad's tenth birthday, April 4, 1863, with a visit to the Army of the Potomac, then encamped on the banks of the Rappahannock River, opposite Fredericksburg. Other business intervened, and it was not until after his birthday (and with it the present of a fine pony) that he got away from Washington. The party consisted of Tad, his father and mother, and several others. The soldiers soon learned of Tad's presence in the army, and wherever he went he divided honors with his father. To men far away from home and their own children, the sight of that fresh-faced laughing boy seemed an inspiration. They waved their hats and cheered like mad.

Later Tad figured in another historic scene. It was the night of April 11, 1863. The news of the fall of Petersburg and Richmond had reached Washington. There was great joy, for we felt that the war was nearly over. On that night the White House was illuminated, and a vast crowd stood outside, cheering and shouting with a roar like that of the sea. A small battery from the Navy Yard occasionally rent the air with a salute, and the clamor of brass bands added to the racket in front of the mansion.

Abraham Lincoln was to make a speech, and he and a few friends lingered at the dinner table until it was time to begin. As the little party mounted the stairs to the upper part of the house, roars of laughter could be heard, mingling with the music and the cheers. At one of the front windows the crowd saw Tad waving a Confederate flag, which had been captured in some battle and given to him. Old Edward, the dignified butler, was struggling with the boy, trying to drag him back from the window.

"The likes of it, Tad!" said the scandalized butler. "The likes of a Confederate flag in a window of the White House! Oh, did I ever!"

The crowd cheered again as Edward finally dragged the boy away.

Just then the President reached the center window that overlooked the portico. With a beaming face, he looked down on the vast assemblage. Another mighty cheer arose, and then the crowd fell silent.

He began with the words "We meet this evening not in sorrow but in gladness of heart." The candles had been placed too low to permit him to see, and a friend who stood behind the drapery of the window reached out and held a candle for him. His speech had been written on loose sheets of paper, and as the President finished with each page he let it fall to the floor. Presently Tad came back and amused himself by chasing the sheets of paper as they fluttered from his father's hand.

"Come, give me another!" he whispered.

The President made a queer motion with his foot toward Tad, but otherwise showed no sign that he had heard.

Below, in that vast sea of upturned faces, all eyes were on the President. Fireworks cast their glow on the tall white pillars of the portico. At the window stood the much-loved Lincoln reading the speech that was to be his last to the American people. Behind him, creeping back and forth on hands and knees, Tad was gathering up his father's carefully written pages.

It was well said of him that for several years he gave the White House the only comic relief it knew. His gaiety and affection illumined the darkest hours of the greatest American who ever lived.

St. Valentine's Day

(February 14)

Some of the practices connected with this popular holiday go back to ancient Rome, when the Lupercalia, a festival dedicated to lovers, was celebrated on February 15. One custom was for the girls attending the festivities to place their names in a box. Each youth then put in his hand, and the name he drew was that of his partner for the coming year. With the coming of Christianity both the name and the date of the festival were changed.

One version of how that came about you may read in the story called "St. Valentine." Other versions tell of three Christian martyrs by the same name who had been put to death because they refused to give up their religion. One of the martyrs left a note to a little girl who had been kind to him during his last days, signing it "From your Valentine." Because he died on February 14, and because he was greatly loved, that date may have been chosen as an appropriate time for sending messages and tokens of affection to our friends.

Several picturesque Roman symbols have survived. One picture that appears on many modern valentines is that of Cupid, the mischievous little Roman god of love. He carries a bow and a quiver of arrows, and any couple feeling the pleasant sting of those arrows is supposed to fall in love. The roses and birds often pictured are a carry-over from other beliefs of long ago. The rose was the Roman symbol of love, and there was an old tradition that wild birds chose their mates on February 14.

All of this makes the holiday more fun, yet it might never have survived had it not been for good Saint Valentine who loved his fellowmen.

Saint Valentine

ANONYMOUS

Once upon a time there lived in a monastery across the sea a humble monk called Valentine. All the other brothers in the monastery seemed to have some special gift.

There was Brother Angelo, who was an artist. He painted such beautiful pictures of the Madonna that it seemed as if she might step down from the frame and bless her children.

Brother Vittorio had a wonderful voice. On saints' days the chapel of the monastery would be crowded with visitors who came from far and near to listen to his beautiful singing.

Brother Anselmo was a doctor. He knew what herbs and roots and drugs would heal the sick. He was busy going about among them, and they followed him with grateful blessings.

Brother Johannes made the most glorious letters on the manuscripts he copied. Brother Valentine used to watch the pages as Brother Johannes wrote the words of some gospel story in a fine hand. Sometimes he would work for days making a big initial letter in bright colors.

Brother Paul was a great teacher in the monastery school. Learned men came from far away to talk with him.

Father John was the wise head of the monastery and had a gift for managing it well.

Indeed, only Valentine seemed not to have any special talent. He felt this keenly. He longed to do some great thing. He had a little garden plot where he loved to work. He used to gather bunches of flowers and drop them down to the children as they trotted to school under the gray walls of the monastery. Many a happy bride in the village wore Brother Valentine's flowers at her wedding. And his lilies and violets were on many a grave in the quiet cemetery.

Somehow he found out the birthday of every child in the village. He liked to hang on the door of the birthday child some little gift he had made himself, and then he would steal away before anyone saw him.

40

Everybody grew to love the good Brother Valentine. So he grew old, loving and beloved. But he did not dream that he, too, had a very special and great talent. When he died, the whole countryside was sad, and hundreds came to his funeral.

After Valentine's death, people said, "Let us, too, give gifts to our friends on good Brother Valentine's birthday." So now on Saint Valentine's Day we send our friends little tokens of remembrance to say we love them.

The Valentine Box

MAUD HART LOVELACE

As Janice walked home to lunch on Valentine's Day, she did not feel happy. It was snowing hard, and once it occurred to her that perhaps her mother would not let her go back to school in the afternoon. Then Janice remembered that her mother would let her go if it were possible at all, because of the valentine box. And that's the very reason I don't want to go, because of the valentine box, Janice thought.

It was very mixed up. What made it harder was that she did not want her mother to know how queer she was feeling inside.

The box itself was beautiful. The fifth-grade children had made it, covering a pasteboard hatbox with red tissue paper, decorating it with white hearts, and cutting a slit in the top through which they would drop valentines that afternoon. The valentine box sat on the teacher's desk looking gay and important, and most of the children could hardly wait for the party. But Janice didn't have a single "party" feeling.

The trouble was that Janice was afraid she wouldn't get any valentines. She was new in the town of Oak Grove. She was going to a new school, and she didn't have any friends.

Back in Chickasaw City she had had plenty of friends, and one very special friend named Mary Lou. Janice and Mary Lou had always walked to school together, and after school they had gone skating, or had played games, or had cut out paper dolls, depending on the weather. Mary Lou was still her friend, of course, and they wrote letters to each other, but Janice needed a friend here in Oak Grove.

There was a girl in her grade she would like to have for a friend. Margaret was her name. Margaret was a large, rosy, smiling girl with a mop of curly brown hair. She looked full of fun and she lived conveniently near to Janice, just in the next block. But Margaret had lived in Oak Grove all her life; she had plenty of friends, so she had hardly noticed Janice, who was small for her age, and dark, and quiet. Janice wasn't quiet after she got acquainted with people. She was as full of fun as anybody. But she didn't get acquainted easily.

I don't believe I'll have a single valentine in that box, she thought now, and hurried through the thickening snow.

In the doorway at home she took off her high boots and carried them into the house. A great gust of snow blew in with her.

"Mercy, what a day!" her mother said, brushing the wet flakes from Janice's snow suit. "If it wasn't Valentine's Day, I wouldn't let you go back this afternoon. And speaking of valentines, see what came in the morning mail!" She held up a big square envelope addressed to Janice.

"It's from Mary Lou!" cried Janice, and after examining the envelope from all sides, she carefully opened it. It was a beautiful valentine, trimmed with paper lace. Inside, Mary Lou had written, "You are my valentine." Janice liked the message even better than the paper lace. She read it over two or three times.

"It's very pretty," said Mother. "And you may get more in the valentine box at school." Then Mother grew serious. "I wouldn't expect many, though, if I were you, Janice. You must remember that you're new in this school."

"Of course," said Janice. "We're going to have refreshments at the party. That's the important thing."

But it wasn't, really. The important thing was getting some valentines from friends who really liked you.

Janice ate her hot soup and sandwiches and an apple, and drank her cocoa. Then she climbed into the snow suit again.

"It's snowing so hard," her mother said, "that I'm going to lend you this old purse to carry your valentines in." She meant the valentines Janice was taking to school to put in the box for other children. Janice and her mother had made them together. They had had fun cutting and pasting and coloring, almost as much fun as Janice and Mary Lou had had making them in other years. Janice was giving one to her teacher and one to Margaret, one to a boy named Bob who had loaned her his eraser twice, and several others to children whom she hardly knew.

"I think I'll take Mary Lou's valentine to school with me," she said suddenly.

"That's a good idea," answered her mother. "You can show it to your teacher."

So Janice put the beautiful valentine into her purse. Then she kissed her mother good-bye and started back to school feeling happier. But the happy feeling did not last.

Across the street three other children were going to school together. They were pushing one another into the drifts, shouting, "Giving me a valentine?"

"Like fun I am!"

That was the way she and Mary Lou used to joke on the way to school on Valentine's Day.

Janice walked primly along on her side of the street with her mother's purse under her arm.

The weather was even wilder than it had been before. The wind was blowing the snow in dizzy circles, whipping the shrubs to and fro, tossing the branches of trees. The snow was beating into Janice's face, and once when she wiped it away she wiped two big tears along with it.

But there wasn't really any chance to cry. She was too busy keeping her feet on the ground and the purse tucked under her arm. The wind was growing stronger all the time, and as Janice reached the corner opposite the school, one terrific gust almost sent her into a snowdrift.

"Oh! Oh!" she heard someone cry behind her.

Turning around, Janice saw Margaret with what seemed at first to be a flock of birds swirling about her head. They were envelopes which the wind had snatched from her hand.

"My valentines!" cried Margaret. "Oh, dear! I've lost them."

"I'll help you pick them up," Janice shouted.

"We can never find them," Margaret shouted back.

"Yes, we can," cried Janice. "Look, here's one, and here's another!" And plowing into a drifted lawn, Janice rescued two valentines, Margaret rescued a third, and Janice a fourth. It was like a game, and they began to whoop with joy.

The wind entered into the fun. It blew one valentine into a pine tree far over their heads.

"I'll get it," shrieked Janice. "I'm good at climbing trees."

"But pines scratch you."

"I'm Wonderwoman," Janice yelled, and dashing in among the needles, flashed up the tree and down.

Margaret chased another envelope down someone's cellar window.

"I'm Wonderwoman, too," she yelled.

They had a glorious time.

"There's one more," cried Margaret. The wind had veered suddenly, and this one was blowing in the opposite direction from the school. The envelope skipped over the drifts like a naughty child turning its back on the school. Margaret and Janice tumbled after the truant. The wind kept the envelope always ahead of them. Sometimes it would rest for a moment on a drift, but just as they caught up with it, the envelope would flutter away. Back at the school, a bell rang.

"Janice," cried Margaret. "Go back to school! You'll be late."

"No later than you'll be," Janice called. "I'm going to catch that valentine if it's the last thing I do."

The valentine blew on, getting farther and farther from school.

On the lawn before one of the houses some boys had made a snow man. He was a big, wonderful snow man, with a pipe stuck into his mouth. Now the wind blew the valentine envelope smack into the snow man. It stuck to his round head, like a jaunty cap. Janice and Margaret stopped to scream with laughter.

Then Margaret grabbed the envelope and took Janice's hand, and they raced for the school.

The hall was warm and unnaturally quiet. From the closed doors of the rooms on either side came a drone of voices. Margaret and Janice brushed the snow from each other, giggling.

"Your feet are sopping," Janice whispered. "How did you get so wet?"

"The snow went down inside my galoshes," whispered Margaret. "Do you think we're very late? Miss Merrill will be furious."

"Ready to snap our heads off," Janice answered.

They both knew that Miss Merrill probably wouldn't be cross at all, but it was exciting to talk that way.

"Did I get all the valentines? Let's count them," Margaret said.

Taking off her wet mittens, she laid the damp envelopes in a row on the hall radiator. Together she and Janice counted them off: One for Miss Merrill, one for Bob, others for John, Susan, Peter, Tom.

There wasn't one for Janice. Janice and Margaret both noticed that at the same moment.

"It's too bad they're wet," Janice said hastily. "Mamma gave me a purse to carry mine—" She broke off in a gasp. "Where is it?"

"What?"

"My purse. I must have dropped it while I was chasing the valentines."

They stared at each other in complete dismay.

"Don't you worry," Margaret said. "We'll go right back and find it."

"No," said Janice. "Anyway, not now. We'd better go and tell Miss Merrill first. We're late enough already."

They hurried off to the fifth-grade room, and Miss Merrill was very sympathetic after Margaret explained what had happened. "Did you have anything of value in the purse, Janice?" she asked.

"My valentines for the valentine box," said Janice. "And one other. It came from Mary Lou, my best friend back in Chickasaw City."

Miss Merrill looked thoughtful. She put her hands on the shoulders of Janice's snow suit, and looked down at the stout rubber boots. "You're perfectly snug," said Miss Merrill. "And there's time enough for you to run back and take a look."

"May I go along to help hunt?" Margaret asked. "It was on account of me that Janice lost the purse, you know."

Miss Merrill put her hands on Margaret's shoulders, and looked down at the galoshes which were oozing snow.

"No," she said. "Because you are wet. But Bob may go to help Janice if he wants to."

"Sure," said Bob.

Bob put on his boots and his warm jacket and cap, and he and Janice went out into the snow. At first Janice felt shy, but as they went up the street, she told him how she and Margaret had chased the valentines, and Bob laughed. They reached the snow man who had worn the valentine hat. And there, at the snow man's feet, Janice found her mother's purse. The snow had not yet covered the purse; it wasn't hurt at all; and the valentines inside were perfectly dry.

"This is the valentine from my friend Mary Lou in Chickasaw City," Janice said, showing it to Bob.

"Gee, that's neat!" Bob said. "Chickasaw City is a swell town, I'll bet. But you'll like Oak Grove, too, after you live here awhile."

Janice began to think that she would.

She was sure of it after they had gone back to the schoolroom and taken off their wraps and put her valentines into the box. For then Miss Merrill asked her to be postman. Janice went up to the front of the room and lifted the cover from the valentine box. Then she took out the envelopes, one by one, and called the names:

"Margaret. Joan. Bobby. Peter. Susan. Miss Merrill."

Three times there were valentines for Janice. She put them on her desk. And after the fun of being postman came the fun of opening them. One was a pink satin heart; it came from Miss Merrill. The second was a picture of a boy on a bike with his basket full of hearts. Janice thought that this valentine might be from Bob.

She hesitated a moment before opening the third one. It was big, and the envelope was made from drawing paper.

Janice opened it and then stared in surprise. The class, she realized, was looking at her. Especially Margaret was looking. In a moment Janice knew the reason why.

The valentine was the picture of a snow man, drawn with black crayon. He was smoking a pipe, and on his head he wore a square envelope cap. There were funny crayon pictures of two girls in snow suits, dancing wildly in the snow. And at the bottom of the page Janice found this message: "For my snowstorm valentine."

"It's from me," Margaret whispered. "I made it while you were out looking for the purse. Isn't it killing?"

"It's wonderful," Janice said.

Smiling, she folded it and placed it in her purse next to the valentine Mary Lou had sent her.

After the valentine box the fifth graders played games. And after the games they had refreshments. They had cookies and little candy hearts. Janice saved some to take home to her mother.

It was a lovely party, but not so nice as what came after. She and Margaret walked home together. It had stopped snowing, the wind had died down, and the afternoon sun sparkled on the drifts. "Can't you come over to my house," Margaret asked, "and play awhile? Maybe we could make a snow man like the one we saw today."

"I'll ask my mother," Janice said. "I think I can."

So they stopped in at Janice's house, and Janice said, "Mother, this is Margaret, my snowstorm valentine."

She and Margaret began to laugh, and Janice's mother laughed, too, as the girls told how they had chased valentines in the snow.

And after that, the two new friends went out to play together.

George Washington's

Birthday (February 22)

George Washington was the first man not a king whose birthday was publicly observed in America during his lifetime. Before the Revolution it was the custom to celebrate the King's birthday, but after the colonists declared their independence of England they had no use for kings. They began to celebrate General Washington's birthday instead. The first time was at Valley Forge, when one of the artillery bands marched to his headquarters and serenaded him.

As the Commander-in-Chief, George Washington somehow managed to hold his ragged and poorly paid army together, and after eight years won America's independence. Later, he was chairman of the Constitutional Convention that worked out plans for a stable government, and as President for two terms he started the new country on its way to becoming a great nation.

The final months of his life were spent on his own plantation. He liked being plain Farmer Washington again, and he loved Mount Vernon better than any spot on earth; but he also owned many acres in the wilderness west of the mountains, and he had great faith in the West. He felt confident that the thirteen states along the Atlantic coast were only a beginning—that the United States was to grow into a much bigger country than most Americans then dreamed.

Washington's last birthday was probably his happiest. On that day in 1799, his adopted daughter, Nelly Custis, was married to his favorite nephew, Lawrence Lewis, and George Washington gave the bride away at a ceremony at Mount Vernon.

Since Washington's death, many legends have grown up around his name. The best-known one is about the time he cut down his father's favorite cherry tree with a new hatchet, and then risked punishment by admitting what he had done, because he was a boy who could not tell a lie. It is an entertaining story even if it isn't true, and it reminds us that the Father of His Country was an honest man. Besides, hatchets and cherries make interesting decorations, and no Washington's birthday party seems complete without them.

On a Bleak Hill

BETTY CAVANNA

With silent monotony the snow had been falling all day. Now, as the grayness of the afternoon and the deeper grayness of the dusk were changing to black, the little campfires on the hillsides winked like lanterns and the thin columns of smoke merged with the night.

To the man who stood with hands clenched behind his back in the doorway of his headquarters, there was no cheer in the lights of the hundred campfires. His eyes were both bitter and sad, and his mouth formed soundless words. "Sickness, madness, starvation, desertion. What else can they expect?" The knuckles of his hands were white, and he closed his eyes to shut out the mockery of the fires.

"General Washington!"

The man's eyes jerked open. The officer who stood before the general had come to inquire about his supper.

Washington waved him off, frowning. Somehow, the thought of food was abhorrent, with his men half starving, huddled around those futile fires. "Later," he said. "I have a letter I want to write."

When the officer had gone, Washington moved over to the desk and sat down. Slowly, still frowning, he drew a clean sheet of paper, with the official letterhead, toward him. He picked up his pen at once, but it was more than an hour before he began to write:

"Valley Forge. December 23, 1777 . . ."

Two days before Christmas! That was all Tom Porter could think about. At home, in Camden, Mom and the kids would be chopping mincemeat, bringing in greens. There might be no traditional fowl this year, but it would be Christmas, nevertheless.

He moved his stiff shoulders inside his torn uniform coat experimentally. Then he worked his fingers, first one hand, then the other. He hitched up closer to the smoking fire, and wondered how long it takes a man to freeze.

Nobody was talking much tonight. They hadn't talked much

50

for a couple of days now. Even the chronic grumblers were too exhausted and miserable to complain.

Tom's eyes, red with fatigue, roved around the circle of faces lighted by the fire. Together, almost opposite, were the Brintain brothers—great hulking brutes of men they had been, before Brandywine; now they looked pinched and pale, in spite of their untrimmed beards. Next to them were two boys from New England, slight lads, both of them gentlemen. They stared into the fire with eyes that saw too much. They couldn't sleep sitting up, the way the Brintains could. Off to one side was old Jim Brown. He was muttering to himself and counting on his fingers, sitting back a bit from the fire, apparently oblivious to the cold. Jim had been with Washington in the French and Indian War, a seasoned campaigner even then. But something had happened to Jim this last week. Every once in a while he'd give a convulsive jerk and throw back his head and croak "Hallelujah!" He did it as Tom watched him, and grinned foolishly.

"Tom! Is he crazy?" The hoarse whisper came from the lad at Tom's left.

Tom shrugged. "Maybe. He wouldn't be the first man to go mad from cold." He turned his head slowly and peered at the boy who had asked the question.

Jeffrey Allen was looking at old Jim, and there was fright in his eyes. Jeffrey was pathetically young—not even eighteen, Tom guessed. Must have faked his age when he joined up. Full of fire and enthusiasm, he had been, before Brandywine, but untrained, like most of the Colonial forces. Perfect target for the enemy! Wonder he was alive today!

At that, Tom reasoned, Jeffrey was only half alive. Thin to the point of emaciation, racked by a hacking cough night and day, the boy was scarcely able to struggle from the fire's side to the nearby grove of trees for his quota of wood. But he never complained. He was a brave little kid. Reminded Tom of his own eldest son.

"Look," said Tom gruffly, after a minute. "Move over and put your head on my knees for a while, if you like. Maybe you can catch a little sleep."

The boy moved over gratefully, curling up against Tom's legs like a forlorn puppy. Tom's chest felt tight. He couldn't look at the youngster. He stared over the boy's head into the fire.

One of the New Englanders got up stiffly and tossed on some more wood, but the cold seemed to creep closer around the huddled men, until Tom believed that even in the middle of the blaze the cold would find him—and freeze him.

He tried not to think about the cold. He tried to think about Mom and the kids, and the fun they must be having, getting ready for Christmas. That was the good thing about kids. They had fun, war or no war, at Christmas. He was glad the kids couldn't know what it was like at Valley Forge. He supposed they thought, still, that General Washington was a great commander. They didn't know he'd betrayed and forsaken his men. He supposed they thought, still, that the Colonial Army was intact and comfortable in their winter quarters located just outside Philadelphia.

Old Jim, opposite, struggled to his feet and staggered off toward the woods, mumbling to himself. Tom made a move to follow him, but the boy's head against his knees was heavy, and he knew Jeffrey was asleep.

"Somebody better go get the old man," he muttered, looking at the Brintain brothers. "He's likely to freeze to death in the woods."

One of the New England boys got up and led Jim back to the fire. Jim alone among them didn't seem to feel the cold. He *is* crazy, Tom Porter thought.

Jeffrey Allen coughed and shuddered in his sleep, and Tom tried to move so that his back would shelter the boy still more from the biting wind. If he only had a blanket! Just one woolen blanket—it didn't seem so much to ask! Surely the civilians, if they knew, would be ready and anxious to spare the soldiers what they could. What was the matter with General Washington? Why didn't he plead for his men?

Tom remembered Washington's face as he had tramped over the hills that morning, inspecting the troops. He had detected, he thought, some pity in it; but if the General felt pity why didn't he act? Could a man who knew pity let his soldiers die like dogs in the snow?

A figure loomed in the darkness beyond the circle of light cast by the fire. "Is Tom Porter here?"

"Here." Tom looked up.

"Report to headquarters at once," came the order.

Reluctantly, Tom awoke the sleeping boy. Jeffrey sighed and sat up, edging still nearer to the fire. Tom arose stiffly and walked away, toward the lighted window of the house occupied by his commander.

The General was alone, sitting at his desk before a bowl of steaming soup and a section of brown bread. The room, warmed by a fire laid on the brick hearth, seemed like heaven next to the biting cold of the night without. The clock on the wall said 9:35. Tom found himself looking at it in surprise. It seemed three times that long since darkness had settled over the hills.

The General had looked up from his food when the man entered. Belatedly, Tom saluted. "You asked for me, sir?"

Washington picked up a square white envelope from the desk and slipped it into a larger brown one before he spoke. Tom noticed the official seal.

"This is to go to the Continental Congress. I've ordered a horse for you. You may start at dawn."

Tom stretched out his hand and walked forward a few paces to take the letter. Then suddenly the aroma of the hot soup seemed to fill his nostrils, and his mouth began to water like a hungry cur's. Something snapped inside Tom's head. As he looked at the General, sitting in such apparent comfort in his chair, his face hardened and hate crept into his smoke-reddened eyes.

"You!" he screamed, dropping the hand that would have taken the letter and pounding with his two fists on the General's desk. "How can you sit here snug and warm while your men starve and freeze? How can you sit here?" Then, as quickly as it had begun, the spasm passed, and Tom was a soldier again, a sane man, appalled by what he had done. "I—excuse me, sir," he stuttered, and his eyes dropped before the General's.

For a long minute Washington said nothing. He sat looking at this man whom he thought he knew, who had served as his messenger many times before. There was no resentment in his look, only distress. If this soldier, whom he had considered loyal beyond question, could thus lose his head, what must the others feel?

Slowly, he pushed the bowl of soup across the desk toward Tom. "Drink this," he said.

Tom shook his head. He couldn't trust himself to speak. The

General's reaction surprised him. He had expected the natural reprimand.

Then, more strangely still, Washington picked up the brown envelope, extracted the white one, and broke the official seal. As he unfolded the sheets within he spoke.

"Tom," he said quietly, "sometimes what seems like well-justified criticism is really calumny. Sometimes it is not within a leader's power to speak plainly to his men." He paused, and looked down at the handwriting on the paper, which was his own. Then he looked up at the ragged soldier standing awkwardly before him. "I need loyalty, Tom," he said. "I need it now, more than ever, from you and men like you. That is why I am going to ask you to read this letter."

Tom took the letter in fingers that still trembled with cold. He had read several paragraphs before the words began to make sense to him, before he realized that General Washington was answering his critics in Congress and defending his naked and starving troops.

"It is a much easier and less distressing thing," he read, "to draw remonstrances in a comfortable room by a good fireside, than to occupy a cold, bleak hill, and sleep under frost and snow, without clothes or blankets. However, although they [these gentlemen] seem to have little feeling for the naked and distressed soldiers . . . from my soul, I pity those miseries, which it is neither in my power to relieve or prevent. . . . It adds not a little to my other difficulties to find that much more is expected of me than is possible to be performed, and that upon the ground of safety and policy I am obliged to conceal the true state of the army from public view. . . ."

Tom was a simple soldier, not an educated man. He read slowly, and then went back and reread the very last part, pondering the words "upon the ground of safety and policy I am obliged to conceal the true state of the army from public view."

"I don't understand," he said bluntly. As he looked up, his eyes, meeting the General's, were only puzzled, no longer filled with hate.

"What is it you don't understand, Tom?"

The soldier read the words, carefully.

General Washington sighed before he answered. "If they

suspected our sufferings—if they so much as guessed the condition of the troops—ill-fed, unhoused, ragged—the British would be upon us in no time!" He got up and strode the length of the room, talking as he walked. "Sometimes a man in a position of leadership must take criticism because in defending himself he would be jeopardizing the safety of others. That's my position now!"

Tom's face cleared, and he nodded. "I never thought of that," he said slowly. "I understand when you say it. To make public our needs would be too great a risk to take."

Tom held out the letter, and the General refolded it. Then, unexpectedly, his thin lips curved in a smile. "Now, will you share my soup?" he asked.

The soldier flushed, and jerked his head toward the door. "If you don't mind, sir," he said, "could I go and get a boy out there who needs it more than I?"

He Believed in the West

JEAN FRITZ

> Ten-year-old Ann Hamilton, her brothers, Daniel and David, and their parents were real people who had started a farm in the wild Western country beyond the mountains. Ann had been warned not to wander too far away from their crude log cabin on Hamilton Hill because of a gang of horse thieves believed to be in the neighborhood. Though often homesick for her old home in Pennsylvania, Ann found pleasure in listening to the stories of a neighbor, Arthur Scott, who had been at Valley Forge and had known George Washington.
>
> "Whenever our courage began to peter out," said

Arthur, "General Washington always seemed to know. I never could figure out how just looking at a man made a person feel bigger and stronger, but that's the way it was."

How wonderful it would have been to have served at Valley Forge, thought Ann—much more interesting than doing chores in this wild Western country! One day when she was gathering grapes, she wandered down the road farther than she intended—farther than she had ever gone alone.

Just then Ann heard hoofbeats. They were coming from the east—not just one horse but three or four, and they were not far away.

Ann ducked down behind some tall grass by the side of the road and made herself into the smallest ball she could possibly squeeze into, wrapping her arms tightly around her knees. She held her breath as the first horse rounded the bend of the road. She must not move—not even a finger. She kept her eyes on the road . . . If four men were traveling together from the East to the West at this time of year, they were probably not settlers. They were likely up to no good. They must be the Doane gang that David had warned her about.

All at once Ann began to tremble all over. The first horse had stopped on the road in front of her. Then the other horses came to a stop. As Ann peeped out between the tall grasses, all she could see was a forest of horse legs. From some place way up high above the legs of the first horse came a deep voice. "Little girl," it said, "I wonder if you could tell me what your mother is having for dinner tonight."

The voice didn't sound like the voice of a horse thief. Slowly Ann lifted her eyes from the legs of the horse to the boots of the rider. Slowly she lifted them to the place where the voice had come from. Then she found herself looking into the most wonderful face she had ever seen.

It was a strong face, kind and good, and there was something strangely familiar about it. It was as if Ann ought to know this man, as if she almost knew him. No matter what David had said about strangers, somehow Ann knew deep inside that he hadn't been talking about this one. She stopped feeling afraid. She stood up.

"My mother is having peas and potatoes and corn bread for our evening meal," she said, "and she's baking pumpkin pie."

The man smiled. He leaned down toward Ann. "Would you tell her," he said, "that General George Washington would like to take supper with her?"

For a moment Ann could not believe her ears. General Washington on Hamilton Hill! Then all at once she knew it was true. This was the way she had pictured George Washington from what Arthur Scott had said about him. This must have been just how Washington looked, riding among the men at Valley Forge. Suddenly Arthur Scott's words flashed into her mind. "He always seemed to be there just when our courage began to peter out."

Ann swallowed hard. She tried to drop a curtsy, but it turned out to be just a stiff little bob. She tried to find her voice, but it didn't turn out any better than the curtsy. It was more like a squeak. "My mother will be pleased," she said. "I'll tell her."

Then Ann found herself and her pail of grapes up on the saddle in front of one of the men in General Washington's party. He said he was Dr. Craik, a friend of the General's, but Ann didn't pay much attention. She didn't even look at the other men. All she could see was the white horse in front of her and the straight back of General Washington going up Hamilton Hill. The road itself seemed almost to be moving them up the hill in a kind of magic dream. Except it wasn't a dream, Ann reminded herself. It was true—gloriously, wonderfully true. For some unbelievable reason, General George Washington was on the western side of the mountains and he was going to have supper on Hamilton Hill.

Suddenly Ann turned to Dr. Craik. "Why did General Washington come here?" she asked.

"He owns land in this county," Dr. Craik replied. "He's come to check on it."

"He owns land *here*—in Washington County?" Ann repeated.

Dr. Craik smiled. "Yes, he can't move here, but he bought land because he believes in this part of the country. Some day this land will be worth a great deal of money. He wants to do all he can to develop this side of the mountains."

Ann fell silent, her eyes on General Washington. Again she pictured him at Valley Forge. A lot of people hadn't believed in a free and independent country, she thought. But Washington had.

And now he believed in the Western Country. It wasn't just fathers and brothers and settlers who believed in it and owned land here. *George Washington did too.*

Ann and Dr. Craik jogged up the hill. The other men called back and forth to each other, but Ann didn't hear them.

Afterward Ann could never remember just how she introduced General Washington and his friends to her mother. When she caught her breath again, they had started on a tour of the farm with David. Ann and her mother were alone in the cabin with supper to prepare.

Mrs. Hamilton's eyes were shining as she stepped away from the door. "Now is the time to use the linen tablecloth, Ann," she said, "and the lavender flowered plates."

Ann was standing in the doorway, her head in the clouds, watching the men put up their horses. At her mother's words, she came quickly down to the world. What a wonderful world it was, she thought, as she flew over to her mother's chest for the linen tablecloth.

"The food is almost ready," Mrs. Hamilton said. "I'll take care of that while you set the table."

Ann spread out the white linen cloth on the table. She smoothed it gently over the rough boards. She pulled it to hang even on all sides. She unwrapped nine flowered plates and placed them around the table. She put knives, forks, and spoons at each place and set new tall candles in the center of the table.

Then Ann stepped back to look at what she had done. Somehow the whole room seemed changed; it seemed larger and more dignified. The clothes hanging awkwardly on hooks along the wall drew back into the shadows. All the light from the fire and from the open doorway fell on the gleaming white party table waiting for General Washington.

"It's more beautiful than any table we ever set in Gettysburg," Ann whispered.

Mrs. Hamilton looked up from the hearth and smiled.

Later the table looked even more wonderful, piled high with steaming food—hot yellow corn bread, round bowls of green peas, roasted brown potatoes, a platter of cold venison, bowls of purple grape jelly, golden pumpkin pies. It was the same meal that they had had nearly every evening all summer on Hamilton Hill, but tonight with the lavender flowered plates, it managed to look different.

"I hope I look different too," Ann thought as she fingered her two blue hair ribbons and hastily tied the sash of a fresh apron.

She felt different. General Washington and Mr. Hamilton led the others into the cabin, and suddenly Ann found herself feeling strangely shy. All the time they were taking their places at the table, she kept her eyes down. It was not until her father was asking the blessing that she stole her first look up from under half-closed eyelashes. When she saw George Washington's head bowed over the white tablecloth and lavender plate, the peas and potatoes, Ann thought she could hardly bear her happiness.

During the rest of the meal, Ann followed the conversation in a kind of daze. She didn't seem to hear anything that anyone said, except General Washington. Everything he said rang out clear, with a special meaning, it almost seemed, just for her.

"If I were a young man," General Washington said, "preparing to begin the world, I know of no country where I should rather live."

"I am determined to find a way," he said again, "that we can join the waters of the West with those of the East so that the two countries may be close together."

Ann held onto every word, turned them over in her mind, locked them away in her heart. It was after the evening meal, after all the thank-you's had been said and General Washington and his party were preparing to leave that he said what Ann was to treasure forever afterward. He stood at the doorway, looking toward the west, his eyes resting on Hamilton Hill, yet somehow going beyond.

"The future is traveling west with people like you," he said to Mr. Hamilton. "Here is the rising world, to be kept or lost in the same way a battlefield is kept or lost"—General Washington turned to Ann and put his hand gently on her shoulder—"through the courage of young girls as much as anyone's. You will live to see this whole country a rolling farmland, bright with houses and barns and churches, some day. I envy you, Miss Hamilton."

Ann felt her heart turning over within her. Even after General

Washington had gone, she went on standing in the doorway, still feeling his hand on her shoulder. She looked out on Hamilton Hill. It seemed to her she had never seen it so beautiful.

That night in the home of a Colonel Cannon several miles west of Hamilton Hill, before he blew out his candle, General George Washington sat down at a table and wrote this in his diary:

"September 18, 1784. Set out with Doctr. Craik for my Land on Miller's Run, crossed the Monongahela at Devore's Ferry . . . bated at one Hamilton's about 4 miles from it, in Washington County, and lodged at Colo. Cannon's."

That night in the cabin on Hamilton Hill, Ann took down from her shelf her deerskin-covered diary. Her heart was too full to write all she wanted. Instead she wrote in big letters across a whole page:

"September 18, 1784.
GEORGE WASHINGTON WAS HERE."

(The above selection is taken from *The Cabin Faced West*. For another story about George Washington, turn to the Hanukkah section of this book.)

Saint Patrick's Day

(March 17)

When the Irish came to America they brought their celebration of Saint Patrick's Day with them. It is believed that a third of the men in George Washington's army had been born in Ireland, and he thought highly of his Irish soldiers. He encouraged them to celebrate Saint Patrick's Day in 1775, while the Continental Army was stationed outside of Boston. During preparations for one battle, the secret password was "Saint Patrick."

March 17 is the anniversary of the death of Ireland's patron saint. He was born, not in Ireland but in what is now England, more than sixteen hundred years ago. When he was sixteen he was captured by pirates, taken to Ireland, and sold as a slave. He soon learned to love the Irish, and he longed to convert them to Christianity.

After six years of tending sheep in the countryside, he managed to escape on a boat sailing for France. Here he became a monk and finally a bishop. The Pope gave him the Latin name of Patrinius, which was shortened to Patrick when later he returned to Ireland as a missionary.

For the rest of his life he worked among the people and founded more than three hundred churches, and many legends grew up around his name. One story told how the shamrock, the little green plant with three clover-like leaves, happened to become the national flower of Ireland. Once, while the good bishop was preaching, he held up a shamrock by the stem to illustrate what was meant by the Gospel of the Trinity. One of the leaves represented the Father, one the Son, and one the Holy Spirit, he said—all three growing from the same stem. This was an explanation the people could understand.

Green is considered Ireland's

special color, not only because the shamrock is green but because Ireland itself is such a green, lush country. Now Irish throughout the world—and many non-Irish, too—like to wear a shamrock or some other "bit o' green" on the day set aside to honor the beloved saint.

The following story is based on the popular old belief that St. Patrick drove all of the poisonous snakes into the sea.

Saint Patrick and the Last Snake

LAVINIA R. DAVIS

Saint Patrick sat down under the shade of an old apple tree. It was a warm day and he was feeling hot and tired. Getting rid of all the snakes in Ireland was not so easy as some people supposed, and Saint Patrick needed a rest.

Some of the snakes he had driven into the sea, some he had driven into the rocks, and some he had magicked away entirely. It was easy enough when the snakes wanted to be driven into the sea or wanted to be driven into the rocks. But sometimes they didn't. Then Saint Patrick had to beg and scold until they minded, and that was what made him hot and tired.

He sat down under the apple tree, and pretty soon he lay back in the soft grass that is so green it makes people call Ireland the "Emerald Isle." The grass was cool, and for a few moments Saint Patrick was at peace. For a few moments, but not for long. Soon a small black spider ran out of the grass and up Saint Patrick's neck. It tickled him.

Saint Patrick slapped off the spider and settled back to his rest. He shut his eyes and thought how peaceful Ireland would be now without the snakes. Just then there was a buzzing in Saint Patrick's ear. It wasn't a loud buzzing, but neither was it a peaceful buzzing, and Saint Patrick sat up again and slapped. It was a mosquito, and Saint Patrick didn't like mosquitoes a bit.

When he was rid of the mosquito, Saint Patrick lay down again, but he had hardly stretched himself out before he felt another thing crawling up the side of his face. This time it was a shiny biting bug and Saint Patrick shook it off very quickly.

"Begone!" he said. "And have done with you. Can't a man have his rest?"

But it seemed a man couldn't, for soon there was the same black bug or another one like it climbing up the back of Saint Patrick's head. This time Saint Patrick sat up very straight and he was as cross as a saint can well be.

64

"Will you be gone," he said, "or shall I never be rid of you? Surely if I free Ireland of snakes, there should be someone to rid me, once and for all, of these bothersome, biting creatures."

And with that Saint Patrick settled back for the third and last time. This time he really went to sleep and not one creeping creature bothered him.

He slept and he slept and at last, when he woke up, he felt better. Now Saint Patrick was rested and cool and ready to go about his business. He sat up and stretched, and stood up and stretched, and he was just starting out on his way when he looked down and saw something that stopped him. There at his feet was the smallest, brownest snake in all Ireland.

"Well," said Saint Patrick, and now he was so well rested that he couldn't be cross. "It's yourself has the nerve. Haven't you heard I'm sending all the snakes out of Ireland?"

The small brown snake said nothing, nor did it look the saint in the face. Instead, it wriggled quickly forward. Saint Patrick looked to see where it was wriggling and there, right in front of the snake on the open part of Saint Patrick's sandal, was another small black spider. The Saint stared and the snake wriggled. The next instant its small sharp tongue darted out and the spider was gone! It was gone without a shadow of a doubt, for the snake had eaten it.

As the snake glided off to a small sunny patch in the grass, Saint Patrick just looked at it.

"Well," he said, and his voice still sounded fresh and rested. "So that's how it is! I rid Ireland of the snakes, and you rid Patrick of biting things."

He stood and frowned, looking down at the snake. It was a very small snake and it never looked at Saint Patrick with its bright unwinking eyes. Instead, it just lay sunning itself. Whenever a bug or a fly, or any kind of a creeping, crawling creature passed near by, out shot the snake's sharp little tongue and the creeping, crawling creature was no more.

"I could drive you into the sea," said Saint Patrick, "or drive you into the rocks, or magic you away entirely." Still the snake said nothing, but lay coiled in the warm sunshine. "Or since you got me my rest," the Saint went on, "I could let you have yours."

Still the snake said nothing, but it gobbled up a mosquito with a little snap.

"That's just what I'll do," said Saint Patrick, and with that he pointed at the snake just as though he were going to magic it away entirely.

But the small brown snake didn't magic away. It lay quite still and as it lay it grew harder and harder to see. It was no longer brown, no, nor nearly brown. It was a bright emerald green, just the color of the grass of Ireland.

"There!" said Saint Patrick, when he could hardly see the snake himself. "There, now you are safe, you and all your kind. Other birds and beasts cannot see you. And as for man, surely no one would harm a little snake that is green as Ireland itself and spends its days adding to the peace of mankind."

The Emigrant Fairy

JEAN MUIR

Paddy O'Flaherty sat on the doorstep of a little thatched cottage in Ireland with a bowl of broth in his lap. He was drinking his broth so fast that it burned his mouth, but Paddy did not care. He wanted to be done with his broth and away to the woods.

It was the eve of Saint Patrick's Day, and a silver moon hung low above the cottage with one lonely star above it. The whole world was still and gray and waiting. It was just the kind of night that the wee people love. Even now, borne on a breeze across the fields, Paddy imagined he could hear faraway piping. It was terrible to have to sit quietly and eat supper while the fairies were dancing by the marshes.

Suddenly Paddy heard a loud thumping of hoofs. That must be the father coming home from town, but what a hurry! In a minute Paddy could see the cart and the old white mare galloping as hard as she could. Then the cart stopped in front of the cottage, and there was the father with his round, smiling face and his bushy red hair.

"Maggie!" the father called. Paddy's mother hurried to the door and stood there wiping her hands on her apron.

"Maggie, alanna," said Paddy's father, "and what'll you be thinking has come for me in the mail?" But he did not wait for her to guess. He waved a big white envelope in the air. "Sure, and it's the passport that'll take us to America!" he shouted.

"Michael O'Flaherty! And is it the truth you're speaking?"

"It is so!" said Paddy's father. He was smiling and Paddy's mother was smiling, too; but Paddy felt his heart sink as if you had thrown a rock in a still black pool. He didn't say a word, but when his father and mother had gone into the cottage, he left his bowl of broth for the cat to drink, and started to run across the fields.

It was true then. They were going away. They were really going on a boat to this faraway America. They were going to leave the cottage and the marshes. They were going to leave Ireland and go to this strange country where there were no fairies.

Paddy felt sure that there were no fairies in America. When his father had first begun to talk about going away to New York, Paddy had asked the cobbler, who knew about such things, if there were fairies in America, too. The cobbler had wrinkled up his nose and shaken his old gray head. "Sure, and I'll not be saying there aren't any, but I'll not be saying there are. All I'll say is that Ireland's the home of the wee people, and what'll they be doing far away from home?"

Paddy crossed the fields and entered the woods. The fairy sounds were louder now, the piping and the dancing. Paddy stepped softly through the bushes and past the tall tree trunks. He made no more noise than a gray moth hurrying on its way through the woods.

He came to the marshes, lying still among the trees, sparkling with the reflection of the stars. Paddy fairly held his breath and sat very still under a great black oak to watch a host of fairies, drifting and whirling. The starlight glinted on their silver wings. The grass scarcely bent under their swift feet, so light they were. There were some who sat cross-legged on the ground and blew magic tunes on pipes of reed. And the marsh grasses bowing before the west wind made music, too—a sad, plaintive music. There were some who danced on the water, skipping lightly from one reflection of a star to the next. And fleetest of all among them danced Patrick O'Flannigan, Paddy's favorite fairy, a small wistful one in a gay green coat.

Paddy heard and saw all this and his heart was heavy. This is the last time you will see the fairies dance. This is the last time you will hear the fairy music. This is the last time you will see Patrick O'Flannigan, he kept thinking.

It seemed to him that he had only sat there a minute when it was time to go back to the cottage. Paddy got up sorrowfully, but he could not go away without saying good-bye to his friends. Paddy began to sing a song of his own, and all the fairies stopped and listened to Paddy's song:

> *Good-bye, fairies,*
> *I am going to a faraway country,*
> *To faraway America where there are no fairies,*
> *And my heart will be that sad without you.*
> *My heart will be sad and will long for the marshes*
> *And the sound of your piping.*
> *Good-bye, Patrick O'Flannigan——*

Paddy wanted to sing some more, but suddenly he was afraid that he was going to cry, so he started to run back to the cottage.

There was great consternation among the wee people. They looked at one another sadly and whispered softly among themselves because they all loved Paddy.

But a fairy's heart is as light as thistledown, and as a rule he cannot be unhappy long. Soon the fairies were skipping among the reeds as merrily as ever.

All but the one little fairy who was fonder of Paddy than all the rest. He could not forget his friend as the others had done. Night after night, week after week, while all the wee people were playing in the marshes, he crept away by himself, to think how lonely he was without Paddy. Finally, one night the fairies missed him and, searching among the reeds, they found him sitting sadly upon a pile of last year's leaves.

"What's ailing you, Patrick O'Flannigan?" they asked.

"Sure, and it's myself is missing Paddy and him in a faraway country and lonely maybe."

"Won't you be piping for us any more, Patrick?"

"That I won't. How can I be piping and my heart that heavy?" The fairy sighed gustily. "Oh, the sweet heart of him, sitting so quiet like and never interrupting the music and the dancing with noisy talk. Sure the marshes are not the same and him not here."

"You won't be thinking of leaving us, too, Patrick?" his friends asked uneasily.

"Aye," said Patrick, "that I will."

"Ochone! Ochone! You won't be leaving the marshes, Patrick?" And when Patrick did not answer, they said again, "You'll not be leaving Ireland, Patrick?"

"Where Paddy is, that'll be Ireland to me," said Patrick O'Flannigan.

Patrick O'Flannigan no sooner had made up his mind to leave the known marshes and to go to New York to find Paddy than he set off on his travels. He started jauntily across the fields, but the way was long and weary, and it was a dusty little fairy that finally came toiling into a great town on the Irish coast. Here were tall ships that had come from strange ports.

Patrick hid himself among a pile of barrels and pondered late into the night. A very serious difficulty beset him. There were such a number of ships, and he had no idea which one would take him to New York. How distressing it would be to travel for days and days only to find that he had been carried to Antwerp or Lisbon or Bombay! And Patrick, in spite of being a very intelligent fairy, did not know how to read.

It was by the merest chance that early the next morning he gathered from the conversation of two passing sailors that the *Shamrock* was bound for New York. A large and pompous cat, who appeared to be someone of importance on the docks by virtue of his age and exceptionally long tail, finally consented to point out the *Shamrock*. Patrick was greatly impressed by the gigantic size and noble bearing of this ship, so, scurrying up the gangplank, he hid himself in the hold.

It was an unpleasant trip, rough and stormy, so Patrick stayed in the hold with the mice. The mice he discovered to be really very charming company. Sometimes the folk on deck fancied they heard a strange, haunting tune, and they would pause in their walks for a moment to listen. Then they would shake their heads wonderingly and walk on, never dreaming that it was Patrick piping for the mice to dance.

And then one day the ship sailed proudly into New York. Patrick saw it, the great, roaring giant of a city, a ragged forest of buildings against the sky, and when the *Shamrock* had finally nosed her way among the other ships at the dock, Patrick said good-bye to the mice and hurried down the gangplank, and there he was in New York!

Patrick had never seen anything like it before—such a moving, rushing place with cars and swift streams of people passing, passing. It was like a mighty wind or a great storm, and Patrick suddenly thought of new songs to pipe, swift-moving and eager, different from the marsh songs.

But then began a weary search. It was a sad task to find one person in all that city, and such a little person as Paddy. Patrick climbed onto a lamp post and peered eagerly into the face of each person that passed, but it was never Paddy. Sometimes far down a street, Patrick would hear a childish clatter of shoes and see a little boy running, and he would dart quickly after him, but it would be Bill or Ted, never Paddy.

Day after day, week after week, month after month went by, and it was the eve of Saint Patrick's Day again. A silver moon hung above the tall houses as Patrick wandered down a street looking up at the bright windows on either side. Suddenly he saw a lonesome face peering out of one of the windows on an upper floor.

"Paddy!" he shouted.

The fairy flew up to the window and hopped onto the sill. There was a little lighted room. Paddy's father and mother were there with smiling faces, but Paddy sat by the window with his chin in his hands.

Patrick rapped softly on the windowpane, but Paddy was so far away in his dreams that he did not hear him. Then the fairy smiled to himself, and sitting down on the window ledge he took out his pipes and began to play the song of the marshes.

Paddy looked up, wondering and unbelieving. Then, as the music grew louder, he knew it was no fancy. He threw up the window joyfully.

"Whisht!" said Patrick.

"Oh," Paddy gasped, "is it yourself?"

"Sh," said Patrick, "don't be making a noise at all, at all, but come to the roof."

Paddy ran out of the room and climbed the steep stairs to the roof, and there was Patrick! Such joyful music as they had there—and such dancing, Patrick sitting cross-legged on the chimney and Paddy dancing among the blowing lines of clothes.

Paddy is a grown man now and a famous composer of music, beloved from coast to coast. Perhaps the next time you hear one of his lovely, haunting symphonies played over the radio or on TV by a big concert orchestra, you will imagine, in the deep notes of the bass instruments, the roaring of a great city. Then up, high, high in the treble, you will hear a tiny, eerie piping. And you will picture a strange little figure dancing against the sky.

Passover

(Celebrated at the
time of the first
full moon in spring)

This week-long festival of freedom recalls for the Jewish people the time when their ancestors were released from bondage in Egypt. Also known as the Feast of the Unleavened Bread, it begins with a ceremony known as *pesaḥ* (Pesach). This is a Hebrew word meaning "to pass over," in memory of the time when the angel of death passed over the houses of the Israelites who had been held as slaves by the Egyptians.

Now after many centuries, Passover is still the most loved of all Hebrew holidays. Throughout the world, Jewish people celebrate by following the old customs, such as the eating of only matzo, or unleavened bread. The following account is taken from *A Pictorial Treasury of Jewish Holidays and Customs*.

The Jewish Festival of Freedom

MORRIS EPSTEIN

To learn the story of Pesach, we must wend our way across the sands of time, to a distant age and to a strange land. There, in ancient Egypt, lived Joseph, the favorite and gifted son of Jacob. Joseph had been sold by his brothers to Midianite merchants, who in turn had brought him to Egypt. One day he was thrown into prison on false charges. Soon afterward, the ruler of Egypt had a strange dream in which seven lean cows devoured seven fat ones. Not a single wise man or wizard in all the land could tell the meaning of the dream. Then Joseph, who had interpreted dreams for the royal cupbearer and baker, was called before the Pharaoh.

"I have dreamed a dream, and none can interpret it," said the Pharaoh.

Joseph answered, "God is the interpreter of dreams. Perhaps through me He shall grant the Pharaoh peace of mind."

Joseph listened and then told the Pharaoh that his dreams meant that seven years of famine would follow seven years of plenty in the land of Egypt.

The king rewarded Joseph by making him governor over all the land. The new governor built huge granaries to be filled during the years of plenty. When the years of famine came, the full granaries saved Egypt from starvation.

While he was governor, Joseph had the good fortune to see his brothers again. They had come to Egypt to buy grain during the famine. Joseph recognized them at once and forgave them for what they had done.

"Take with you as much grain as you need," he said. "And—promise me this: you shall bring our father here, so that he may spend his last years in this great land of plenty."

So the family was reunited and Jacob lived out his days together with his favorite son.

74

Many years passed. Pharaoh and Joseph and his father and brothers died. Generations came and went. A new Pharaoh rose, who did not know of Joseph and his good deeds. The new Pharaoh feared that the Israelites might grow so numerous that they would overrun the land. To avoid this, he determined to enslave them and oppress them, so that their numbers would diminish.

For many years, the Children of Israel toiled under the taskmasters of Egypt. And then it happened that this Pharaoh, too, dreamed a dream. He saw an old man with scales in his hand: on one side was a small, tender lamb; on the other, all the great men of Egypt. And the little lamb outweighed all the Egyptians.

The next morning, one of Pharaoh's wise men interpreted his dream. He warned the king that the lamb represented the Israelites and that a child would be born to one of them who would overthrow the Kingdom of Egypt and set all the Israelites free. This child would excel all men in wisdom and his name would be remembered forever.

In panic and desperation, Pharaoh commanded that every baby boy born to the Israelites be cast into the Nile. Thousands of children were drowned by this decree and there was great mourning and weeping among the Israelites.

There lived among the Israelites a man named Amram, of the tribe of Levi. Jocheved, his wife, had given birth to a boy. Wishing to save the child from the hands of the cruel Egyptians, his mother hid him well. Now Pharaoh had sent out spies to search for all the newborn babes. Jocheved made a cradle of bulrushes, the long weeds at the river's edge, and daubed pitch over the cradle to make it waterproof. She put the child into the cradle and set it afloat. Miriam, the child's sister, watched by the river bank, her heart throbbing with anxiety.

Then it happened that Thermuthis, the daughter of Pharaoh, came to the river to bathe. She heard a child crying and rescued the little boy. Miriam timidly approached the princess and offered to call one of the Hebrew women to nurse the child. Receiving the princess' permission, Miriam soon returned with her mother. Thus little Moses was reared by his own mother. Afterwards, the princess took the child Moses to the palace.

Although Moses grew up in the palace of the Pharaoh, he never forgot that he was an Israelite. When he saw his people slaving in the hot sun, he determined that he would help end their misery. Once, after he had grown to manhood, Moses saw an Egyptian taskmaster beating an Israelite. Moses struck down the officer and buried him in the sand. When Pharaoh discovered this, he became angry and sentenced Moses to death.

Moses fled to Midian. There he sat down to rest near a well where shepherds gathered. Among them were the seven daughters of Jethro, priest of Midian. Moses helped the girls water their flock, and Zipporah, the eldest daughter, invited Moses to her father's home.

Moses married Zipporah, and for many years he tended the flocks of Jethro. One day he came near the mountain called Sinai. While grazing the sheep, he saw a fire spring up in a thornbush. Amazingly, the bush was not consumed. Moses wanted to approach but the voice of God called out to him from the fire and ordered him to stand still. Then God commanded Moses to go to Egypt and set the children of Israel free.

With his brother Aaron, Moses appeared before the king and asked him in the name of God to free the Israelites. Pharaoh laughed and said that he had never heard of the god of the Hebrews. Moses threw down his rod, and it became a snake. Pharaoh laughed; his magicians could perform the same feat. And even though Moses' rod swallowed all the other rods, Pharaoh remained unconvinced.

Moses told Pharaoh that if he would not set the Israelites free, God would turn all the waters of Egypt into blood. The plague took place but the king's heart remained unsoftened. Then came the plagues of frogs, of darkness, and of wild animals. Each time Pharaoh offered to let the Israelites free if only the plague would cease, and each time he refused to fulfill his promise.

Then came the final plague that broke the will of Pharaoh, the plague that brought death to every firstborn in every Egyptian home. In the dead of night, Pharaoh, whose own son lay dead, called for Moses and begged him to take his people out of the land. Moses gathered the Hebrews and left Egypt in great haste. They baked unleavened bread because they had no time to allow the dough to rise. Thus were prepared the matzoth which were to become such an important symbol in the celebration of Pesach.

The Israelites marched for three days. Meanwhile, Pharaoh summoned his army and began to pursue them. On the sixth day he found the Israelites resting near the Red Sea. The fleeing Israelites were terrified. The sea was in front of them and the mighty Egyptian army behind them. How were they to escape?

Moses prayed to God for aid, and the Lord parted the waters and left dry land upon which the Israelites could go across. Pharaoh followed them into the sea. Then another miracle occurred: the waters became as they had been before and swallowed the entire army of Pharaoh. Only Pharaoh himself was saved so that he might live to see and hear the glories of God.

The Israelites wandered for forty years until they reached Canaan, the Promised Land beyond the River Jordan. In Canaan, with the Ten Commandments that God had given them through Moses on Mount Sinai, they began a new life. They built homes and planted vineyards and celebrated their harvest festivals.

Since those days, the Jewish people have celebrated Pesach beginning with the eve of the fifteenth day of Nisan. During the eight days they eat unleavened bread to remind them of the bread their fathers baked in haste when they left the land of Pharaoh.

Easter

(Sunday following the first
full moon after March 21)

Long before there was a Christian religion, the awakening of the earth after a long winter's sleep was a time for gladness. During the season when flowers bloomed again and birds filled the days with song, the early Anglo-Saxons set aside a day to honor Eostre, their goddess of springtime.

When Christianity came it was natural for Christians to choose the name Easter for a special spring Sunday in commemoration of Christ's Resurrection. The New Testament tells of the day, now called Good Friday, when Jesus was crucified, and of the following Sunday, when he arose from the dead. That event has become the most solemn and joyful day in the Christian calendar.

Many early Christians believed that the sun danced at dawn in praise of the Resurrection. This legend doubtless inspired the sunrise services of today. The worship ceremony held since 1921 in the Hollywood Bowl in California is attended by more than thirty thousand worshipers. Members of the Moravian faith have held a sunrise service in Winston-Salem, North Carolina, since 1773, and there are now similar services in various parts of the United States.

Although Easter is a Christian festival, many of its customs date back to pagan times. Some pagan peoples used to eat little buns as a sacrament in honor of Eostre. Later, the buns were given a Christian meaning by decorating each one with a cross, and we still eat hot cross buns today. Another ancient practice that survives is wearing new clothes for Easter. The earth blossoms in the spring, so why shouldn't people dress up, too?

One of the customs most popular with children is hunting Easter eggs. The Easter bunny is supposed to hide them the night before, but why he was chosen for this agreeable chore no one is quite certain. The hare, which is born with its eyes open, was an ancient symbol of the moon, and the full moon determines the date of Easter Sunday. The egg has long been considered a symbol of new life, and all kinds of eggs —beautifully decorated eggs, candy eggs, and eggs boiled and tinted in gay colors—are still an exciting part of our Easter celebration.

79

Easter Eggs
A Story of Hungary

KATE SEREDY

But for her long black braids anybody would have taken Kate from Budapest for a lanky little boy. Ever since she had arrived at the farm to live with her aunt and uncle and her cousin Jancsi, she had been perfectly satisfied with Jancsi's old clothes. "I'd rather be a boy, anyway," she said.

Kate was always trailing after Jancsi now, following him from house to barn, from barn to pasture, asking a million questions. Pretty soon she began to help him. She liked to drive the geese and ducks to the brook or feed the chickens. She loved horses. Whenever Kate was missing, she could be found in the stables. Jancsi taught her to saddle, feed, and currycomb the horses. He was very proud of the way she rode. After the first painful lessons, she listened to his sound advice and was rewarded one day by her uncle.

He was looking on while Jancsi and Kate put the horses through all their paces. "Pretty good," he said. "Kate, the first week after Easter I'll take you with me when Jancsi and I ride out to inspect the baby lambs—providing you keep out of mischief."

She was off her horse and in her uncle's arms before he knew what had happened. She was hugging and kissing him until he gasped for breath.

"Uncle Márton! Oh, I'm so happy! I'm so glad you'll take me because—I'd have sneaked after you, anyway."

"And gotten a boy's size licking for it!" laughed Uncle Márton.

"Let's see, it's a whole week until Easter. Wish it wasn't so long. I don't like Easter anyway. You have to be all dressed up and nothing to do," said Kate.

"Oh, but Easter is wonderful!" cried Jancsi. "We make Easter eggs, and everybody goes visiting. There are millions of good things to eat and—!" Jancsi gasped for words to describe the wonders of Easter.

Kate interrupted, "Make Easter eggs? How can you make an egg?"

80

"Mother just dyes them, silly, and we write all kinds of flowers and patterns on them."

This was something new for Kate. She contemplated it in silence for a while. "What else do you do?" she asked.

"Go to church, and sprinkle the girls, an' everything. Wait and see—it's fun!"

"Sprinkle—what—sprinkle the girls?"

" 'Course. All the boys and young men go to all their friends who have girls to sprinkle them with water. The girls and mothers give them meat and cakes to eat and Easter eggs to take home."

"Oh! but that's silly. Slosh water on girls for no reason at all and get cakes and everything. What do the girls get for getting wet?"

"Wait a minute, Kate," laughed Uncle Márton. "It does sound silly if you put it that way, but there is a beautiful reason for it. Do you want me to tell you?"

"A story?" asked Jancsi eagerly.

"No, Jancsi, the truth," said his father. "Come on, let's sit under the apple tree and I'll tell you." He spoke seriously, almost as though he were thinking aloud.

"Easter is a holiday of joy and love and giving. We welcome our friends and offer them the best we have. For us, who live on the land, Easter means the real beginning of spring—and spring for us is new hope, new life after the long, bleak winter. Spring brings warm sunshine, life-giving soft rain. Every living thing depends on sunshine and water. So we celebrate Easter by giving each other the sunshine of hospitality, and we sprinkle each other with fresh, pure water. How does your Easter greeting go, Jancsi? Say it for Kate!"

Jancsi recited:

> "My song is the song of hope,
> The voice of spring is my voice,
> All my dear friends, let us rejoice;
> God gave us sunshine, God gave us *rain*,
> Our prayers have not been in vain.
> Gone is the cold, cheerless winter,
> Here is glorious Easter again!"

Kate nodded. "I like it, Uncle Márton, only I—well—I can't understand why only the girls get sprinkled."

"You can sprinkle us on Tuesday after Easter. That's when girls have a good time," laughed Jancsi, jumping up. "Come on, the horses are waiting for a rub."

The last days before Easter were busy and exciting ones. Uncle Márton and Jancsi whitewashed the house inside and out. They painted the window boxes and shutters a bright blue. Jancsi and Kate selected the largest, most perfect eggs, and they were laid aside for decorating. Auntie made piles and piles of nutcakes and poppyseed cakes, baking them in different shapes. Some of them looked like birds or lambs, some were crescent-shaped, some looked like stars and crosses. The cousins were always sniffing around the kitchen, waiting for "tastes."

Evenings Auntie got out her dyepots, and the fascinating work of making dozens and dozens of fancy Easter eggs kept the family busy. There were two ways to decorate them. The plainer ones were dyed first. When they dried, Uncle Márton and Jancsi scratched patterns on them with penknives. The fancy ones were lots of work. Auntie had a tiny funnel, with melted beeswax in it. With this she drew intricate patterns on the white eggs. After the wax hardened, she dipped them in the dye. Then she scratched off the wax and there was the beautiful design left in white on the colored egg. In this way she could make the most beautifully shaded designs by covering up parts of the pattern again with wax before each dipping. The finished ones were placed in baskets and put on a shelf until Easter morning.

"I'll make some extra-fancy ones for Kate. She can give them to the boys she likes best," Auntie said, smiling.

"Could I try to make one or two myself?" begged Kate. "All by myself. I don't want anybody to see them."

"Look out, Kate, you'll get all messed up, and this dye doesn't wash off. You have to scrub it off with sand," warned Jancsi.

Kate went to a corner with her dyepots and labored for a long time in silence. When she finally put her eggs away and came back to the table, she was a sight!

"Oh, Kate, you clumsy!" cried Jancsi. "Now you look like an Easter egg. Oh, you look funny!" She was red paint from head to toe. Her fingers were dripping; her nose looked like a red cherry.

Jancsi's hands were wet with the dye, too, but he carefully kept his face and clothes clean.

Kate looked at him seriously.

"Jancsi, dear, there's just a little smudge of black on your nose," she said, pointing a red finger at an imaginary spot.

"Don't touch me! I'll wipe it off," cried Jancsi, and forgetting his wet hands, he rubbed his nose vigorously.

"M-m-m. That's off, but your forehead is smudged, too. The smoke from the candle, I imagine," said a very sweet and solicitous Kate.

Jancsi rubbed his forehead.

"Your chin, too. My, my, these old-fashioned candles."

Jancsi rubbed his chin. His father and mother were laughing hard, but he didn't know why.

"It's perfect now, Jancsi," smiled Kate. "Now you look like an Easter egg yourself."

"Oh, my boy," laughed Uncle Márton, "won't you ever learn the ways of our sweet pussy? You are decorated for Easter all right."

Jancsi ran to the mirror. He couldn't help laughing.

"I should have known better," he admitted. "She had her angel face on. I'll tell the boys to scrub your face for you; sprinkling isn't enough."

Saturday, Auntie packed all the meats, bread, and cakes in big baskets lined with snow-white napkins. They would take them to the church Sunday to be blessed by the priest. She put the finishing touches on the family's Sunday clothes. Kate didn't pay any attention to her own dress Auntie had promised for Easter; she was satisfied with her boy's clothes.

On Sunday they started to dress after a very early breakfast. Kate's clothes were laid out on her bed. Suddenly, a wail came from her room. "Oh, Auntie, which skirt shall I wear?"

"Which skirt? All of them, of course; it's a holiday!"

"But there are eighteen on my bed!"

"That's because you're only a little girl. I'm wearing thirty-six, but I'm a married woman," said Auntie, appearing in the doorway. She completely filled it. Her pleated and starched skirts were all the colors of the rainbow, standing away from her body like a huge umbrella. She wore a white shirtwaist, with puffed sleeves, and a tight black vest laced in front over red buttons. Her head was covered with a fringed, embroidered shawl tied under her chin. She wore tight black boots with high heels. Kate gazed at her with awe.

"I'm really very young," she said meekly. "Couldn't I wear just one or two skirts?"

"All nice girls wear at least ten," was Auntie's firm answer.

When Kate finally emerged from her room, she looked like a small replica of her aunt. Her dress was even more colorful, with a scarlet red vest. Her sparkling, shimmering bonnet had long red and green ribbons on it, cascading almost to her knees. But Kate's face was sad. "My old boots—" she said, "they look awful with this pretty dress."

"Oh, you poor lamb!" cried Auntie. "We clean forgot your boots! Father! Jancsi! We forgot Kate's boots."

Uncle Márton came in, solemnly shaking his head. "Hm-hm. Think of it! Our pussy hasn't any boots. What can we do? She will have to wear mine!"

He went to the cupboard. When he turned around, he held the prettiest, trimmest pair of little red boots in his hand.

"Oh!" said everybody. Kate flew to him, crying, "Uncle Márton! You are the sweetest, best, dearest uncle!" She was trying to hug him and put her boots on at the same time.

Uncle Márton left to get the wagon while Kate was still dancing around happily. She was kissing her aunt and she even attempted to kiss Jancsi. But he balked at that. "Only girls kiss," he declared, and stalked out after his father.

They drove to church in great state. The wagon had been freshly painted, the horses were brushed until their coats shone like black satin. They overtook and passed more and more wagons as they approached the village. "Our wagon is best of all!" said Kate proudly.

The streets around the village church were lined with vehicles. The church square was packed with people. They were dressed in brilliant colors, the women in immense skirts, swaying, their hair-ribbons floating in the breeze. The men all had bunches of flowers in their hats, and wore snow-white pleated shirts and pants and black, blue, or green sleeveless jackets. It made the prettiest picture Kate ever had seen. "Like a big flower garden," she whispered.

Slowly the church filled, and the service began. After the last prayer and hymn, the priest blessed the food in the church square. Groups of friends stood around for awhile, talking. Kate was introduced to many people. Here was a city girl, and she was the subject of open admiration from the village boys and girls.

"We'll come to your house tomorrow!" promised the boys.

When Kate woke up Monday morning, Jancsi and his father had already left for the village. Auntie and Kate spread the best white tablecloth on the big kitchen table and placed huge platters of meat, bread, and cakes on it. "What a beautiful tablecloth," exclaimed Kate. "I never saw anything like it in the stores."

"I made it myself, Kate, when I was your age," said Auntie. "I planted the flax, reaped it, prepared it, spun the thread, and wove it into this cloth. It's more than twenty-five years old now, but it's as good as new." Kate wanted to know more about spinning and weaving, but Auntie was too busy. She promised Kate to teach her all about it in the winter.

They were still arranging the baskets of eggs when the first wagon drove in. The men and boys walked in, and one of them spoke a piece:

> *Glory be to the Holy Father*
> *Who gave us food and pure water.*
> *As we water the rose to make it bloom,*
> *We sprinkle the rosebud in this room.*
> *May you love long,*
> *Old and young.*
> *Peace be with you on this holy day of Easter.*

They all repeated the last line. Kate saw the flasks of water in their hands. It won't be so bad; the bottles are very small, she thought. Just the same, she squealed and ran when the boys stepped forward and began to throw water on her. There was great shouting and laughing in the kitchen. "We want eggs! Give us some eggs, Kate. We'll stop sprinkling if you do," cried the boys. She ran to the baskets and gave them handfuls of eggs. Auntie invited them to eat anything they liked. Another wagon drove in. Young men came on horseback. It was great fun for Kate! She was pretty wet by now but didn't mind it. Visitors came and left; the kitchen was always full of people and laughter. She liked the verses they spoke; she liked the boundless hospitality; she liked ever so much to be there and enjoy it all!

The food supply was almost exhausted when the last wagon drove off. There weren't any more eggs. She slumped in a chair, tired but happy.

Jancsi and Uncle Márton came home in the afternoon, loaded with eggs. "Well, Kate," asked her uncle, "did you give everything away? Not one egg left for us?"

"I saved one for you and one for Jancsi," said Kate, walking to the small basket where she had hidden the eggs she had made all by herself.

"You said I had to give the best ones to people I like best." She smiled, holding out her hands.

"Mine has a nice flower on it and—oooh—little ducks! Aren't they, Kate?" said Jancsi.

"Yes, I drew them for you because we had such a good time with the duckies."

Her uncle took the egg offered to him. It wasn't a very good Easter egg, being a tiny bit smeary, but to him it was the most beautiful gift in the world. This is what Kate had written on it: "I like you best of all, Uncle Márton!"

Pinney's Easter Hunt

LAVINIA R. DAVIS

It was Easter Sunday, but there was nothing very Eastery about the farm. The wind was cold and raw, the tan fields were still hard with frost, and only the maples in the south pasture were bright with buds.

Pinney shivered as he pulled on his old wool jacket and went out to do the chores. You felt colder when you knew it was meant to be spring and still the world didn't warm up. It was always knowing about things that made them seem bad, like knowing about the Easter Hunt over at Wainbridge that very afternoon.

Pinney hurried up to the barn and tried not to think about the Easter Hunt, but that was impossible. You just couldn't help thinking about an egg hunt where they were going to give two live Bantam chickens to the boy who found the most eggs. Pinney waved to Grandpa and tried to chase away his thoughts. It wasn't Grandpa's fault that he had to milk all the cows and couldn't spare the time to drive all the way over to Wainbridge. And it wasn't Grundy's fault that she was just getting over the grippe and couldn't drive Pinney over, either.

Pinney fed the chickens and the pigs. It certainly wasn't his grandparents' fault, but that didn't help. If only he hadn't known that there was even a chance of his winning a pair of Bantams, he would have been better off.

When Pinney was all through his chores he suddenly had a good idea. Though the upper meadows were still frozen it was much warmer in the lowlands, and he might find some bloodroot or hepatica. He would transplant some into a little pot and give it to Grundy for an Easter plant. If somebody had an Easter surprise that afternoon Pinney thought he would feel better.

Pinney picked up a trowel and a basket in the woodshed and went into the woods. The twigs still snapped frostily underfoot as they had in December, but at least now there were birds chirping, and as Pinney got near the swamp there were green pincushions of skunk cabbage to show that it wasn't midwinter.

After a little while Pinney dug his hands in his pockets and began to whistle. He hoped he would find the hepatica soon. He was cold and what he really wanted to do was to go home and read in front of the big pot-bellied stove. But he wanted to please Grundy, too, even if the spring wind that cut in under his collar seemed colder and more unpleasant than any wind all winter.

Pinney kept on and on. He passed over Grandpa's boundary and walked onto Mr. Leggett's farm. Mr. Leggett was one of Pinney's friends and never minded his trespassing, but reaching his farm made Pinney realize how far he had gone from home. If he hadn't gotten any hepatica so far there wouldn't be another chance until he got to the shelter of Leggett's ledge, which was right in the middle of the woodlot.

When he finally reached the ledge Pinney's marching whistle suddenly quickened. Hepatica! Lots of it. Pale, pale lavender flowers with a deep green leaf. Pinney looked around at the sheltering arms of the rock ledge approvingly. Nothing but the warm south wind could blow in here. It was a perfect, natural shelter.

Pinney picked out three good plants, dug them carefully, and placed them in his basket. They had good long roots so Grandma could transplant them later into her flower garden. He was just covering the roots when he heard the little noise behind him.

Ba, ba, ba. It was such a feeble little noise Pinney wasn't even sure he'd heard. *Ba, ba,* the sound was repeated, and Pinney shot around on his heels. For a second he didn't see anything and then, as its little black nose wriggled, he saw the lamb!

It was small, and woolly, and Pinney knew it must be very newly born! He patted its little round head and wondered why its mother had left it. Grandpa didn't raise sheep, and Pinney knew it was one of Mr. Leggett's flock. Perhaps Mr. Leggett or Jake MacTavish, his shepherd, had overlooked it. Except for its nose and its black-stockinged legs, the lamb was a perfect match with the gray rock behind it. Even if the lamb had been overlooked, Pinney was sure someone would be back soon to carry it home.

He petted it for a moment, held it in his arms. It nestled close to him and trembled as if it needed his warmth. But Pinney put it down again. It stood uncertainly on its wobbly legs, looking very forlorn. He mustn't get fond of it. It would probably be safe here, and surely Jake would come back soon.

Pinney started picking up his trowel and basket, but he didn't feel like leaving. He wished Mr. Leggett or Jake would come back while he was there. He'd feel better if he saw them starting off with the lamb in their arms. Right now it looked awfully lonely and pathetic, even in the shelter of the deep ledge.

Just before he started off Pinney turned to have one more look at the lamb. It was much too weak to try to follow him. It lifted its little head, but even that took too much strength and it dropped against its woolly chest. Pinney tried to move. But then, all of a sudden, he knew he wouldn't leave the lamb.

He couldn't take a chance on Jake or Mr. Leggett's not finding that lamb. He'd have to bring it home to them tonight. Even if the Leggett barn was still a long, long walk away, Pinney knew he would have to get there. He just couldn't leave the lamb by itself.

Pinney picked it up in both arms, tucked it under his coat, and somehow gripped the basket in his finger tips. It was an awkward load, but Pinney was sure he could manage. He started his marching whistle again, only louder and quicker this time so that he would walk faster. He had a long way to go, and it was getting late. Left, right, left, right! Pinney went as fast as he could along the edge of the ledge, out of the protection of the woods, and across the windswept fields, up the long hill to the farmyard.

More than once he had to stop to repack his load. Either the lamb would move in his arms or the basket would slip in his stiff fingers. Then he would readjust his burdens, straighten his shoulders, and march on. It might have been safe to leave the lamb in the home field where Jake or Mr. Leggett would be sure to find it. It seemed safe. It probably was safe, but Pinney wasn't taking any chances. The little animal nestling in his arms was so small, so helpless! He spoke to it reassuringly and thought that it seemed to tremble less at his words.

Jake was milking when Pinney finally reached the barn. The place was warm and steamy with the breath of the feeding cows.

"Here's one of your lambs," Pinney said. "Found it by the ledge. Guess maybe it was lost." Carefully he unbuttoned his coat and displayed his small charge.

Jake took the lamb in his big gnarled hands. "Must be a twin to the black lambie the big ewe bore this morning," he said. "I brought home the blackie and couldna understand why the mither fashed herself so at leaving the ledge."

Pinney nodded understandingly. He touched the lamb in farewell.

"Good night," he said and started for the door.

"Good night," Jake said, still bending over the lamb. "You'll like be hearing from the master."

Pinney never even wondered what Jake could mean. There were other more important things to think about. In the first place he had to run home to keep from being late, and in the second place Grundy and Grandpa were waiting for him, anyhow. Besides, he wanted to forget about the lamb. He was glad that it was safe.

Grundy was up and about for the first time in a week and all dressed in her best blue silk that always meant a party. Grandpa was all through milking and was already fussing about in the kitchen making flapjacks, which were his own particular specialty for birthdays and Christmas and Easter.

Pinney potted his plants in red pots he found in the cellar. He gave them to Grundy as they sat down to their supper. She hugged him and thanked him just as if he'd brought her three dozen store roses all for herself. Finally, she gave him another hug and nodded to Pinney's own place. There were two very specially hand-painted eggs that Grundy had dyed for Pinney herself. Then there was a chocolate rabbit that Grandpa had bought at the store, and a shiny new nickel lay beside it.

Pinney said his thanks, and as he poured sirup on Grandpa's flapjacks he promised himself he wouldn't ever think about the Wainbridge Egg Hunt and the Bantams again.

But it was an easier promise to make than to keep. The very next morning he woke up with an empty disappointed sort of feeling hanging all over him.

Resolutely he jumped out of bed and pulled on his clothes. He wasn't going to think about it. He really wasn't.

He hadn't even started his breakfast before Grundy called to him. "Been up to the barn yet, sonny?" she asked, and her voice sounded as mysterious as Santa Claus. "Been up to the barn yet to feed the pigs?"

When Pinney was all through his oatmeal and his fried eggs and bacon, he went up to the barn. Grandpa was tinkering with the tractor in the shed, but when he saw Pinney he dropped his tools. "Been over to the barn yet?" he asked, and he, too, sounded mysterious.

Once Pinney was inside the barn he understood. There, right in front of him, was the little lamb he'd returned to the Leggetts yesterday!

The lamb's little black nose was the same. Its black-stockinged legs were the same. Its round tennis ball head was the same. It just looked a little stronger, and around its neck on a piece of green raffia was hung an envelope. Pinney went nearer and saw his name on the outside.

He pulled it open and looked inside. "Happy Easter," he read. "And good luck. See if you can bring this lamb up as well as you brought him home."

"He's yours to keep," Grandpa said. "Tom Leggett brought him over this morning. Said any boy had the gumption to take so much trouble to bring a lamb home ought to own one. He brought along a nursing bottle for you to feed him with."

For a long time Pinney couldn't say anything. He just hugged the lamb and thought how it made a better pet than even the finest Bantams.

The lamb tried to lick his hands, and then suddenly Pinney spoke. "Just think! Suppose I'd gone to Wainbridge and nobody had found the lamb!"

Pan American Day

After the United States won its independence, the efforts of South American countries to follow its example aroused a great deal of sympathy among the people of our own country. In December, 1823, President James Monroe sent a message to Congress warning that the United States would not permit any European government to interfere with the government of any country in the Americas. This message, known as the Monroe Doctrine, enabled the new South American republics to maintain their independence.

Many years later, on April 14, 1890, representatives of twenty-one republics in North, Central and South America met in Washington, D.C. and passed a resolution to form a Pan American Union. Later, it was decided to celebrate that date as Pan American Day. *"Pan"* is the Greek word for "all," and it was hoped that by observing the same holiday the peoples of the Americas would come to understand one another better. In 1931 the new holiday was observed by schools

92

and cities throughout the nation, and there was a gala celebration in Washington, D.C.

The Pan American Union's handsome building in Washington serves as headquarters for OAS (Organization of American States). The purpose of this organization, begun in 1948, is to promote peace, justice and further cooperation among Amer- ican republics. In the following story you will read about Simón Bolívar, the hero born in Ven- ezuela, who was among the first to suggest a union of independent American nations. He has been called the George Washington of South America because he helped to bring liberty both to his native land and to several neighboring countries.

They Heard a Horseman Singing
The Story of Simón Bolívar

BRASSIL FITZGERALD

That was a school that some of you who read this would have liked attending. The seats were saddles, and the schoolyard stretched windswept miles to the mountains. There was but one student, a boy of fourteen with a wide-smiling mouth. He rode a high-stepping gray horse. His black eyes studied the distance, where dust hung in the clear, bright air. A faint bawling of cattle came from the dust, and around it black dots moved swiftly. Those dots were cowboys, the llaneros, his llaneros.

The boy's teacher rode with him, a middle-aged man and stout, both hands gripping his saddle horn, and between jounces he lectured his student.

"Every caballero, Simón, should know the history of the illustrious don George Washington. Are you listening?"

"Yes, señor, with deep interest," the boy answered politely, but his eyes were wistful, watching the cowboys.

"Mark me now," the teacher continued, "when he was a boy, George Washington was not at all like you, Simón. Not at all. He was serious. It is told that when a child, at the family hacienda at Virginia, he cut down a fruit tree. When questioned, little George said to his father—" Teacher stood in his stirrups and shouted, "You shameless rascal! Whoa! Come back here." School was out. Simón had spurred his gray, and was fast away. His voice drifted back, rollicking over the drumming hoofs. The rascal rode singing.

When George Washington died at Mount Vernon, Simón Bolívar was a lad of sixteen, in Caracas, the principal city of Venezuela. Simón was an orphan, a very wealthy one. A slim, handsome youth, he sang ballads under the grilled windows of the girls of Caracas. He danced at the governor's palace in the splendid uniform of a junior lieutenant in the local militia, the White Guard. One evening, his uncle, don Carlos, called him into the tapestried, candlelit drawing room.

94

"His Excellency the Governor is displeased with you, Simón," don Carlos said. "He complains that you are a disturbing influence among your brother officers of the White Guard."

Simón shrugged a velvet shoulder. "I'm sick of the White Guards, my uncle. Have you heard what the Spanish officers call us? The White Mice!"

Don Carlos lifted his hands in a gesture of helplessness, and he said to the clergyman who sat listening, "You see how he answers me! He's stubborn, Father Andrea, and willful!"

The little priest said gently, "Beware the sin of ingratitude, Simón. You have much to be thankful for."

"Your reverence," the boy answered sullenly, "the poorest North American is more fortunate than I, being free."

Father Andrea's eyes were sad. "Only the good are truly free, my son. Those who serve evil are slaves. We ask for true liberty, Simón, when we ask our father, 'Deliver us from evil.' "

"We must deliver ourselves from evil, as the North Americans did," the boy said bitterly.

No one answered that, and the silence was troubled, for men of Caracas had died in cages for such talk. Don Carlos broke the long silence. "I want you to go abroad, Simón, to Europe. Your Uncle Esteban in Madrid stands high in her Majesty's favor. A year with him will complete your education."

"And make me a courtier, Uncle? No, thanks. I'd rather be a llanero."

His uncle's face flushed, but he kept his temper. "When you tire of Madrid you can go to Vienna. That fat, bald scamp of a teacher, Rodriguez, who used to visit the ranches with you—he's in Vienna, I've heard. But you've doubtless forgotten him."

"Simón had not forgotten. He smiled. "It is my duty, my dear Uncle Carlos, to obey you in all things. When do I sail?"

He sailed on January 17, 1799. . . .

When Simón returned to Venezuela, he brought a bride—the lovely young Maria. When the sunlight went out of the garden, Maria would put down her sewing to watch for Simón. Then the quiet would end with a clatter of hoofs and a gay voice singing. He would call her his princess, his little white flower. His happiness filled the house.

After dinner the two would be alone where a fountain tossed

silver spray in the moonlight. Simón would talk of the day's work, or of politics. He explained to Maria that all Spanish America was ruled by two viceroys responsible only to the King of Spain. From Mexico City a viceroy ruled Mexico and Central America. From Lima, in Peru, another ruled the Spanish colonies of South America. Under these viceroys were assistant tyrants, called captains general. There was one in Caracas. In all Venezuela his word was law.

Simón's voice would quicken as he talked. "He could put me in chains, Maria, for buying a book or for owning a printing press. Were I to plant olive trees or wine grapes, he would send his soldiers to root them up. That's because Spain has olives and wine to sell us."

Simón's voice was dry and bitter. "Do you know what Pizarro told his king?" Maria didn't know, but Simón told her of Pizarro, who had conquered the Indians of Peru more than two hundred years before. "The New World is a cow for our milking," Pizarro had said.

In the moonlight Simón's great eyes would burn like coals. "But someday, Maria, we shall find a patriot leader like don George Washington. Then we will break our chains. Then we will say to the king of Spain, to all Europe, what our brothers of the north have said." Simón's voice was fierce and proud. "Listen, Maria, for this is the answer to tyrants. This is democracy's credo: 'We hold these truths to be self-evident, that all men are created equal, that they are endowed by their Creator with certain unalienable rights, that among these are life, liberty, and the pursuit of happiness . . .' "

Simón and Maria were happy for ten months. Then Maria fell sick of a tropical fever. She died in Simón's arms. And Simón sought escape from his grief in Europe. He wandered from city to city, until he met his old teacher, Rodriguez, again. With eyes like wet stones in a white, sick face, Simón looked at his friend and asked humbly, "Can you help me?"

Rodriguez could, and did. Together they walked the roads of France, eating in farm kitchens the coarse food of the peasants, sleeping in humble inns. Rodriguez was a wise teacher. Trudging happily along in the roadside dust, he talked of the friends he visited in books. He boasted of his friends, making them live again for Simón. So down the long pleasant roads of France, Joan of Arc walked beside them; and Horatius, who had held the bridge at Rome;

a bulb-nosed and bearded Greek named Socrates, who kept asking questions; and little ragged Saint Francis, whistling through two fingers to the roadside sparrows.

There came a day, a hot noon in the shade of a haystack, when Simón said thoughtfully between bites of bread and cheese, "Rodriguez, I'll never drink or gamble again. Life's too short. There is too much to do."

He's cured, thought his friend and teacher.

One summer evening in 1805 the two travelers climbed the Holy Mount on the outskirts of Rome. In the city below, the church bells rang, long golden notes in the hushed golden air. Simón was thinking aloud. "I swear by the God of my fathers, and by my native land, that my hands will never tire, nor my soul rest, until I have broken the chains that bind us to Spain."

When Bolívar went home to Venezuela to begin his lifework, no crowd cheered, no bands played. To the patriots meeting in secret to plan resistance to Spain he was just another recruit. When the fighting started in 1811, it was General Francisco de Miranda who commanded the patriot forces. This General Miranda was a true patriot, but unwise. He told his men they weren't soldiers. They believed him. So he failed. He surrendered. And the first Republic of Venezuela died ignobly under the boots of the Spanish regulars.

Simón Bolívar, his estates and fortune taken away by the government, fled to Cartagena, where the patriots of New Granada held a strip of the seacoast. There he was given command of two hundred men, Negroes, Indians, and half-breeds. Bolívar smiled, told them he was proud to command them, that each of them was worth three Spaniards. They grinned back, shuffling their bare feet in the dust, believing. In six days, with these untrained soldiers, who thought themselves heroes, Bolívar fought six battles and won six battles.

At one time the Spaniards caught him in a mountain valley, a deep narrow canyon between a wild, rushing river and steep rock walls. All one long afternoon, from the higher ground, the Spaniards poured fire into the rebels trapped below. In the late afternoon the sun went out of the canyon, and the triumphant Spaniards rested. Between shouts of laughter, a captain offered gold to the man who would bring him Bolívar's ears.

Somewhere close in the fog a new voice spoke, a clear bold

voice. "Here are my ears, señor. Come and get them." Then Bolívar's men charged out of the mist. They had crawled up a thousand-foot cliff. Driving their bayonets into the crevasses, they had pulled themselves up, hand over hand. Bayonets and brains won that battle.

Yet Bolívar was often and long defeated, and in 1814, after three years of struggle, he was an exile on the British island of Jamaica. He was a sick man, but he would not surrender. With two hundred borrowed dollars he sailed again for his native land. In 1819, he led his army across the continent toward the main range of the Andes.

As the men climbed, the trails grew steep. The air turned thin and cold. They began to suffer from the dread mountain sickness, headaches that turn swiftly to drowsiness; and those who sleep die.

One night, thirteen thousand feet high in the mountains, they camped on a rock-strewn plateau. There was no food. There was no wood for fires. Wrapped in his horse blanket, Bolívar moved from group to group, sharing all that was left to him, his will to endure. No one can know his thoughts that long, dreadful night.

But on some such night, Bolívar dreamed of a brotherhood of all the free nations of the Americas. More than any statesman of his generation he foresaw the destiny of the Americas. A sick man moaned, then sighed without waking, feeling the warmth of Bolívar's blanket.

With morning came hope, for the rocky trail turned downward. Far below, as the dawn clouds rolled away, the men saw the green of the timberline and the silver of streams flowing westward. They had done the impossible. They had crossed the main range of the Andes.

The villagers of Socha saw them coming, skeletons and scarecrows led by a ghost. "El Libertador!" the natives cried. "El Libertador!"

"The Liberator" met and defeated the army of Spain three days later. That was the turning point. He marched from victory to victory until, between the two oceans, his people were free.

The Silver City
The Story of a Mexican Boy

MARGARET PHELPS

On the seventh day of his journey, Pico reached the top of the silver mountain and there was Taxco. Its houses were white with gay, red-tiled roofs and they stood one upon the other, against the mountainside. There, too, were the silver mines. The earth gave up the silver and Taxco men and boys hammered it into splendid objects.

Pico looked about him with delight. He forgot the many weary miles his sandaled feet had trudged from Mexico City. He had reached the far-off mountain. Here his parents, Nahua Indians, had lived when they were children, and Pico's dream was to become a silversmith, a good one, so he could earn enough pesos to bring his mother and father back to their mountain. In Mexico City they worked very hard but were very poor.

The boy pushed his faded green serape higher on his shoulder and began to stroll through the town. Here, truly, work is pleasure and pleasure is work, he thought, looking intently at everything. The streets were cozier than any he had ever trod; streets whose shops bulged outward, their tiny windowpanes patterned with silver goods.

Pico turned right and he turned left—and whichever way he turned he could still find himself confronting a vista of silver.

He tried to count the objects as he came upon each tiny shop, but he lost the number among the crooked cobbled streets.

Everywhere Pico went he saw leaning inns and clustered white stone houses one on top of the other, and then he saw more small shops with shelves, tables, counters and glass cases all filled with silver objects—rings, bracelets, pins, teapots, and platters—and splendid silver necklaces and wise-looking masks hung in rows.

Pico came suddenly upon a shoemaker's shop where an old man worked over a bench. The dark little room smelled of musty leather. Just around the corner, above the shoemaker's shop, was the largest silver store in Taxco.

Pico stared up. The full name of the silver shop was *Taller de las Delicias*. Did he dare climb the steps to ask for work? It would be splendid indeed if he could become a silversmith in this fine shop.

He removed his plaited straw hat; then he went up the flight of rustic steps.

At the top Pico's feet wanted to run away.

Would a man who owned such a big silver shop bother with a small, hungry boy? Pico's dark eyes peered inside the door.

At the far end of a long room he saw a man standing behind a counter. The boy wondered if that man was the master of the shop.

He stepped inside the doorway. Silver everywhere! Solid silver from Taxco mines.

As Pico walked down the long narrow room he passed a low table. A gray fawn rested on a pile of red blankets on top of the table. The fawn looked up at him with gentle eyes and Pico stopped. If this man will hire me I will design a silver fawn, he thought, stroking the fawn's gray fur. The fawn wiggled its short tail, and Pico went to speak to the man.

The man said, "The master of this shop is gone to a faraway city. He is making quite a trip. Come back later."

Pico turned away. He couldn't wait to get work until the master came back from his long trip. Pico was hungry. He had to earn food at once. As he stood, it came upon Pico with a rush that he did not have a friend in Taxco. How did he expect to make money to send for his parents when he could not even get work to buy food for himself?

Pico walked slowly out through the narrow room.

When he reached the pavement he cupped his hands to drink from a dripping pipe he found hidden near a little balcony. Then he sat down to rest, across the cobbled street, facing the shaded plaza.

This was a charming little plaza. American tourists went in and out of shops, and in the sunlight the bright colors of the Indians' clothes splashed lovely designs against white house walls. Every so often a blue shawl floated between Pico and rows of silver necklaces displayed behind small-paned windows on the square.

Surely there was much to do in Taxco. All around the plaza were little stores where boys and men worked. Silversmiths! Only Pico did not belong to Taxco. No one spoke to him. Not even the two green parakeets, close together on their perch in a round cage hanging in a doorway, paid attention to Pico.

So Pico left the plaza. He entered the shops one by one. He spoke shyly to every person who would listen. "Please," he would say, "will you hire me? I want to become a silversmith."

But nothing came of his asking. Some silversmiths said they had all the boys they needed. Other masters shook their heads. "No," they said, "we do not need you."

Pico left the plaza section to trudge up and down narrow, hidden streets. If he walked far enough he thought he might come upon some kind old man who needed a boy.

He climbed another flight of steps. Halfway up Pico stopped to lean over a tile wall. His hungry stomach pressed itself tight against the tile as Pico looked down at two men making adobe bricks in wooden frames. "Will you hire me?" called Pico. "I will help set bricks to dry in the sun."

One man shook his head no, and the other fellow threw a baked brick at a pig that was leaving its footprints in the drying clay.

As Pico climbed another flight of steps, shadows came swinging down the mountain to meet him. Pico smelled onion soup, and soon he saw supper smoke rising from all the red chimneys.

He turned back to go down the mountain to the plaza.

Pico sat down on the pink church steps to eat his last dulce. He thought of his mother, and as he ate her farewell gift his eyes roved the plaza. After a while he spied a tin can. He went over to get it. When he came back to the church step he worked a long time before he got the top off the can. But it finally loosened, and Pico dropped the can top in the purple basket he had brought from home.

When complete darkness came, Pico slipped down a narrow street to curl up in a passageway.

He stuck his hand into his purple basket. In the darkness he found the tin can top and his fine nail tucked under the little white napkin. The ball of green maguey string was there, too. He was still hungry.

He pulled his faded green serape up until the fringe touched his chin. He heard a cricket's notes clicking in his ears like silver castanets making a song. And so Pico fell asleep . . .

He sat up straight. The narrow cobbled street was empty. He blinked his eyes several times before he realized he had slept the night in Taxco.

Down the alleyway to his left Pico saw a cluster of dawn-sprinkled banana leaves. He wondered if he could find a banana.

But when he reached the tree he found no fruit. So he wandered in and out of cobbled streets until he came upon the market place.

Already the mountaineers had spread their wares for sale.

No one spoke to Pico. He could see that here no one needed a boy. Never before had he been so hungry, he thought, as he turned into a tiny, cobbled street he had not yet seen. The air blew crisp against his cheeks as he walked between the white houses. Pico breathed deeply. He was not sure he could climb this steep street.

He leaned back against the wall to look at the pavement soaring up and up above him. His legs trembled, and overhead the houses seemed to turn suddenly into jagged white peaks, and all the chimneys became up-and-down smudges against the bright blue sky.

"Will I find my master on this street?" Pico asked himself, feeling hunger tugging under his belt.

He clutched the handle of his purple basket and tried to steady his legs.

I must keep walking, Pico told himself.

As he climbed, sounds from the faraway market nibbled at his ears. A woman met him carrying a water jar on her dark head.

His purple basket jounced against the white walls and a flaming trumpet vine scraped his plaited straw hat.

At last he reached the top—and there the narrow street twisted down suddenly. Before Pico knew what had happened he again found himself in front of silver shops.

He went down four stone steps and quite unexpectedly he spied a snug little shop.

This was a special nook with wide blue steps in front.

Pico's heart beat like a pulsing bell clapper as he peered inside the door.

The room was not too large and not too small. It is just right, thought Pico.

At the far end of the room a tiny fire burned. Smoke went up like a silver web.

Pico blinked.

The little man who owned this place stood behind a counter.

He looks kind, thought Pico.

He mounted the blue steps to get a better view.

The master of this shop was yellowish-brown, like aged leather, and he had a white mustache and a little pointed beard. His black velvet cap let a fringe of white hair escape over his ears, and the velvet of his black blouse was dusty.

The man was talking with two American tourists who stood in front of him. He was showing them a splendid silver tray. This man does fine work with his fingers, Pico thought. Instantly, he was sure he wanted the little man with the dusty blouse for his master.

But Pico knew a small boy must not disturb a silversmith when he is busy with customers, so he sat down on the edge of the blue step to wait.

After a while Pico turned and peered over his shoulder.

Inside the little shop, smoke still floated up like a silver web, and now Pico's nose smelled beans, hot with chili.

Ah, thought Pico, gazing at the silversmith, if he takes me, I will brush the dust from his velvet blouse for him.

Suddenly Pico's dark eyes widened.

There at the far end of the snug room stood a bench. Near, on a small table, were tools. Silversmith tools! Tools for Pico, perhaps!

The two women tourists passed out through the blue door. Then, quite near him, stood the little old silversmith, his black velvet cap nodding good-bye to the American ladies.

Pico jumped up.

"Please—" he grabbed off his plaited straw hat—"please, I will dust your velvet blouse for you."

His voice trembled. For those were not the words Pico had intended to say.

He dropped his purple basket. It went tumbling down the blue steps.

Now, thought Pico, he will think I am careless.

His throat choked as he rescued his basket and stumbled back up the blue steps to stand in front of the little old silversmith.

The man said, "I have a wife. She usually dusts my blouse."

He looked down at his creased velvet jacket and his lips were smiling. "Lately," he said, "she has been busy with her tulip bed."

Pico looked up into the yellowish-brown face above him, scarcely seeing the white mustache and the little pointed beard. For suddenly he remembered his fine nail!

"Please," he said, reaching into his purple basket, "I wish to make something for you."

He could feel the eyes of the old silversmith on him. His hand moved quickly as he pulled out his nail.

"Ah!" said the silversmith. "So you wish to make something for me?" and he smiled down at Pico as he brushed his velvet blouse with his narrow right hand.

Pico sat down then, for suddenly his legs would not hold him up. For a moment everything was jumbled. Pico felt as if he would topple off the blue step. Oh, he thought, if I had only one nibble from a tortilla perhaps my legs would stiffen!

The silversmith said, "Come inside, boy. Customers are coming," and he put his hand on Pico's shoulder.

When they were inside the snug shop, Pico felt himself being set down in front of the table where all the tools lay. He gasped.

There were pointed steel tools and blunt ones, too, and big and little hammers. On Pico's right stood a small charcoal burner for heating metals and tools.

"You can work here," said the old silversmith as he turned to wait on the customers who were entering the door.

Pico stared down at the fine tools, his fingers itching to touch them. But he kept his mind on what he wanted to do. He must make something for the old silversmith.

If what I make turns out well, thought Pico, perhaps he will take me for his boy.

He reached into his basket to grasp the tin can top he had found near the plaza the night before.

Pico laid the top on the table in front of him. What should he make for the silversmith? So much depended now on how well he worked with his nail.

Suddenly Pico knew what he wanted to make. He bent over the tin can top, his nail poised. I shall make a turtle, he thought. This turtle shall be the finest I have ever made.

First, Pico outlined a round fat body. He was a long time shaping it to his satisfaction. Next, he carved four stubby legs. His fingers quivered as he outlined the legs. He was determined to make them look as if they wanted to start walking immediately. This was hard to do. But after a while Pico was satisfied with the turtle legs. They seemed just right.

Pico held up the carving, staring at it. Perhaps it would turn out well if he could keep his trembling fingers steady. But he had not eaten all day, so it was hard to steady his hands when so much depended upon what he was doing.

Pico glanced over his shoulder. The old silversmith was wrapping up bundles. Soon he would come to the workbench.

"Work fast!" Pico whispered to his unsteady hands. "Work fast." His dark eyes glowed as he carved crisscross marks on the turtle's back. Now the tin turtle was crisscrossed like a real turtle's hard-shelled back. Next Pico carved a round-looking head, with a short neck. Then he carved a short, pointed tail. When he had finished the tail, he reached into his basket and brought out the green maguey string. Swiftly Pico punched a hole in the tin turtle's neck, threaded it, and tied the two ends of green string together.

"Where did you learn to carve with that nail?" asked a voice.

Pico gave a start. For the old silversmith stood over him. Pico's heart hammered against his small ribs and his legs were striking the stool. He tried to stand.

"Sit down, boy," said the silversmith, and Pico felt the man's hand on his shoulder. "Let me see your work."

Pico handed up the small turtle he had made. There was nothing more he could do. Everything depended now on what the old silversmith thought.

"So," murmured the kindly voice, "so, you would dust my blouse for me." The old silversmith was looking intently down at Pico's work.

The man turned the small turtle around and around as though he were thinking. "An excellent turtle," he said, "an excellent turtle."

Pico closed his eyes because once again everything suddenly jumbled. He clutched the stool.

"Let me see your hands."

Pico opened his eyes and held out his trembling hands.

"Why," said the man, "you should work with silver, boy! How would you like to be a silversmith?"

"That is what I wanted to do all this time!" exclaimed Pico, his thin voice sounding as if it were amazed that anyone in all Mexico didn't know Pico wanted, more than anything, to be a silversmith.

The old master said solemnly, "Now that my hands are getting old I need a good boy."

"I will be a good boy!" cried Pico.

"Come," the silversmith touched his arm. "Come, boy. The hour is late. Let us eat."

Pico felt himself being led to a small round table where a woman stood dishing beans, hot with chili, into blue bowls.

The woman wore a wide white apron over her dark-brown dress and a red rose tucked in her thick black hair.

The old silversmith said, "Sit down, boy."

Pico sat down and the woman passed him a steaming blue bowl full of beans.

When they were seated, the silversmith said to his wife, "My velvet blouse is dusty."

But the woman tossed her head, laughing. She said, "Now that the tulip bed is finished, I will dust your velvet blouse three times daily."

The man said, "From now on you will have two black velvet blouses to dust. Mine and this boy's."

Pico felt the kindness in the old silversmith's voice as he stared across the table at the white mustache and little pointed beard. He let his eyes glance shyly at the red rose tucked in the woman's dark hair. The woman seemed a jolly person, and he could tell by her manner that she also welcomed a small boy. She said, "He must go to school."

The silversmith nodded, and Pico cried, "I will study hard!"

Then he was silent for a long time, thinking. Finally, he said, "I wish to send for my parents. How can I make money enough to bring them from Mexico City to Taxco in a coach?"

The old silversmith looked thoughtfully at Pico. "I will pay you to help wait on my customers," he said, "and if you work hard, I will make you the best silversmith in all Mexico."

"Thank you," said Pico, his dark eyes filled with wonder as he stared down at his two brown hands.

When supper was over and the empty ache in Pico's stomach troubled him no more, the silversmith's wife said, "Come." And Pico followed her outside into a small patio.

On one side red geraniums guarded a wall, and across a square of grass Pico saw the neat tulip bed. The woman led him to a coffee bush and there on the damp earth lay a small gray fawn.

Pico stopped breathing, his lips partly open.

The fawn under the coffee bush looked so much like the one he had seen yesterday. Yet it was not the same. This gray fawn had brown ears.

The silversmith's wife said, "He shall be your fawn."

Pico knelt and slipped his arms around the fawn's graceful neck. Could this be true? A gray fawn for Pico!

The woman left him and now he was alone with the small fawn.

Pico put his brown face close against the soft gray fur.

The coffee bush was very quiet above them.

"We will be friends," Pico whispered into the fawn's brown ear. The small animal pushed his damp nose against the boy's warm brown throat.

Pico stared up. He could see the tall church spires, like silver nails against the dull blue sky and high up to the east the silver mountain peaks dozed on a plum-colored couch. The gray fawn nestled closer.

I am glad I came to the silver mountain, thought Pico, his dark eyes shining at the moon coming up like a big silver wheel behind the plum-colored mountain. Now I can be a silversmith.

Arbor Day

(Various dates)

"There is beauty in a well-ordered orchard which is a 'joy forever.' It is a blessing to him who plants it, and it perpetuates his name and memory, keeping it fresh as the fruit it bears long after he has ceased to live."

These words are from a speech made by J. Sterling Morton, a resident of the new state of Nebraska, which was an almost treeless state when it joined the union in 1867. Most of the few trees that had once grown there had been cut down by settlers in need of building materials.

But Sterling Morton was a man of vision. He knew that trees were necessary to retain moisture in the soil, to serve as windbreaks on the flat prairie country, and to add beauty to the landscape. He set out fruit trees and shade trees—hundreds of them—urging others to do the same. When he became president of the State Board of Agriculture, he suggested that a special day be set aside for planting trees. On April 10, 1872, more than a million trees were set out in Nebraska, and the state legislature made tree-planting day an annual event. Later, the date for Arbor Day—so called because *arbor* is the Latin word for tree—was changed to April 22, Mr. Morton's birthday.

Arbor Day is now celebrated throughout the United States and in many other countries as well. Through the efforts of such public-spirited men as Sterling Morton and Presidents Theodore and Franklin Roosevelt, the country has come to realize that forests are among the nation's most valuable resources.

A much earlier American who urged the planting of trees was John Chapman, better known as Johnny Appleseed. In the days when the nation was young, he wandered through the backwoods country carrying seedlings for the new settlers so that they and their children and their children's children might have orchards.

109

The Birthday Orchard

A Story of Johnny Appleseed

EMILY TAFT DOUGLAS

Ada Bartlett stole out of the cabin and ran pell-mell along the path to the spring. This was her favorite place in the whole clearing, but this morning she buried her head in her arms and lay on the ground sobbing. It was her birthday, but nobody cared.

She remembered her birthdays back in Boston, before she was a backwoods girl—the cake, the gifts, the little birthday guests in white dresses and ribbons. Even last year, on her first birthday in the Indiana country, her mother had given her a beautiful doll—a doll which, unknown to her, had traveled with them the whole way in the covered wagon. And then her mother, smiling and rosy as she was in those days, had somehow stirred up a birthday cake to make it a real party. The whole family had played games, and it had been a lovely day.

Then came the winter, and what a winter! Ada shivered as she remembered how the wind had roared across the prairies and how, in spite of the chinkings of moss between the logs of their cabin, the cold had swept in. Her eyes filled with tears as she thought about her little brother, who took sick and faded away, without a doctor or proper food. It was then, Ada thought, that her mother forgot how to smile and her father became afraid. He was afraid that he could never tame his wilderness and that his whole family might perish.

Once, when she had said that her birthday was coming, he had replied, "Your mother has enough on her mind without worrying about birthdays. Besides, there aren't any birthdays in the wilderness."

For a long time Ada lay on the ground beside the spring. She felt very empty and tired. Then something caught her attention. There, facing her, stood a man. He was the strangest-looking man that she had ever seen. His gray hair touched his shoulders. He wore a burlap coffee sack for a shirt, and his bare legs stuck out below short, faded overalls. This funny outfit was topped by a wide-brimmed hat made of cardboard. And yet, after her first glimpse of his curious costume Ada forgot all about it. The man's eyes and his smile told her that he would never do anyone any harm.

"Do you care if I sit down and rest here a spell?" he asked. Without waiting for an answer, he sat down on the ground, his back against a tree. "You and your folks must be new settlers in these parts."

"We've been here more than a year," Ada told him. "We came all the way from Boston. It seems like a thousand years ago."

"I'm from Boston, too," the man told her. "But by your count I left there a million years ago. Well, how are you making out on the frontier?"

Tears welled up again in Ada's eyes as she thought of their troubles.

"Hm," the man said. "I reckon the drought last summer burned your father's corn?"

Ada nodded. "And a wolf killed Daisy, our cow," she managed to tell him. "Then my little brother took sick and couldn't live any longer. My mother has never been the same since."

"The wilderness likes to test folks," the man declared. He gave Ada a long look and asked, "About ten years old, aren't you?"

"Ten today, but of course birthdays don't count in the backwoods," she said. Then she turned her head away, for she could not manage her chin that day.

"So that's the way of it," he said. "Your birthday! Now just a moment. I may have something here." He dug into his knapsack and burrowed around for a moment. Then he pulled out a parcel.

"I carry little things here in case of need. Yes, here's what I have for girls on their tenth birthdays." He took out a piece of pink silk ribbon and handed it to her.

"It's not really for me?" Ada asked. After all, when her own parents forgot about presents, why should a stranger give her one?

The man nodded.

"It's beautiful," Ada told him as she smoothed the ribbon tenderly across her lap.

"It's the color of apple blossoms," the man pointed out. "That's why I always choose pink."

Again he burrowed in his knapsack. "There's something else I'd like to give you," he said. "It's the finest present in the world." He pulled out a large package.

When he unwrapped it, Ada saw dozens of small bags made of deerskin. The man chose one of these bags and held it up. "This is my treasure," he announced. "And the most wonderful thing about it is that every year it will give you more gifts."

"What is it?" Ada asked, for the words had a magic sound.

"Want to see?" The man plucked open one end of the bag and took out a small black object.

"A seed!" Ada exclaimed. She was both puzzled and disappointed.

"An apple seed," the old man nodded gleefully. But before he had a chance to go on, Mrs. Bartlett and Ned, Ada's older brother, appeared, carrying buckets to fill with water from the spring. The man scrambled to his feet.

"Don't fear," he told Mrs. Bartlett. "It's only me. I was just passing through these parts and stopped for water."

"Are you going far?" she asked, with a glance at his bare feet.

"Yes, I'm aiming to go farther west into the Illinois country this trip. Maybe I'll push on as far as the Mississippi."

Mrs. Bartlett looked at the stranger again, and with more interest than she had shown for weeks. "You're not settling here? You're just traveling through the wilderness for—for pleasure?"

The man nodded. "I like the wilderness. Ever since I was a little chap I've loved the woods. But now, of course, I've got my work." He showed her what was in the little deerskin bags. "I follow the frontier, preaching orchards. Everywhere I go, I carry seeds to start orchards in the wilderness."

"Oh," cried Mrs. Bartlett with sudden recognition, "then of course I know who you are! You're Johnny Appleseed!" And she, too, sat down to rest against a tree.

"That's what folks call me," he said.

To Ned, Johnny Appleseed's job was still a mystery. "But who wants an orchard in the backwoods anyhow?" he asked.

The old man did not answer at once. Then he murmured in a low, tantalizing tone, "Do you remember large, red-cheeked, juicy apples?"

"Oh, I want one!" exclaimed Ada, half expecting him to pull apples from his knapsack.

Johnny Appleseed's eyes were still on Ned as he went on, "An apple would taste mighty good right now, wouldn't it? And do you like roasted apples on a winter evening? Or maybe you would prefer a mug of cider in the fall, or a deep-dish apple pie?"

"Oh, stop!" cried Ned, his mouth watering. "Ma, do you remember the pies you used to make back in Boston?"

Mrs. Bartlett only sighed.

Johnny Appleseed turned toward her. "Maybe you would like an orchard by your house. How would it be to look out every spring on an orchard in bloom? It's the most beautiful sight God ever made, and you can have it right here."

"It sounds almost like heaven," Mrs. Bartlett murmured.

She smiled as she stood up—her first smile since her little boy had died. "You'll stay to dinner with us, of course," she said. "We've no apple pie or anything tasty, but you're welcome to share with us."

"I'll be proud to share," Johnny Appleseed accepted. "And maybe we can start an orchard here as, well—as a sort of birthday gift for this little girl."

Johnny Appleseed not only stayed to dinner but spent the night. Outside it was raining in earnest. Rainy days in Boston had been cozy, Ada thought, but who could feel cozy with greased-paper windows and leaks between the logs where the moss stuffing had fallen out? Besides, the cabin was too small to hold Ned's noise, her mother's sadness, and her father's restlessness. Already Tom Bartlett was pacing the floor like a caged lion. He refused to listen to talk of an orchard. He was already doing the work of two men.

"If you want it to rain in this forsaken country," he grumbled to Johnny Appleseed, "you have a drought for weeks, but if the earth is already soggy, you can count on it to pour every day."

Johnny Appleseed did not say anything. He took a small black book from his knapsack and squatted down beside the hearth. "Do you care if I read aloud?" he asked.

Tom Bartlett stared without answering, and Johnny Appleseed opened his book. His voice was one that Ada never forgot. It had the roar of the wind and the sea at times, and again it was as gentle as a rustling breeze. It was the familiar Twenty-third Psalm that he was reading.

When he was through, Mrs. Bartlett wiped her eyes, but she looked less sad than usual.

The lines of bitterness on Tom Bartlett's face had faded.

"What with hostile tribes and heat," he said, "I suppose those shepherds had as hard a time in Bible days as we settlers have now."

"It takes faith now as it did in the Bible days," Johnny Appleseed told them. "But you have green pastures and still waters. You shall not want."

"You think there is a living for us here?" Tom Bartlett asked.

"I know it," said Johnny Appleseed. "You can make this land blossom like a garden. I've seen it happen all the way from Pittsburgh to the Illinois country. The frontier has been turning into rich farmland."

"But it's not just a living I want," Mrs. Bartlett broke in. "Our children are growing up ignorant, like all backwoods children. They don't have schooling, and they'll never have a real chance in the world."

"I was just thinking," Johnny Appleseed went on, "that in a few years, when more settlers come, you'll have a school right here to give the trimmings to your children's training or to ready this boy for college, if you want. In the meanwhile you'd make a first-rate teacher yourself."

Mrs. Bartlett shook her head. "How can we ever hope to have a real school here?" she asked.

"Schools follow settlers mighty fast," Johnny Appleseed told her. "First there are only wilderness, wild beasts, and Indians. Then a few families try out the land. They make good farms and that draws other settlers. They have corn and wheat, and sometimes orchards."

Tom Bartlett raised his head, and Johnny Appleseed hurried on. "Soon they have crops to trade, and one fine morning they will find a little store sprouted up like a mushroom overnight. Then the mothers start planning for a school. I've seen it happen up and down this frontier land."

Mrs. Bartlett put aside her work. She was watching Johnny Appleseed now as if he were a strange new creature, just come within her sight. "You sow, but you never reap," she murmured. "Didn't you ever have a home and orchard of your own?"

He nodded. "Yes, I had both of them once, long ago."

"That was in Boston," Ada broke in, "a million years ago."

Johnny Appleseed chuckled. "No, but I was born in Boston, two million years ago by your count. It's easy to remember, because I was born within sight of Bunker Hill in 1775—the year before the Declaration of Independence was signed. But I got the woods in my blood, and as soon as I was grown I began to follow the Indian trails. Where Pittsburgh now stands was frontier. I settled there and built a house. I had a farm and an orchard that was the wonder of the wilderness."

"Then why did you leave?" asked Mrs. Bartlett.

Johnny Appleseed thought for a moment. Then he answered, "It was the covered wagons and the settlers going west. I grew sorry for the travelers. They were so needful of comforts when they came to my house."

Johnny Appleseed went on to tell how so many people stopped for a bite to eat or for lodging that his neighbors said he ran a free tavern.

"Poor, bedraggled creatures they came," he said, "the men and older children toiling along the road with the horses and cows, and the great, creaking wagons swarming with little ones. They were tired and dirty and hungry when they reached my door."

Ada watched Johnny Appleseed's face light up as he told how he helped those poor travelers. "They smacked their lips over my good bread, fresh butter, and wild honey," he boasted, "but most of all they relished my apples. On cool evenings the guests roasted apples at my hearth. And they always asked, 'When shall we ever taste another apple?' "

Johnny Appleseed told the Bartletts how he planned to spread orchards in the backwoods. He planted several nurseries in Ohio, and later some in Indiana. But for the settlers in the lonely parts, he said, seeds were the only answer, for seeds were a safe and handy way to carry the makings of an orchard.

"Once I realized this," he declared seriously, "I was ready for my lifework in the wilderness."

"You left your fine house and your orchard," exclaimed Mrs. Bartlett, "to help strangers in the wilderness!"

"Some folks say I was crazy to leave a good living in the East and peddle apple seeds out here," the old man admitted. "Well, maybe they're right. But I've been following the frontier for thirty years now. I help make the wilderness blossom. I help make it fit for settlers and their families."

"You do a good work," Tom Bartlett admitted gruffly.

"Nothing gives folks such a home feeling as an orchard," Johnny Appleseed went on. "If you've started an orchard, you know you're settled, because you want to see it bear fruit. Then you start making the best of things. Besides, the apple is the king of fruits. Think of fresh apples in the fall and of roasted apples on winter evenings. Think of cider, apple butter, pies, tarts, jelly, and dumplings."

He unrolled the list slowly, temptingly, "There's a host of pleasure in that one fruit. And the orchard itself! Do you remember the blessed shade in the summer and the pink blossoms in the spring?"

"Oh, Tom, do you remember the full moon shining on my father's orchard?" suddenly broke in Mrs. Bartlett. "We used to walk there and we thought that it was heaven."

"Pa," Ada whispered, "Ma is smiling!"

Tom Bartlett looked at his wife. "An orchard means that much to you?" he asked.

"It would be like a little bit of home," she said.

"Please, Pa," begged Ada. "I've seen his little bags of seeds. He wanted to give me one, and I'd love it more than anything."

"I was only thinking of a birthday present," Johnny Appleseed apologized. "She's ten years old today, and that's an age for presents."

Tom Bartlett flushed. "All right," he agreed out loud. "It will be Ada's birthday present."

Ada jumped up and flung her arms about her father's neck, and Ned shouted for joy.

Johnny Appleseed beamed. "I was figuring on staying over and helping you get started." He burrowed again in his knapsack and took out one of the deerskin bags for the birthday girl. "It's my treasure," he told her. "Take care of it, and you will have an everlasting treasure for yourself and for your children."

It was late April several years later. There had been a week of warm weather, then a day of showers, and the next morning the sun shone brightly. Ada was hanging out some dish towels. She was shaking out the damp cloths when a breeze brought her a whiff of something sweet. She glanced over her shoulder and saw the miracle. The apple trees had burst into bloom!

For a moment she stood there, clothespins in her hand, and stared. She had known this would happen someday. The swollen buds had promised that it would happen soon. But she had waited so long that now she could scarcely believe her eyes. The promise of the small black seeds was fulfilled in this blossoming!

"Johnny Appleseed, you are right," she whispered, letting the clothespins fall to the ground. "This is the most beautiful sight on earth."

Why the Old Man Planted Trees

DAN MURDOCH

A nobleman was once riding along the road and saw a very old man digging in his garden. Beside the old man, on the ground, lay a sapling tree, ready to be planted. The nobleman stopped to watch, and after a few minutes called out to the old man, "What kind of tree are you planting there, my good man?"

The old man wiped his brow and picked up the sapling. "This is a fig tree, sir," he said.

"A fig tree?" cried the astonished nobleman. "Why, how old are you, may I ask?"

"I am ninety years old," said the other.

"What!" cried the nobleman. "You are ninety years old, and you plant a tree that will take years and years to give fruit?"

"Why not?" replied the old man.

The nobleman pointed to the tree. "Surely you don't expect to live long enough to get any benefit from the hard work you are doing with this sapling."

The old man leaned on his shovel and looked around his garden. Then he smiled and said, "Tell me, sir, did you eat figs when you were a boy?"

"Certainly." The nobleman sounded puzzled. "Why?"

The old man smiled again. "Then tell me this," he said, "who planted the trees from which those figs were picked?"

The nobleman hesitated. "Why—why, I don't know."

"You see, sir," the old man continued, "our forefathers planted trees for us to enjoy, and I am doing the same for those who come after me. How else can I repay my debt to those who lived before me?"

The nobleman was silent for a moment and then said, "You are very wise, old man, and I have been foolish."

"Thank you, sir," said the old man. "May I ask your name?"

"It doesn't matter," said the nobleman. "You are far more important than I am. Good-bye."

The old man nodded his head in farewell and began to dig again, while the nobleman clucked to his horse and rode off, one arm raised in salute to the wise old man.

Patriots' Day

(April 19)

This holiday, celebrated in Maine and Massachusetts, is the anniversary of the battles fought at Lexington and Concord in 1775, marking the beginning of the American Revolution. Ralph Waldo Emerson was referrring to the battle at Concord in his famous poem telling of "the shot heard round the world." The American experience was an inspiration to men everywhere who yearned for freedom.

Today a visit to Boston on Patriots' Day is like stepping back into history. The lantern in Old Christ Church is hung again in a special ceremony. Two men are selected to take the parts of Paul Revere and William Dawes, of whose daring ride the night of April 18, 1775, you will read in the following story. The men who reenact the roles leave Boston in broad daylight, sped on their way by cheering crowds. Other crowds greet them when they reach Lexington and Concord.

In each of these towns there is an elaborate celebration. The original heroes, if they could come back, might be surprised to see the parades with very modern floats. It is all great fun. But the Minute Men drilling on the village green are dressed in colonial clothes, like those of the real Minute Men. And they look just as serious as they reenact some of the scenes that started our nation on its way.

121

The Midnight Rider, Paul Revere

CARL CARMER

"One if by land. Two if by sea."

These words echo in our minds when we hear the name of Paul Revere. We see a figure on horseback galloping through the night, calling out, "The British are coming!" Perhaps we even remember a stanza or two of Longfellow's poem:

> Listen, my children, and you shall hear
> Of the midnight ride of Paul Revere. . . .
>
> A hurry of hoofs in a village street,
> A shape in the moonlight, a bulk in the dark,
> And beneath, from the pebbles, in passing, a spark
> Struck out by a steed flying fearless and fleet. . . .

Paul Revere. A patriot on horseback, yes, but also an artist and craftsman whose designs were to become treasured heirlooms. He was to found one of America's great industries.

But how did men see him while he lived? That Boston patriot Dr. Joseph Warren, for one. He was Paul Revere's friend and admirer. What might he say of him? "A dark, stocky, sturdy figure of a man. Paul was of French stock. His hands were strong. A craftsman's hands. Strength—that was the keynote of Paul's mind and body. Above all, he was trustworthy, utterly trustworthy."

Dr. Warren had good reason to value trustworthiness. Along with such Massachusetts leaders as Samuel Adams, John Hancock, and Isaiah Thomas, he was active in the colonists' growing movement toward rebellion against the British. One April evening as he started toward Revere's shop, he knew the threatening explosion could not be far off.

Apparently the redcoats were up to something, too. Only last

122

night, in Boston Harbor, the small boats on the British transports had been lowered and made ready for action. At any moment, those boats might be filled with armed soldiers. The most ominous sign of all was that the British grenadiers and light infantry had been ordered off guard duty.

The bell above the shop door tinkled as Dr. Warren entered Revere's shop and found its owner still at work. Warren looked around cautiously.

"Clemmens has gone to supper," Revere assured him. "We can talk freely." Ike Clemmens, whom Revere employed as an engraver, was a Tory.

"Sam Adams and John Hancock have gone to Lexington," Dr. Warren said. "So has John Adams. Unfortunately, General Gage, the British commander, seems to have learned of this. Gage will certainly try to seize them, as well as our military stores at Concord."

"Hancock and Adams must be warned," said Revere.

"Yes," Dr. Warren agreed. "Will you go to them, Paul?"

Paul nodded.

"And then to Concord," Doctor Warren went on. "All our cannon and ammunition must be hidden deep in the swamps, where the British can't find them. On your way back, stop to see Colonel William Conant in Charlestown. Tell him if the British make a move we'll give him warning. Signal lanterns will be hung in the belfry of Christ Church. One lantern if the British march by land. Two lanterns if they embark in the boats for Cambridge."

Not long after that night, Dr. Warren, only thirty-four, was to die at Bunker Hill, slain by a British musketball. Revere lived on for many years, but people remembered his midnight ride to warn the patriots that the British were coming. They couldn't stop talking about it. His wife, Rachel, would pretend to be annoyed, but her pride in her husband showed through.

"That precious ride again!" she sometimes exclaimed. "Will I never hear the end of it? I'll tell you this, though—I tried to stop him."

Then she might explain: "Paul was a widower with six children when I married him. And I had one of my own. So that night, when Paul told me he must ride a second time, I thought of our seven children——

"Oh, have I confused you when I say a *second* ride? Well, he had already gone to Lexington and warned Adams and Hancock, then on to Concord and home. After that, if the British moved, he was to inform Bob Newman, the sexton at Christ Church, from whose belfry the warning lantern would hang. Then Paul was to ride *again*, this time ahead of the British. That first ride was bad enough, but the second! Why, it was almost like asking Paul to put his head into a noose! If the British caught him, I'd be a widow—with seven mouths to feed.

"So I said, 'Why is it *you're* the one who is always asked to risk his neck?'

" 'Not me alone,' he said. 'Billy Dawes is riding tonight. And he goes the most dangerous way, by land across the Neck. And Josh Bentley and Tom Richardson will row me over to Charlestown——'

" 'Under the guns of the enemy fleet?' I was half weeping. 'Oh, no, Paul!'

" 'Don't you fret. We'll be quiet about it, Rachel,' he said. With that he gave me a kiss and was out the door before I could argue any more.

"It was but a short time after he departed that someone came rapping on the door with the news that the British had posted men on the road to Lexington to stop any warning rider! And Paul had known that before he left!

"Well, I don't suppose *I would* have stopped him, even if I could have. For if you love a man like Paul, you don't come between him and the doing of what he believes is right."

In later years, Paul wrote about that fateful night when he, Josh Bentley and Tom Richardson shoved a boat into the water at full tide. The oars were muffled in a flannel petticoat borrowed from Richardson's sweetheart, the petticoat still warm—said Paul—when they ripped it apart to bind the blades. Past His Majesty's ship the *Somerset*, with her sixty-four guns, they let the tide take them gently onto the Charlestown shore. Here Colonel Conant waited, holding the reins of a horse.

"Jim Larkin's finest," the colonel said, giving the horse a pat, "and Charlestown's best. Good luck to you, Revere!"

Good luck . . . perhaps Paul had it, that night. But he also had courage and devotion to his country's cause.

For most of us that's the Paul Revere story, and that's all we know about Revere. But he was to enjoy forty-three prosperous years. They were also years of service to his country.

When the Continental Congress needed someone to engrave and print its paper currency, it turned to Revere. When Massachusetts needed a commander for the militia defending Boston, Revere accepted the dangerous position. When cannons were needed, it was Paul Revere who, in a short time, learned how to make them.

And when peace came and the Second Church required a new bell, it was Paul who cast it. From his Boston shop, beautiful silver work—museum pieces today—continued to pour. More and more children came to him and Rachel.

In 1798, Revere wrote to the Secretary of the Navy, suggesting he be allowed to make copper sheathing for ships of war. But how could he do this, he was asked, since only the British knew the secret of making sheet copper. In the second place, America did not have the rolling mills that would be necessary. Well, in the first place, Revere said, about this "British secret," "I do not believe it's a secret at all. We'll experiment until we find out how to make it. And in the second place, I'll build the mills myself, even if I have to borrow the money."

Let the log of the U.S.S. *Constitution* speak for his craftsmanship: "June 26, 1803. The carpenters gave nine cheers, which was answered by the seamen and caulkers, because they had in fourteen days completed coppering the ship with copper *made in the United States of America!*"

(This selection, edited by Carl Carmer, was based on a program in the "Cavalcade of America" radio series.)

Paul Revere Rides Again

JACK BECHDOLT

"A horse?" asked Mr. Crane. "What's all this about a horse?"

He set down his cup of coffee and looked inquiringly at his family gathered about the breakfast table.

Nelson, the younger of the Crane boys, choked with excitement and became speechless. Many times he had rehearsed to himself just how he would make this request. Now that the moment had come, he was tongue-tied.

His brother John came to his rescue. "Nelson wants to rent Mullins' old white horse," John explained. "He wants to be Paul Revere in the Patriots' Day pageant and he can't do that very well without a horse, can he?"

"Pageant?" Mr. Crane exclaimed. "What pageant?"

"Nonsense, Richard," said Mrs. Crane. "Don't pretend you haven't heard of the pageant. Your children have talked of nothing else for a week. It's to be a historical pageant. The children will impersonate various characters in American history. Nelson's choice is Paul Revere. So he wants to rent Mr. Mullins' horse."

"It's only five dollars," Nelson said, quivering with eagerness. "Mullins says I can have the horse all day for that price and he won't charge me anything extra for a saddle and bridle. And I'll pay for it out of my pocket money!"

Mr. Crane stared thoughtfully at his son. "You think you know how to ride?"

"Yes, sir, I do," said Nelson. "I've been practicing."

Mr. Crane glanced at his wife. She smiled and nodded. "Go

ahead, my boy," he said. "But remember, in the words of Nathan Hale, you have but one neck to break honoring your country!" Smiling at his own joke, he got up from the table.

"Thanks a lot, John," Nelson gasped when he was alone with his brother. "I was scared he'd say no."

"When did you learn to ride? I don't believe you can." John was skeptical.

"I can ride this horse. Mullins let me try it the other day and I didn't fall off once. It's a swell horse, John! It's really beautiful—or it will be with a little fixing up!" Nelson's eyes glowed with a vision of himself in wig and greatcoat, booted and spurred like Paul Revere.

John smiled his big-brother smile and said, "Let's have a look at this wonderful horse and talk to Mullins."

Mr. Mullins was the village odd-job man. He trimmed hedges, mended broken furniture and sharpened lawn mowers. He was a huge, hairy person who went about in all weathers clad in a torn undershirt, baggy overalls and sneakers. He lived in a little shack he had built on the outskirts of the village.

In a nearby pasture Mr. Mullins' horse, Captain, roamed at will.

The two boys and Mr. Mullins leaned on the pasture fence.

"There's an awful lot of him," John said doubtfully.

There was, indeed. Captain was a great beast, a noble old ruin. To Nelson, who contemplated riding him, he loomed as big as a church.

"Think you can stick on his back?" John asked. Nelson swallowed hard. "He acts friendly," he said.

"Why, that hoss is gentle as a kitten!" said Mr. Mullins. "Captain knows the route of that parade better than you do. Me and Captain used to deliver milk in that part of town. Get up on his back, Nelson. Show your brother how you can handle him."

John and Mr. Mullins boosted Nelson onto Captain's broad back. Nelson took firm hold of the long white mane and softly said, "Giddap, Captain." Captain moved a few steps, stopped and fell into a doze.

"What did I tell you?" Nelson beamed. "Isn't he noble, John?"

John started to say that he hoped Captain wouldn't die of old age before the parade. But he held his tongue. He felt it would be cruel to make fun of his kid brother. Nelson had set his heart on riding that horse.

"Let's take him home and work on him a bit," John suggested.

With Captain reluctantly plodding behind them, the two brothers left the pasture. Their arrival in the Crane's back yard drew out the family.

"Here he is!" Nelson shouted. "Gosh, isn't he something?"

"He is indeed," Mr. Crane agreed. "Quite a museum piece."

"I thought you said it was a white horse," said Sister May.

"He will be when he has had his bath," said John.

"He needs it," said May, and turned up her nose.

Their sister Agatha, who was wheeling Horace, the baby, in his buggy, murmured, "See Nelson's horsey, Horace. Nice horsey?"

"Blub," said Horace and blew derisive bubbles. The family giggled.

"Go ahead and laugh! A lot any of you know about horses," Nelson burst out. "You wait till we get him fixed up and you'll see."

"Of course we will. And he is a very fine horse!" It was Mrs. Crane who understood Nelson's hurt feelings. She knew how much this parade meant to him. "We'll be proud of Nelson."

Mrs. Crane rubbed Captain's velvet muzzle and fed him a cube of sugar.

"You boys get Captain all fixed up pretty, and I'll have Nelson's costume ready for him."

Undoubtedly Captain had not been bathed for a long time, if ever. John and Nelson used the garden hose and bars of laundry soap and spent hours in scrubbing. They combed out Captain's flowing mane and tail and when he had dried they dusted him liberally with some of Mrs. Crane's white talcum powder. The powder was perfumed.

Nelson gazed on their handiwork with pride. Now Captain gleamed like a horse carved from pure white marble.

Directly after lunch the parade began to form at the north end of the village. The bands and floats and marchers watched with surprise the appearance of Captain, ridden by Paul Revere wearing a wig and three-cornered hat and looking not unlike Nelson Crane.

"Splendid!" exclaimed Professor Etheridge, the school principal. "You are our only horseman, Nelson. You shall lead the procession."

Whistles blew. Commands were shouted. The school band blared out a military march as Captain moved to his place at the head of the column.

"There, Captain," Nelson whispered in the old horse's ear. "Didn't I tell you you'd make a hit?"

Captain started out jauntily when the bugles sounded. He even tried prancing a little as the procession turned into Main Street.

And then it happened! In Captain's muddled old mind, Main Street meant milk to be delivered. He made his usual first stop at the Adams place and stood patiently for the time it used to take Mr. Mullins to carry in the bottles.

Shouting at him did no good. Frantic kicking from his rider had no effect.

The parade stood still. The line buzzed angrily. "Is this a Patriots' Day parade or are we waiting for the Fourth of July?" yelled one of the paraders.

As unexpectedly as he had stopped, Captain started off again at his gentle, ambling gait. Behind him the paraders fell into step and the band played with renewed vigor. But only briefly.

They reached the home of Dr. Farraday. Captain halted again.

Paraders and spectators tugged at his bridle, shoved from the rear and offered a great deal of advice. Nelson shouted commands and drummed his heels on Captain's ribs. Captain stood his ground until old habit told him it was time to move again.

The third time this happened Professor Etheridge lost patience.

"To the right oblique, march!" he shouted. He spoke to Nelson as the column detoured around Captain. "We can't wait for that old nag any longer. This is a parade, not a milk delivery!"

Nelson's cheeks flamed. He heard the sniggers of his fellow-paraders and could not meet their eyes.

Somebody shouted, "Ride 'em, milkman!"

Another humorist squeaked, "Leave me a bottle of whipping cream."

Nelson gritted his teeth and writhed in silence. It seemed as if the parade would never be done passing. The memory of those grins and jibes burned.

But parades do end. The last float rolled past the disgraced horseman. Nelson and Captain were alone on an empty street. Captain dozed.

Nelson could not be angry with him, he looked so peaceful and innocent. "Oh Captain . . . how could you?"

Looking up, Nelson saw John running down the road. "For goodness sake, hurry up," John panted. "You'll miss the whole show."

"You try hurrying the old fool," Nelson groaned. "I give up."

"Then you'll have to get off and walk, that's all."

"Whoever heard of Paul Revere walking! People will laugh at me the rest of my life." Nelson winced at a new thought. "I've disgraced the family. Mother said you'd all be so proud of me and now . . ." Emotion overcame him.

"I'm not going to stand for it," Nelson declared suddenly, his tone very different. "I said I'd ride this horse and I'm going to! Mother went to a lot of trouble making this costume. I'm going to ride if I have to wait all day for Captain to change his mind."

"Now you're talking," his big brother exclaimed. "Don't let him get you down! Look, here comes Mullins. Maybe he can get him started."

Mr. Mullins seemed more interested in Captain's extraordinary intelligence than in Nelson's troubles. "Think of him remembering that milk route all these years," he marveled. "Watching him make his stops took me back to those frosty mornings long ago when we made the regular rounds. I tell you, boys, that horse has a brain!"

The ringing of the village fire bell interrupted Mr. Mullins. Captain, too, heard that loud alarm. He quivered. His big ears pricked forward. His aged eyes brightened.

A red fire truck swung into Main Street and went roaring up that thoroughfare with siren screaming.

The bridle was snatched from Mr. Mullins' hand. Captain lunged forward, uttering a shrill neigh. He was off at a gallop, with Nelson clinging for dear life. John and Mr. Mullins were left far behind.

"By gorry," marveled Mr. Mullins, "I clean forgot about that blasted fire bell. When he was a young fellow, Captain used to belong to the fire department. He never forgets to go to a fire if he can get loose."

Up the main street roared the fire department. Up the main street, far behind but gaining by the second, charged Mr. Mullins' wonder horse bearing Paul Revere.

Captain's mane and tail streamed out behind. His big, iron-shod hoofs struck sparks from the cobbles. Flat on his back, arms about his charger's neck, rode Nelson. His three-cornered hat blew off. The braided pigtail of his wig streamed straight behind.

The paraders scattered to let the red fire wagons pass. Before they could form ranks again, the fiery white steed roared past with Nelson Crane still in the saddle. Now they were leading the column.

Nelson's hands froze about the reins. He pulled hard for dear life and shouted, "Whoa." To his intense astonishment Captain slowed down.

Captain was not the sturdy young horse he had been in his fire department days. His lungs were roaring like an old bellows, and his knees wobbled. The fire wagons were out of sight now; the alarm bell had ceased its clangor. Captain slowed down to a walk.

At last, Nelson managed to catch his breath. His body felt beaten and bruised from top to toe. His head reeled with giddiness. But he and Captain were leading the parade and all the marchers had fallen in behind him. Nelson jerked his wig straight, wiped his steaming brow, and pulled down his coat.

As they drew nearer the grandstand, Nelson saw the spectators clapping their hands and heard cries of encouragement and admiration.

"Hooray for the parade," cried a small boy in the first row.

"Hooray for Paul Revere," shouted Mr. Crane, waving his hand wildly.

"Hooray for Nelson Crane," his mother yelled excitedly.

Nelson looked straight ahead, a broad grin on his face. He swelled out his chest, pulled in his stomach, and tried to look every inch a hero as he led the parade into the park.

Mother's Day

(Second Sunday in May)

The suggestion that one day should be set aside each year to honor all mothers came from Miss Anne Jarvis of Philadelphia. In 1907, on the anniversary of her own mother's death, she arranged for a special service in her church, and during the years that followed other churches began to observe the day. By 1914 the idea had become so popular that Congress, in recognition of the influence mothers have in the making of better citizens, recommended that the second Sunday in May be called Mother's Day. President Woodrow Wilson then issued a proclamation, asking that the American people display the flag on that day, "as a public expression of our love and reverence for the mothers of our country."

More recently, in connection with the annual celebration, an American Mothers Committee selects a woman of outstanding accomplishments as "Mother of the Year." It is the custom to wear a carnation on Mother's Day—a white one if one's mother is dead, a red one if she is living. As an expression of their love, the children in a family present their mother with greeting cards and gifts, and grown sons and daughters frequently phone or pay her a visit. People had found happiness in such reunions long before there was an official Mother's Day, and there is an old saying:

He who goes a-mothering finds violets in the lane.

Mama and the Graduation Present

KATHRYN FORBES

Winford School had become the most important thing in life to me. I was finally friends with the girls and was invited to all their parties. Every other Wednesday they came to my house and we would sit up in my attic, drink chocolate, eat cookies, and make plans about graduation.

We were enthralled with our superiority. We were going to be the first class at Winford to have evening graduation exercises; we were having a graduation play; we were making our own graduation dresses in sewing class.

And when I was given the second lead in the play—the part of the Grecian boy—I found my own great importance hard to bear. I alone, of all the girls, had to go downtown to the costumer's to rent a wig—a coarse black wig that smelled of disinfectant but made me feel like a real actress. At every opportunity, I would put it on and have Papa listen to my part of the play.

Then the girls started talking about graduation presents.

Madeline said she was getting an onyx ring with a small diamond. Hester was getting a real honest-to-goodness wrist watch, and Thyra's family was going to add seven pearls to the necklace they had started for her when she was a baby. Even Carmelita was getting something special; her sister Rose was putting a dollar every payday onto an ivory manicure set.

I was intrigued and wondered what great surprise my family had in store for me. I talked about it endlessly, hoping for some clue. It would be terrible if my present was not as nice as the rest.

"It is the custom, then," Mama asked, "the giving of gifts when one graduates?"

"My goodness, Mama," I said, "it's practically the most important time in a girl's life—when she graduates."

I had seen a beautiful pink celluloid dresser set at Mr. Schiller's drugstore, and I set my heart upon it. I dropped hint after hint, until my brother Nels took me aside and reminded me that we did not have money for that sort of thing.

"I don't care," I cried recklessly, "I must have a graduation present. Why, Nels, think how I will feel if I don't get any. When the girls ask me——"

Nels got impatient and said he thought I was turning into a spoiled brat. And I retorted that since he was a boy he naturally couldn't be expected to understand certain things.

When Mama and I were alone one day, she asked me how I would like her silver brooch for a graduation present. Mama thought a lot of that brooch—it had been her mother's in Norway.

"Mama," I said reasonably, "what in the world would I want an old brooch for?"

"It would be like a—an heirloom, Katrin. It was your grandmother's."

"No, thank you, Mama."

"I could polish it up, Katrin."

I shook my head. "Look, Mama, a graduation present is something like—well, like that beautiful dresser set in Mr. Schiller's window."

There, now, I had told. Surely, with such a hint——

Mama looked worried, but she didn't say anything. Just pinned the silver brooch back on her dress.

I was so sure that Mama would find some way to get me the dresser set that I bragged to the girls as if it were a sure thing. I even took them by Schiller's window to admire it. They agreed with me that it was wonderful. There was a comb, a brush, a mirror, a pincushion, a clothesbrush, and even something called a hair-receiver.

Graduation night was a flurry of excitement.

I didn't forget a single word of my part in the play. Flushed and triumphant, I heard Miss Scanlon say that I was every bit as good as Hester, who had taken elocution lessons for years. And when I went up to the platform for my diploma, the applause for me was long and loud. Of course, the aunts and uncles were all there, and Uncle Ole and Uncle Peter could clap very loudly, but I pretended that it was because I was so popular.

And when I got home—there was the pink celluloid dresser set!

Mama and Papa beamed at my delight, but Nels and my sister Christine didn't say anything. I decided that they were jealous and felt sorry that they would not join me in my joy.

I carried the box up to my attic and placed the comb and brush carefully on my dresser. It took me a long while to arrange everything to my satisfaction. The mirror, so. The pincushion, here. The hair-receiver, there.

Mama let me sleep late the next morning. When I got down for breakfast, she had already gone downtown to do her shopping. Nels was reading the want-ad section of the paper. Since it was vacation, he was going to try to get a job. He read the jobs aloud to Papa and they discussed each one.

After my breakfast, Christine and I went upstairs to make the beds. I made her wait while I ran up to my attic to look again at my wonderful present. Dagmar, the little sister, came with me, and when she touched the mirror I scolded her so hard she started to cry.

Christine came up then and wiped Dagmar's tears and sent her down to Papa. She looked at me for a long time.

"Why do you look at me like that, Christine?"

"What do you care? You got what you wanted, didn't you?" She pointed to the dresser set. "Trash," she said, "cheap trash."

"Don't you dare talk about my lovely present like that! You're jealous, that's what. I'll tell Mama on you."

"And while you're telling her," Christine said, "ask her what she did with her silver brooch. The one her very own mother gave her. Ask her that."

I looked at Christine with horror. "What? You mean—did Mama——?"

Christine walked away.

I grabbed up the dresser set and ran down the stairs to the kitchen. Papa was drinking his second cup of coffee, and Dagmar was playing with her doll in front of the stove. Nels had left.

"Papa, oh, Papa!" I cried. "Did Mama—Christine says——" I started to cry then, and Papa had me sit on his lap.

"There now," he said, and patted my shoulder. "There now."

And he dipped a cube of sugar into his coffee and fed it to me.

We were not allowed to drink coffee—even with lots of milk in it—until we were considered grown up, but all of us children loved that occasional lump of sugar dipped in coffee.

After my hiccuping and sobbing had stopped, Papa talked to me very seriously. It was like this, he said. I had wanted the graduation present. Mama had wanted my happiness more than she had wanted the silver brooch. So she had traded it to Mr. Schiller for the dresser set.

"But I never wanted her to do that, Papa. If I had known, I would never have let her——"

"It was what Mama wanted to do, Katrin."

"But she loved it so. It was all she had of Grandmother's."

"She always meant it for you, Katrin."

I stood up slowly. I knew what I must do.

And all the way up to Mr. Schiller's drugstore, the graduation present in my arms, I thought of how hard it must have been for Mama to ask Mr. Schiller to take the brooch as payment. It was never easy for Mama to talk to strangers.

Mr. Schiller examined the dresser set with care. He didn't know, he said, about taking it back. After all, a bargain was a bargain, and he had been thinking of giving the brooch to his wife for her birthday next month.

Recklessly, I mortgaged my vacation.

If he would take back the dresser set, if he would give me back the brooch, I would come in and work for him every single day, even Saturdays.

"I'll shine the showcases," I begged. "I'll sweep the floor for you."

Mr. Schiller said that would not be necessary. Since I wanted the brooch back so badly, he would call the deal off. But if I was serious about working during vacation, he might be able to use me.

So I walked out of Mr. Schiller's drugstore not only with Mama's brooch but with a job that started the next morning. I felt very proud. The dresser set suddenly seemed a childish and silly thing.

I put the brooch on the table in front of Papa. He looked at me proudly. "Was it so hard to do, Daughter?"

"Not so hard as I thought." I pinned the brooch on my dress. "I'll wear it always," I said. "I'll keep it forever."

"Mama will be glad, Katrin."

Papa dipped a lump of sugar and held it out to me. I shook my head. "Somehow," I said, "I just don't feel like it, Papa."

"So?" Papa said. "So?"

And he stood up and poured out a cup of coffee and handed it to me.

"For me?" I asked wonderingly.

Papa smiled and nodded. "For my grown-up daughter," he said.

I sat up straight in my chair, and felt very proud as I drank my first cup of coffee.

My Mother Is the Most Beautiful Woman in the World

BECKY REYHER

Once upon a time, long, long ago, when the harvest season had come again, the villagers were all busy cutting and gathering the wheat. Marfa and Ivan went to the field early each day, as did all their children. There they stayed until sundown. Varya was Marfa and Ivan's youngest little girl, six years old. When everyone went to the fields in harvest time, Varya went, too. Her legs were so short she had to run and skip to keep up with her mother's and father's long steps.

"You are a little slowpoke!" her father said to her. Then, laughing loudly, he swung her up on his shoulder where she had to hold tight to his neck, for his arms were full carrying the day's lunch and the long scythe to cut the wheat.

In the field, in the long even rows between the thick wheat, Varya knew just what she must do. First, she must stay at least twenty or thirty paces behind her father, who now took even greater and bigger steps, so that he might have plenty of room to swing wide the newly sharpened scythe.

"Stand back, Varya! Mind the scythe!" he warned. Swish, swish, swish, went his even strokes, and down came the wheat, faster and faster, as he made his great strides.

Soon Marfa began to follow Ivan. She gathered the wheat in sheaves or bunches just big enough to bind together with a strand of braided wheat. Varya, eager to be useful, helped gather the wheat, and held each bunch while her mother tied it. When three sheaves were tied, they were stacked against each other in a little pyramid.

"Careful, little one!" her mother cautioned. "The wheat side up!"

After a while, instead of long rows of wheat, there were long rows of sheaves, standing stiffly.

Sometimes Varya forgot to follow her mother. On very hot days she stopped to rest upon the warm ground, and let her tired, bare feet and toes tickle the dark, moist earth. A while later she ran and caught up with her mother, and then her mother hugged her to her and wiped her dripping face. Even though her mother's arms and bosom were hot and damp, they felt cool and restful to Varya.

Day after day, Ivan, Marfa, and Varya went to the field, until all the wheat was cut and stacked and none was left growing in the ground. Then a big wagon came and everyone pitched the wheat up to the driver, who packed it in solidly and carefully and took it to the threshing barn.

The villagers worked tirelessly throughout the summer. Finally it was the last day before harvest. Marfa and Ivan worked more quickly and harder than ever. They did not seem to notice the hot sun. The wheat swished almost savagely as it came rushing down.

But to Varya the day seemed the longest she had ever lived. The sun seemed hotter than on any other day, and her feet seemed almost too heavy to lift.

Varya peered into the next row of wheat that was not yet cut. There it was cool and pleasant and the sun did not bear down with its almost unbearable heat. Varya moved in just a little farther to surround herself with that blessed coolness. "How lucky I am!" she thought, "to be able to hide away from the hot sun. I will do this for just a few minutes. Surely, Mama will not mind if I do not help her all the day."

Soon Varya grew sleepy, for in so cool a place one could curl up and be very quiet and comfortable.

When Varya awoke, she jumped to her feet and started to run toward her mother. But her mother was nowhere in sight.

Varya called, "Mama, Mama," but there was no answer.

Sometimes her mother got ahead of her and was so busy with her work she did not hear.

Maybe if I run along the row, I will catch up with her, Varya thought. She ran and ran, and soon she was out of breath, but nowhere could she see her mother.

"Maybe I have gone in the wrong direction," she said to herself. So she ran the other way. But here, too, there was no trace of her mother.

Varya was alone in the wheat fields, where she could see nothing but tall pyramids of wheat towering above her. When she called out, her voice brought no response, no help. Overhead the sun was not so bright as it had been. Varya knew that soon it would be night and that she must find her mother.

Varya cut through the last of the wheat that had not yet been cut, breaking her own pathway, which bent and hurt the wheat. She would not have done this had she not been frightened.

When it was almost dark, Varya stumbled into a clearing where several men and women had paused to gossip after the day's work. It took her only a second to see that these were strangers, and that neither her mother nor father were among them.

The little girl stared ahead of her, not knowing what to do. One of the men spied her and said in a booming voice that he thought was friendly, "Look what we have here!"

Everyone turned to Varya. She was sorry that with so many strangers looking at her she had her hair caught back in a tiny braid with a bit of string, and that she was wearing only her oldest, most faded dress. Surely, too, by now her face and hands must be as streaked with dirt as were her legs and dress. This made her burst into tears.

"Poor little thing," cried one of the women, putting her arms around Varya, "she is lost!" But this sympathy, and the strange voices, made Varya want her mother all the more. She could not help crying.

"We must know her name and the name of her mother and father. Then we can unite them," said the women.

"Little girl, little girl," they said, "what is your name? What is your mother and father's name?" But Varya was too unhappy to speak.

Finally, because her longing for her mother was so great, she sobbed out:

"My mother is the most beautiful woman in the world!"

All the men and women smiled. The tallest man, Kolya, clapped his hands and laughingly said, *"Now* we have something to go on."

This was long, long ago, when there were no telephones and no automobiles. If people wanted to see each other, or carry a message, they went on their two feet.

From every direction, friendly, good-hearted boys ran to village homes with orders to bring back the beautiful women.

"Bring Katya, Manya, Vyera, Nadya," the tall man, Kolya, called to one boy.

"Ay, but don't forget the beauty, Lisa," he called to still another boy.

The women came running. These were orders from Kolya, the village leader. Also the mothers, who had left the fields early to get supper for their families, thought perhaps this was indeed their child who was lost.

As each beautiful woman came rushing up, blushing and proud that she had been so chosen, Kolya would say to her: "We have a little lost one here. Stand back, everyone, while the little one tells us if this is her mother!"

The mothers laughed and pushed, and called to Kolya: "You big tease! What about asking each mother if this is her child? We know our children!"

To Varya this was very serious, for she was lost and she was desperate without her mother. As she looked at each strange woman, Varya shook her head in disappointment and sobbed harder. Soon every known beauty from far and near, from distances much farther than a child could have strayed, had come and gone. Not one of them was Varya's mother.

The villagers were really worried. They shook their heads. Kolya spoke for them. "One of us will have to take the little one home for the night. Tomorrow may bring fresh wisdom to guide us!"

Just then a breathless, excited woman came puffing up to the crowd. Her face was big and broad, and her body even larger. Her eyes were little pale slits between a great lump of a nose. The mouth was almost toothless. Even when she was a young girl everyone had said, "A homely girl like Marfa is lucky to get a good husband like Ivan."

"Varya baby!" cried this woman.

"Mama!" cried the little girl, and they fell into each other's arms. The two of them beamed upon each other. The smile Varya had longed for was once again shining upon her.

All of the villagers smiled thankfully when Varya looked up from her mother's shoulder and said with joy:

"This is my mother! I told you my mother is the most beautiful woman in the world!"

The group of friends and neighbors, too, beamed upon each other, as Kolya repeated the proverb so well known to them, a proverb which little Varya had just proved: *"We do not love people because they are beautiful, but they seem beautiful to us because we love them."*

Cornelia's Jewels

Retold by
JAMES BALDWIN

It was a bright morning in the old city of Rome many hundred years ago. In a vine-covered summerhouse in a beautiful garden, two boys were standing. They were looking at their mother and her friend, who were walking among the flowers and trees.

"Did you ever see so handsome a lady as our mother's friend?" asked the younger boy, holding his tall brother's hand. "She looks like a queen."

"Yet she is not so beautiful as our mother," said the elder boy. "She has a fine dress, it is true; but her face is not noble and kind. It is our mother who is like a queen."

"That is true," said the other. "There is no woman in Rome so much like a queen as our own dear mother."

Soon Cornelia, their mother, came down the walk to speak with them. She was simply dressed in a plain white robe. Her arms and feet were bare, as was the custom in those days; and no rings or chains glittered about her hands and neck. For her only crown, long braids of soft brown hair were coiled about her head; and a tender smile lit up her noble face as she looked into her sons' proud eyes.

"Boys," she said, "I have something to tell you."

They bowed before her, as Roman lads were taught to do, and said, "What is it, Mother?"

"You are to dine with us today, here in the garden; and then our friend is going to show us that wonderful casket of jewels of which you have heard so much."

The brothers looked shyly at their mother's friend. Was it possible that she had still other rings beside those on her fingers? Could she have other gems besides those which sparkled in the chains about her neck?

When the simple outdoor meal was over, a servant brought the casket from the house. The lady opened it. Ah, how those jewels dazzled the eyes of the wondering boys! There were ropes of pearls, white as milk and smooth as satin; heaps of shining rubies, red as the glowing coals; sapphires as blue as the sky that summer day; and diamonds that flashed and sparkled like the sunlight.

The brothers looked long at the gems.

"Ah!" whispered the younger. "If our mother could only have such beautiful things!"

At last, however, the casket was closed and carried carefully away.

"Is it true, Cornelia, that you have no jewels?" asked her friend. "Is it true, as I have heard it whispered, that you are poor?"

"No, I am not poor," answered Cornelia, and as she spoke she drew her two boys to her side, "for here are my jewels. They are worth more than all your gems."

I am sure that the boys never forgot their mother's pride and love and care; and in after years, when they had become great men in Rome, they often thought of this scene in the garden. And the world still likes to hear the story of Cornelia's jewels.

Armed Forces Day

(Third Saturday in May)

A Department of Defense created in 1947 combined all of the American armed forces under a single authority. The first Armed Forces Day, proclaimed by President Harry S. Truman in 1950, replaced several anniversary holidays that had been celebrated separately by the Army, Navy Air Force, Marine Corps, and Coast Guard. Their combined efforts, the President said, were "vital to the security of the nation and to the establishment of a durable peace."

Of the different branches of the armed services, the Army is the oldest. After the battles at Lexington and Concord, many New Englanders rushed to join the companies of militia that hoped to drive the enemy out of Boston. In June, 1775, the Continental Congress, meeting in Philadelphia, voted to adopt this informal force and call it the Continental Army, and also authorized recruiting additional soldiers. The commander, General George Washington, was much concerned over the lack of any ships to protect American shores. In response to his plea, the Congress voted to outfit four merchant vessels as warships.

These small sailing vessels, sent out to fight the mighty British Navy, were the beginning of the powerful American Navy of today. One of the early commanders, John Paul Jones, provided an example of courage and bold action that has inspired Navy men ever since. In a sea battle between his vessel, the *Bonhomme Richard,* and the much better equipped English warship, the *Serapis,* it did not seem possible that the Americans could win; but when Jones was called on to surrender, he threw back the defiant words, "I have not yet begun to fight." After three hours of hard fighting, it was the English who surrendered.

Marines, America's soldiers of the sea, also fought gallantly during the Revolution. After the nation won its independence, a permanent Marine Corps was established by the new Congress in 1798. Two years later, the Coast Guard was founded.

The Air Force, of course, did not come into existence until the present century.

Each branch of the armed forces has had a record of great deeds. Each branch has had many heroes. Two heroes of World War II later became President of the United States. One was Lieutenant John F. Kennedy, whose story you may read in the section on Veterans' Day. The other was General Dwight D. Eisenhower, the Supreme Commander in charge of the successful invasion of Nazi-held Europe in 1944. His story follows.

Dwight Eisenhower, Hero

ELIZABETH L. CRANDALL AND FRANCES CAVANAH

"I'm here, Dwight. They said you wanted to see me."

Edgar Eisenhower stood beside the bed, looking down at the flushed face of his younger brother.

A few days earlier, Dwight had fallen and skinned his knee. With six boys in the family, a skinned knee was nothing unusual, and the fourteen-year-old boy had not even mentioned the injury. But then an infection had set in, his leg began to ache, and he realized he must tell his parents what had happened.

When they saw that his leg was swollen and that dark streaks of purple were spreading from his knee, they sent for the doctor. He was now in the hall talking with Mr. and Mrs. Eisenhower. Dwight, tossing feverishly in his bed, had asked for his brother.

Edgar was not quite two years older than Dwight. Though both boys had quick tempers and often settled their frequent arguments with their fists, they were devoted to each other.

"I'm here, Dwight," Edgar repeated. "Did you want to see me?"

"Listen, Ed," Dwight said. The boy's lips were parched and his voice was weak, but his words were clear and emphatic. "Don't let them do it!"

"Do what?" asked Edgar. "What do you mean, Dwight?"

A flash of anger lit up Dwight's fever-dulled eyes. "The doctor says they'll have to cut off my leg!"

In those days there were no wonder drugs to fight infections. When blood poisoning in an arm or leg threatened to spread to other parts of the body, amputation was usually the only means of saving the patient's life.

"Don't let them do it!" Dwight demanded again. "Promise me you won't. No matter what happens! I'd rather die than lose my leg. Promise me, Ed!"

Cut off Dwight's leg! Edgar could think of nothing more terrible. He knew how he himself would feel—how any boy in their

148

home town of Abilene, Kansas, would feel about an amputation.

By the time the Eisenhower boys were growing up, the cattle drives were over, and Abilene—the old railroad shipping point at the end of the Chisholm Trail—had become a quiet, pleasant town of some five thousand people. But stories of the cowboys and of the deeds of the famous town marshall, Wild Bill Hickok, were still told there. The boys who heard such stories grew up feeling they must be physically strong in order to make their way in life. Yes, Edgar knew exactly how his brother would feel about losing a leg.

Edgar pulled a chair to the side of Dwight's bed and sat down firmly. "I won't let it happen," he said. "Word of honor."

As the hours passed, Dwight's fever rose higher and higher. He became delirious with pain. Edgar allowed the doctor to examine Dwight and give him medicine, but that was all he would let him do. Again and again the doctor appealed to the boys' parents.

"Make Edgar leave that room. Let me operate if you want Dwight to live."

Mr. and Mrs. Eisenhower also realized what the loss of a leg would mean to Dwight. Besides, they were a little afraid of surgery. There had been very little illness in their home. Good food and rest and prayer could cure most ills, they believed. And yet the doctor should know, they told each other anxiously. In this crisis they simply did not know what to do.

But Dwight had made a decision, and Edgar had made a promise. For two long days and nights, the older boy stayed beside his brother's bed. On the third day when the doctor entered the room, he gave Edgar an angry look. Then he took Dwight's temperature and carefully examined the infected leg.

Slowly the doctor turned to the parents who were standing, whitefaced, in the doorway.

"I can't understand it," he said, and there was awe in his voice. "The leg is much less swollen, and the fever has gone down. Your son is going to be all right."

In the years ahead Ike did prove to be "all right." After graduating from the United States Military Academy, at West Point, with the rank of second lieutenant, he had a distinguished career in the Army. In 1942, shortly after the United States entered World War II, Dwight D. Eisenhower, by now a general, was placed in command of the Allied troops in North Africa. The Germans there were finally driven out, and later they were also defeated in Sicily and on the Italian mainland.

Meanwhile, preparations had been going on in England for the great Allied invasion across the English Channel. By the fall of 1943, it had been decided that this invasion, known by the code name of Overlord, was to take place the following spring. The expedition, made up of American, British, and Canadian troops, as well as a number of other units formed by men who had escaped from their Nazi-conquered lands, was to serve under one over-all command. Inasmuch as the United States would be supplying the largest share of the manpower and equipment, Winston Churchill, the British Prime Minister, had suggested that an American should be named as the Supreme Commander, and Ike was selected.

No soldier in history had ever been given a more difficult assignment than Dwight D. Eisenhower. Hitler had had four years to turn western Europe into a great fortress. But a successful Allied invasion would shorten the war and put an end forever, it was believed, to the Nazi tyranny. That being the case, Ike told his old West Point friend, Omar Bradley, the invasion would succeed— because it had to. General Bradley was one of the numerous officers commanding soldiers from a number of different countries, all serving under General Eisenhower. The success of Overlord depended on their willingness to work together.

"I am almost fanatic in my belief," Ike once said, "that only as we pull together, each of us in the job given him, are we going to defend and sustain the priceless things for which we are fighting."

By March, 1944, secret headquarters had been set up on a wooded estate near the English Channel. Ike's office was a trailer, and he often met with his officers in a manor house almost hidden among the trees. Most of England looked like an armed camp. Airports had been built. Ports were jammed with ships. In many of the villages there were more American soldiers than Englishmen. There was a feeling of tenseness in the air. The troops realized there was to be an invasion soon, but few knew where and when it would take place. The decision to try to invade Normandy on the northwest coast of France was still a carefully guarded secret.

In making final plans General Eisenhower and his staff officers were helped immeasurably by members of the French resistance movement. At great risk to themselves the "underground" sent short-wave messages—in code, of course—giving the Allied commanders important information about the enemy. At one of the meetings, where the Supreme Commander and his staff were making final plans, Winston Churchill was present.

"Generals," he said, "I have every confidence in you. The destiny of the world is in your hands."

The date for the invasion—"D-Day," the officers called it—had been tentatively set for June 5, 1944. On that night there would be a late-rising moon, which would make it easier for paratroopers and other airborne troops to be dropped behind the lines. The tide would be right for the landing of the thousands of soldiers who would cross the channel on ships. And then because of weather—the worst weather on the channel in twenty years—D-Day had to be postponed.

On the night of the fourth, General Eisenhower and his staff officers met with three meteorologists from the British Royal Air Force. What were the weather prospects for June 6? Would the skies clear by then? the general asked. The meteorologists replied that the forecast was for better flying weather the night of the fifth and the following morning. During that period the planes could take to the air, but by noon the next day the skies would be overcast again. There would probably be a very rough sea, making it more difficult for the seaborne troops to reach the Normandy beaches.

The general hesitated. Whatever he decided, he would be taking a grave risk. Bad weather might cause the expedition to fail, even after months of careful planning. But if he postponed D-Day another time, it would be several weeks before there would be the right combination of moonlight and tides for the invasion of the Normandy coast. With thousands of soldiers feeling tense after weeks of waiting and curious as to what was going to happen next, the secret could not be kept much longer. And secrecy was necessary for the success of the plan.

"I don't like it," said General Eisenhower slowly, "but what else can we do? I am going to give the order to go ahead."

On the night of the fifth, the general visited headquarters again. With several companions he climbed to the rooftop where they stood looking up at the dark sky. The first planes were taking off for

France to drop parachute fighters behind the lines. The task of the parachute troops would be to capture the crossroads and open the way for the main body of the invaders. By dawn of June 6—D-Day—hundreds of ships would have crossed the channel.

How many of the men disembarking from those ships in the face of enemy gunfire would reach the shore? How many would never come back? The general's face was white and drawn when he returned to his trailer.

After that there was nothing to do but wait. Nor was the general the only one who waited. With the invasion launched, there was no longer any reason to keep it a secret. Londoners heard the news as they were going to work the next morning. The American people read it in their newspapers, a few hours later. In Philadelphia the Liberty Bell began to toll as it had on another historic day in July, 1776.

Seated in his trailer, General Eisenhower sat hunched over his radio hour after hour. At last came the news that he had been waiting for. Details were still lacking, but the Allied Troops had established a beachhead on the Normandy coast. He immediately broadcast a message, beamed to the captive countries across the channel.

"People of western Europe," he said, "a landing was made this morning on the coast of France. This landing is part of the concerted United Nations plan for the liberation of Europe. . . . Although the initial assault may not have been made in your country, the hour of your liberation is approaching. . . . Great battles lie ahead. I call upon all who love freedom to stand with us. Keep your faith . . . together we will achieve victory."

After the general established his headquarters in France, the Allied soldiers continued to win victories. Town after town—in France, in Belgium, in Holland, and in Luxembourg—was liberated by the Allied troops.

The Allied victories did not come easily. There were desperate counter attacks in which many lives were lost. Still General Eisenhower's troops pressed on, until they entered Germany from the west. Russian troops were battering the country on the eastern front, and in May, 1945, the once-powerful Nazis were forced to surrender. Western Europe was free after years of slavery. The people rejoiced, and the man they desired to honor above all others was General Ike.

When Dwight D. Eisenhower returned to the United States in June, a few weeks after Germany's surrender, he received a hero's welcome. In New York City more than four million people lined the jampacked streets to cheer the man who had led the Allies to victory in Europe.

"Ike! Ike! We like Ike!" the people cried, and the cry was repeated in city after city that he visited. Perhaps what pleased the general most was his enthusiastic reception in his home town of Abilene, Kansas. Had it not been for the hard decision he made there at the time he injured his knee, he could never have had a military career. Now the people who had known him as a boy were also shouting, "We like Ike!"

Those words were to become a campaign slogan that in a few years would help to elect him President of the United States.

(Adapted from *Meet the Presidents*.)

Memorial Day

(April 26 in four Southern states; May 30 in all others.)

In 1866, when the Civil War had been over little more than a year, Union soldiers were still occupying Columbus, Mississippi, in the defeated South. In a cemetery on the outskirts of the town, both Confederate and Union dead lay buried—men who had been killed in the battle of Shiloh, not many miles away. On April 25, a group of women in the town came there to decorate the graves with flowers—not only the graves of the soldiers who had worn the gray uniforms of the Confederates, but also those of the Union soldiers who had worn the blue.

Many people in the North read about this generous act and were deeply touched. A young lawyer, Francis Miles Finch, wrote a poem called "The Blue and the Gray," which became popular and helped in some measure to heal the bitter feelings between North and South. One stanza of the poem reads:

From the silence of sorrowful
  hours
  The desolate mourners go,
Lovingly laden with flowers
  Alike for the friend and the
  foe:

Under the sod and the dew,
  Waiting the judgment day;
Under the roses, the Blue,
  Under the lilies, the Gray.

The women of Columbus were not the first to place flowers on the graves of the war dead, but it is believed that they inspired the establishment of an annual Decoration Day, now usually referred to as Memorial Day.

In 1868, General John A. Logan, commander-in-chief of the G.A.R. (Grand Army of the Republic), an organization of Union veterans, designated May 30 as a day for strewing flowers on the graves of fallen comrades, and there was an official celebration at Arlington National Cemetery, across the river from Washington, D.C. Since that time Memorial Day has been regularly observed throughout the nation with ceremonies and parades. With the passing of years there were fewer and fewer Civil War veterans left to march, and those who still lived were all the more eager to take part. The following story is about such an old soldier and his fifteen-year-old nephew who found a way to celebrate, even in the desert.

155

Memorial Day in the Desert

A Story of the Old West

RALPH D. PAINE

The new station where an occasional stagecoach stopped was set down in the heart of the Nevada desert. There was not even a house within thirty miles—only two tents—and the white sand and sagebrush stretched desolate to the bare brown mountains that cut the skyline along the rim of Death Valley. A boy in his early teens came out of one of the tents, blinking in the glare of sand and sky. He shaded his eyes with a battered sombrero and looked across the desert toward a cloud of dust in the distance.

"Here comes the stage, Uncle John," he called. "I hope there are some passengers for us to feed. If they'd only bring just *one* boy through, and I could talk to him for half an hour. Wouldn't it be great! I haven't seen a boy since we came to the desert to live."

Captain John Bright, the "boss" of the station, poked the tent flap aside. "This desert don't sprout youngsters," he said. "That's a fact, Jimmy. We're lucky if we get a stray man to pass the time o'day with. Help me get the relay horses ready, and then dust off an extra plate and cup. Jake may have a hungry passenger. It's about time. Nobody's been here in two days."

The boy led a pair of lanky grays out of the little corral by the well, tied them to a post in front of the tents, and scurried inside with an excited air as if great things were about to happen. His few duties were soon done and he was perched on the well box waiting long before the stage emerged from its curtain of dust. Two straining horses pulled a battered Concord wagon through the sand at a snail's pace. Their slow walk quickened a little as they drew near the tents, and the boy saw with a pang that the bent and white-whiskered driver was the only occupant. The driver grinned through the mask of dust that covered his wrinkled face.

"Nothin' doing, Jimmy," he said, noticing the boy's disappointment. "This route ain't as popular as if it had Pullman sleeping cars. I've been eight hours makin' thirty miles. Grub ready?"

156

Jimmy followed the driver to the mess tent and peppered him with questions about the news from the big outside world beyond the desert. The old man fished a newspaper from a pocket.

"Here's a *Los Angeles Times* that was passed along from Las Vegas," he said. "It's four days old, but it may cheer you up some."

Jimmy acted as waiter while the driver bolted his beans, bacon, canned corned-beef and coffee, and then the two shifted the harness to the fresh team of horses. A few minutes later the stage moved on like a boat steering out of sight across a lonely sea, and Jimmy felt the isolation of the desert closing down around him again. His uncle stretched out on a blanket in the sleeping tent and soon began to snore, leaving the boy with no one to talk to. He sat down in the mess tent, spread the newspaper on the rough plank table, and slowly read the headlines. It was hard for him to realize that men and women and boys and girls were still working and playing in crowded city streets. Though he had been in the desert only three months, it seemed a lifetime. As he looked through the newspaper, one brief item caught his eye:

> The Phil Sheridan Post, G.A.R., has completed its arrangements for the Memorial Day exercises and parade. There is much regret among the veterans in blue that their old Post Commander, Captain John Bright, will be absent from the ranks. For ten years he had led the Memorial Day pilgrimage to the graves of the heroes who fought for Old Glory. He left the city recently to take up his residence in Nevada, but the old soldiers are hoping that if Captain Bright is alive, he will get here to take his old place at the head of the thinning column.

The boy ran into the other tent, waving the newspaper. "Uncle John! Wake up! They haven't forgotten us back home."

Captain Bright sat up on his blanket and rubbed the sleep from his eyes. He read the paragraph and his gray beard could not hide the quivering lip. "The thirtieth of May," he said slowly, "just two days off. Not that I've lost track of the date for Memorial Day. Not for a minute, but we can't leave the station."

The old soldier who had served in the Union Army picked up the paper and read the paragraph aloud. His voice trembled a little when he came to the mention of "Old Glory." Then, as if ashamed of his show of feeling, he rose to his feet and stood very erect.

"We'll have to make the best of it, Jimmy," he said, resting his hand on the boy's shoulder. "There isn't much chance for a celebration out here, but it is good to know they haven't forgotten us back home. Pshaw, it's tougher for you than it is for me to be stuck out here a hundred miles from nowhere. Don't you hate me for it sometimes?"

"Of course not. I get kind of lonesome at times," the boy admitted, "but you are all I've got, Uncle John. We're partners. Maybe next year you can go back and lead the Grand Army parade."

The old man shook his head; he felt that he had made a failure of his life. A dishonest partner had wrecked the business he had toiled for years to build up. On the brink of old age, and without capital, he had been unable to make a new start in the crowded commercial life of the city. The help offered by his friends had seemed to him little more than disguised charity, and he had grasped the chance to take charge of one of the stations of the stage line flung across the desert to reach the new gold camps in southwestern Nevada.

The care of his dead sister's only boy had sorely perplexed him, and it seemed best to take Jimmy with him through the first summer. By autumn he might have saved enough from his wages to outfit the boy for school and keep him there. A touch of selfishness had swayed this decision, and he sighed over his weakness. But he could not bear to face the lonely life without a companion, at least not for a while. Jimmy was the pluckier of the two, the old man thought to himself. The boy was so eager to help.

No more was said about Memorial Day, but after supper they sat together under the stars that blazed low in the velvet sky. The old man talked of Antietam and Fredericksburg, of forlorn hopes, and of thin lines of blue and gray hurled in desperate charges. Jimmy listened, thrilled as he always was, by his uncle's stories, and suddenly the desert seemed peopled with marching men.

Through the forenoon of Memorial Day, Captain John Bright was restless and absentminded. His thoughts were back with his comrades in the G.A.R. Last year, because he was one of the youngest and strongest, he had led the parade, and he wondered who would take his place this year.

Jimmy wrestled with a problem of his own. He was too young to give up the idea of some kind of a celebration. There were no soldiers' graves, there were no flowers, but he did find a small American flag that they had brought with them.

"I don't think it's right to let the day go by without doing something, honest I don't," he said, "You know that prospector's grave about two miles over toward the Funeral Range? I mean the man that got lost and died of thirst last year and you and the stage driver buried him under a little heap of rocks. For all we know he may have been an old soldier. You can't say he wasn't. Anyhow he was a brave man, or he wouldn't have been going into Death Valley alone. I'm going to ride my burro over and stick this little flag on his grave."

Captain Bright looked pleased and touched, but replied with a slightly worried air, "I think I can see you all the way from here, but be sure to fill your canteen, Jimmy, and don't get out of sight of camp. I'd go with you, but there's a freight outfit coming in from the southward and they'll want water."

The boy hurried over to the corral and saddled his mouse-colored burro. With the little flag tucked inside his shirt, he marched off behind the stubborn little beast, which kicked up its heels in protest. For the first mile at least, Jimmy decided, it might be easier to go on foot through the deep sand. As he trudged along, he was thinking of the unknown prospector whose bleached bones had been found. Perhaps the prospector had discovered a mine and was trying to get out of the desert with the news when he got lost and ran out of water. Or maybe he had gotten sick and his burro had run away.

Was there a boy waiting for him somewhere at home? It was very sad and mysterious, but there were many sad stories and mysterious stories about the Death Valley country. This one was especially vivid because of the heap of rocks his uncle had placed over the grave instead of a tombstone.

What if the lost prospector *had* been an old soldier? the boy thought again as he trudged over brush and sand. What if he had been a Grand Army man, like Uncle John, who had fought bravely in battle? It was hard to think of an old soldier losing his life in a fight with heat and thirst and with no one to mourn him.

Anyway, Jimmy could place a flag on the grave. He took off his hat while he stuck his flag between fragments of lava on the rude mound. He also decided to gather some more stones to mark the spot, and by the time he had finished the burro had wandered off several hundred yards. When he caught up with the little beast, he cinched up the saddle and gazed across the desert toward the Funeral Range. Beyond those bare and ragged walls lay Death Valley. He was glad that Uncle John was not a prospector, toiling among those forbidding-looking mountains.

As Jimmy mounted the burro and was about to turn back toward camp, he thought he saw something move toward the mountains. Shading his eyes, he stared at some little whirls of dust that rose above what appeared to be a black dot in the distance. The dot seemed to flounder, stood erect, then floundered again as it moved closer. It looked like a man, but what was a man doing on foot in the desert and coming from that direction? If it was a man, it meant he was in distress and needed help. Jimmy dug his heels into the burro's flanks and moved closer.

At length the object ceased to move. When the boy drew near, he saw a man, naked to the waist, lying face down. His shoes were gone. He had no canteen and no hat, and his hands and feet were bleeding where he had been crawling and falling in his struggle to move on. The boy fell on his knees and tugged at the blistered shoulders until he half-turned the helpless man so that his face was clear of the choking sand.

Then Jimmy wet the blackened lips with water from his own canteen, and managed to unlock the clenched teeth and pour a few drops on the swollen tongue. Finally the man swallowed, once, twice. The effect was magical. His eyes opened; he groaned and tried to raise himself on his hands and knees. But he lurched forward and fell.

Jimmy was frightened. It seemed impossible that he could raise the dead weight to the back of the burro, but he was afraid to leave the man here while he went to camp for help.

"It's only a little way to our camp, he said. "I'll help you. Can't you get up?"

Another drink from the canteen, and the man's wits began to clear a little. "I'm all in," he muttered. "But I'm not dead yet. Bring the burro."

For a wonder the burro stood docile in its tracks while the man made a desperate effort to pull himself up by the stirrup. Then he fell, doubled across the saddle like a sack of meal. It was all Jimmy could do to hold him there, as he walked beside the burro with its silent burden. Fortunately, long before they drew near the camp, Uncle John saw that something was wrong and came running toward them. He dragged the unconscious stranger into the tent and laid him on a blanket.

"You were just in time, Jimmy," said Uncle John. "Open a can of that beef tea and put the kettle on. Another hour and you wouldn't have been a bit of use."

The pink and azure twilight was falling when the lost prospector sat up on the blankets, his head in his hands, and said brokenly, "I'm alive, and I ain't gone plumb crazy. Thank God for His mercies. I wonder where my burros are. Is this here camp in the Death Valley, pardner?"

"You were twenty miles out of the Valley when my nephew found you."

"What was a kid doing way out there?"

"I was celebrating Memorial Day," Jimmy explained a little bashfully. "There is—there is a grave out there."

"There came blame near bein' another one alongside of it," was the reply. "Celebratin' Memorial Day in this God-forsaken hole? Well, you are a lively young patriot! And lucky for me!"

Jimmy did not want to claim too much credit. "It was all on account of Uncle John—I mean Captain Bright here." he said. "He's a Grand Army man, you know, and I couldn't let the day go by without doing something to let him see that I remembered."

"Say, stranger," Uncle John broke in, "I see a scar across the bald head of yours. Maybe you were one of the boys in blue."

A smile lit up the cracked and blackened face of the old prospector as he stretched out a bandaged hand. "No, I reckon I did my fighting under Jeb Stuart, I wore a gray uniform, and one of *your* troopers put that dent in my *cabeza*. We ain't going to fight the war all over again, are we?"

Captain Bright smiled back and took the old Confederate's hand in both of his.

"Here's where we celebrate the day together," he said, "and we'll thank God that your grave isn't ready to be decorated tonight.

You came mighty near giving me an excuse for a parade all by myself."

From outside there came the rattle of trace-chains, and the creaking of wagons, and the noise of a driver shouting at his weary mules. Captain Bright hurried out and found a freight outfit pulling up to the well. Its crew made camp near the corral, and that evening they sat by the campfire while Captain Bright and Daniel Yake, late of the Army of the Confederacy, swapped stories of the great days when they were foemen in arms.

Then one of the freighters, a tall Texan burst into song, and in full chorus the little company, North and South, the Blue and the Gray, swung from "Dixie" into "The Star Spangled Banner." But the crew of the freight outfit remained silent while the two old soldiers sang together, "We're Tenting Tonight on the Old Camp Ground."

When at last the fire died down and the freighters said good night, Jimmy murmured drowsily, "We did celebrate after all. We had our Memorial Day even in the desert."

> (This selection was condensed from "Old Glory in the Desert," published in *St. Nicholas Magazine* more than sixty years ago.)

Flag Day

(June 14)

When the American colonists revolted, they fought under flags with various designs, and months went by after independence was declared before there was an official flag to represent all thirteen states. On June 14, 1777, the Continental Congress passed the following resolution:

Resolved. That the flag of the United States be thirteen stripes, alternate red and white, that the "Union" be thirteen stars, white in a blue field, representing a new constellation.

Each star and each stripe represented one of the thirteen original states. It soon proved impractical to add a stripe each time another state was admitted to the Union, but the plan was maintained to add an additional star for each new state. Now that there are fifty states in the Union, there are fifty stars in the flag.

New York was the first state to observe Flag Day. That was in 1897. Now the holiday is generally observed throughout the nation. One of the legends that have grown up around the flag concerns Betsy Ross, an upholsteress, whose little house and shop may still be seen in Philadelphia. It is known that she did make flags, but there is no historical record that General Washington ever visited her or suggested that she make a flag of a special design. Though it is one of those stories we like to read about, it may or may not be true.

The story of Francis Scott Key, who wrote "The Star-Spangled Banner," is a different matter. Mr. Key was a lawyer living in Baltimore during the War of 1812. On September 13, 1814, he was rowed out to a British ship in the harbor to arrange an exchange of prisoners. Though treated with courtesy, he was not allowed to return to the city because, as he soon realized, the British were about to bombard Fort McHenry. All through the night he anxiously awaited the outcome of the attack, but with the coming of morning he saw that the American flag still waved over the fort. Deeply stirred, he wrote "The Star-Spangled Banner," which many years later, in 1931, Congress designated as the National Anthem. The flag that inspired the song is now preserved, though partly shot away, in the Museum of History and Technology, in Washington, D.C.

"The Star-Spangled Banner Girl" is the true story of how that flag came to be made.

Star-Spangled Banner Girl

CAROLYN SHERWIN BAILEY

Caroline Pickersgill had learned to sew as soon as she could hold a needle. While her mother kept their little red brick house in old Baltimore spotless and shining, while she polished the brass candlesticks, scoured the floors, and spread the linen out on the garden grass to bleach, Caroline sat beside her grandmother Rebecca and stitched—first the long seams of hand-woven sheeting, so long and stiff for little fingers to hold; then a calico dress for her wooden doll. That was fun! After that, she embroidered scallops for pantalets and petticoats, and matched the countless tiny squares of colored cloth that made the pattern of patchwork quilts. Caroline could hardly have been patient enough to sit sewing, quiet and industrious, in her small red rocking chair, if old Rebecca, her grandmother, had not told her stories to shorten the work. They were thrilling stories, for Rebecca Young had made a flag for General Washington to carry when the American army took part in the siege of Boston.

The story always began with Rebecca's description of her Philadelphia flag shop. She had even advertised her craft in the *Philadelphia Ledger* in the days of the Revolution:

Colours

For the Army and Navy, made and sold at the most reasonable terms,

REBECCA YOUNG

In Walnut Street, near Third Street, and next door but one to Mr. Samuel McLane's.

N.B. Any person having Bunting for sale may hear of a purchaser by applying as above.

That was how her advertisement had been printed. Then Caroline's grandmother Rebecca would go on to tell of the visit of General Washington to her shop, of his order for a flag which should have thirteen stripes of red and white, one for each of the Colonies. In the corner of this flag was a "grand union" of the old British flag, a blue field with the red and white crosses of St. Andrew and St. George.

Soon after this flag was delivered to General Washington, Rebecca had been obliged to flee with her children in an ox cart going West. Her silver spoons and the Bible had been lost in the forest. There had been her struggle in the wilderness of western Pennsylvania and then their return to this pleasant home in Baltimore. The entire countryside remembered how Rebecca had made General Washington's battle flag. Beautiful needlework was their family pride, Rebecca told Caroline. Her own fingers were too stiff now to take the tiny stitches for which the family was celebrated, but Caroline's mother, Mary Pickersgill, who had been only a baby when they fled from Philadelphia, still made beautiful flags. Perhaps some day Caroline also would stitch well enough to sew together stripes of red and white bunting, her grandmother said.

Peace and happiness filled the house where these three, Rebecca, Mary, and Caroline, lived alone. Caroline's father was dead, but they owned their brick house near the waterfront in Baltimore, and Mary made a fair living for them stitching more and more of the banners that Caroline watched going out toward the sea, flying above merchant ships and sailing vessels. The American Revolution was nothing but history to the little girl, hard to believe when the bees hummed drowsily in their garden and the hens clucked contentedly over their nests. But Caroline often wondered at what she saw from the Baltimore wharf.

She loved to go down to the wharf, just a step from their front gate, and follow with her eyes the crimson trail her mother's flags made as the ships bearing them put out to sea from Chesapeake Bay. For almost two years many of these flags had been pulled down before they were out of sight; seamen had been taken from the American ships by British cruisers, and sometimes the ships were claimed as the property of England if captured on the high seas.

Still, this War of 1812 meant very little to Caroline Pickersgill. Other matters seemed to her vastly more important. Bonnets were much fancier in Baltimore than ever before because the girls and ladies were copying the clothes of the French Court. Caroline was making wreaths and bunches of silk flowers, a bombazine frame, and a piped green silk covering for her doll's bonnet. From scraps of her mother's bunting she had made the doll a blue cloak with a red lining, the stylish French colors. It was now fully two years since her mother's banners had first been torn from ships' rigging, and the small town of Baltimore still dozed beneath its white church steeples, its elm trees and flowering hedges. Caroline had come to think that the British and American ships were playing a game out there at sea, and by means of it helping to give her mother more work. For Mary Pickersgill made a new flag for every one torn down and tattered, and Grandmother Rebecca folded each one carefully, sending it to sea with her blessing.

It was August of the year 1814. Caroline had never been so happy before. She was a tall girl now, with a flowered bonnet of her own, and with daintier dimity and muslin dresses billowing about her silk slippers than almost any other girl in Baltimore had. She was fourteen years old, and she could sew better than any of her friends. She made all her own clothes, from her embroidered chemises to the lace mitts that reached from her slender wrists to the edge of her puffed sleeves.

Sewing was not Caroline's only hand skill, either. Her mother spent all her time in their flag shop, too busy to do the housework. Rebecca was seventy-five years old and growing blind. She sat in the garden all summer long, trying to see the colors on the ships as they sailed out, and in the winter she huddled by the fireplace, telling over again the story of General Washington's visit. Caroline did the family sewing, baked bread, tended the garden, kept the pewter plates and the silver spoons shining, and raised the largest potatoes and the brightest hollyhocks in Baltimore. She also sold honey and eggs and was always invited to quilting bees because she could quilt faster than most women. Her days were filled from morning till night with things to do and be happy about.

But all Baltimore was not as peaceful as the Pickersgill flag shop on Albermarle Street. What seemed at first to be the thunder of a summer storm was the roar of British and American ships' guns. After two years of sea warfare and the capture of American seamen by British captains, American ships had begun to imitate the methods of pirates. Many of the vessels sailing up and down the Atlantic coast were now privateers, a polite name for prize-runners. If British ships can impress our sailors, we will take their cargoes, these privateers said. A quarrel between nations that might have been peacefully settled two years before had blazed into warfare, and at last Baltimore was threatened. British ships seeking a fleet of American privateers were on their way to attack and hold the tiny brick fort built in the shape of a star, which stood, surrounded by cow pastures and hay fields, on a low peninsula guarding the town. There seemed no hope for Baltimore. Danger such as the townspeople had not known since the Revolution stalked at their very doorsteps.

But it was adventure, not danger, that lifted the brass knocker of Caroline Pickersgill's front door on that long-ago August day. She ran to open it, and curtsied as three townsmen entered in haste and excitement. They were the three officers in charge of the few troops that Baltimore had been able to muster. According to old records of this visit, these neighbors were Commodore Barney, General Stricker, and Lieutenant-Colonel MacDonald. Their swords hung at their sides. Their anxious faces were gray in the candlelight as they spoke to Caroline's mother.

"Fort McHenry will not stand a day's siege from British guns," they said. "Our only chance is to trick the enemy into thinking us stronger than we are. We desire, Mistress Pickersgill, that you make at once a great American flag. We want this banner to measure at least thirty-six feet long and twenty-nine feet wide. Four hundred yards of bunting will be delivered to you here in a few hours if you consent to help us. What say you? Can you deliver this flag to the fort before we are attacked from the sea? We hope that so large a flag will speak to the enemy of the high courage of our land."

"At once, good sirs," Mary Pickersgill answered. "As soon as the bunting arrives, I will begin cutting."

"Do your best, Mary," urged Rebecca, tapping the brick hearth with her cane. Then, going back to her dream world, she said: "Do you not see General Washington and his aides there in our doorway, come to us for a battle flag?"

"Couldn't I help with the sewing?" begged Caroline, her eyes shining with excitement. "Surely, Mother, you can trust me to stitch stripes together." So the three, old Rebecca, young Mary, younger Caroline, daughters of the Stars and Stripes, promised to do their part in protecting their town.

The mammoth rolls of bunting were delivered at their house promptly that night, but, alas, it was soon discovered that there was not a room large enough for cutting out the flag. The parts had to be cut to fit exactly, mostly upon the floor. Much of the sewing also had to be done on the floor, Mary Pickersgill kneeling down and stitching each stripe, each star. What should they do? At last, in the early morning, with the help of soldiers, they carried the bunting to a deserted malt house that stood near the fort. There, on the great floor, Mary cut, basted, and stitched. Caroline ran between the malt house and their home, taking stripes to be stitched, caring for old Rebecca, and returning to kneel beside her mother to add her fine seaming to the completion of the flag.

The flag had not been started a moment too soon. Disturbances in Baltimore had begun. A group of British soldiers had broken into the garden of Dr. Beans, a well-known townsman, while he was serving tea to some friends. The intrusion had resulted in the arrest of the doctor, who was imprisoned on one of the enemy ships as a British prisoner of war. Ladies in crinoline and silks had scattered, leaving their jasmine tea, sponge cakes, and ices untouched. A gentleman guest, young Francis Scott Key, a Baltimore attorney, had gone at once with a flag of truce to attempt the doctor's rescue. He was now aboard the American cartel ship, the *Minden*, in Chesapeake Bay two miles from the town. Should the attack upon Baltimore from the water be successful, it was rumored that the town would be set on fire.

But the flag was finished—red, white, and blue, six times as long as a man is tall, secure against storms because of the firm hand-stitching of Caroline and her mother, and bright with the courage of patriotism. They watched it being carried to Fort McHenry and raised upon a tall pole behind the guns.

In the early morning after the flag-raising, the attack upon Baltimore from the water began. For twenty-four hours British mortar ships poured bombs, rockets, and red-hot shot against the little fort, tearing gaping holes in the earth and piercing the brick walls. A few rents were made in the flag, but it waved bravely in the sunshine. Never had such a flag taken part in battle. Aloof and peaceful, it floated above the fire of the attack. After a day of terrible shellfire and a night of the same horror, the fort still stood. The great banner stitched by Mary and Caroline Pickersgill billowed in the wind as the attacking fleet sailed away, defeated as much by the seamstress's art as by the brave militia of Baltimore.

From the water, Mr. Francis Scott Key watched the flag all that night, as it flew above the red of the rockets and the smoke of the bombs. He could not tell whether the British or the American forces were victorious. The next morning he saw the flag still waving over the fort; and after he and Dr. Beans had been released and were safe on land again, he wrote his famous song.

Oh, say can you see by the dawn's early light,
What so proudly we hailed at the twilight's last gleaming?

There were many stanzas to the poem, but each ended:

The Star-Spangled Banner, oh, long may it wave,
O'er the land of the free and the home of the brave.

Soon, everybody in our country was singing Mr. Key's song about the flag that Caroline had helped to stitch. We still sing "The Star-Spangled Banner," and the old flag itself is kept as one of our most precious relics of American history in the Museum of History and Technology in Washington, D.C. The boy or girl who visits the museum will marvel at the tiny stitches Caroline set in the Star-Spangled Banner.

(This selection is taken from *Children of the Handicrafts*.)

Father's Day

(Third Sunday in June)

In 1910 a special day to pay tribute to fathers was set aside by the Ministerial Society of Spokane, Washington, at the suggestion of Mrs. John Bruce Dodd of that city. The following year a Chicago committee, of which Jane Addams was a member, met to consider a similar celebration.

"Poor father has been left out in the cold," said Miss Addams, the well-known social worker of Hull House. "He doesn't get much recognition."

She felt that Father, like Mother, deserved a special day, and the members of a men's Bible class in Wilkinsburg, Pennsylvania, also endorsed the idea. One of them suggested that the official flower should be the dandelion, because "the more it is trampled on, the better it grows."

That remark was made in jest, of course. The rose, not the dandelion, is the official flower for Father's Day, which is now observed throughout the United States and Canada. On that day, at least, Father receives the appreciation he deserves.

Father's Day

GLADYS TABER

One of the very best holidays of all is Father's Day. At least, I always thought so, because Father was especially important to me. It was not as easy as Mother's Day, for Mother was pleased with anything that was a gift, no matter whether she needed it or not. As long as there was a card saying, "To My Dearest Mamma with love," or "Grace from Rufus," Mother loved anything at all.

But Father liked things that suited him, and when he had his day his presents had to be the right ones.

Also, he liked to be surprised, and yet he was practically impossible to surprise because he kept looking in drawers and opening closet doors all the time, and rummaging in the attic.

"What's this big box in the coat closet?" he would call to Mamma. "I haven't seen this before!"

Or if we had his gift delivered, and worked and worked to get it sent when he couldn't possibly be home because he had a class at that time, he always bolted in after some papers just as the men carried his present up the walk.

"I haven't ordered a desk chair," Father would say snappily. "You have the wrong address. Take it away!"

Once we planned a surprise dinner of his favorite food—and as Mamma piled the frosting high on the Lady Baltimore cake, in came Father hungrily looking for an onion sandwich. "What's all this?" he said. "Company coming? You didn't tell me!"

So it kept us pretty busy.

One thing I always gave him was a blue tie, because blue was our favorite color. Father had racks and racks of blue ties, all the same shade of blue.

He did not smoke, so all those lovely smoking gadgets were no use, and he did not care for handkerchiefs. He used his to wipe off the stock of his gun or polish his shoes, or whatever needed doing. One time I saved up and gave him a blue silk lounging robe, and he wore it once.

174

He liked guns and specimens and hunting equipment and scientific books, which we never could pick out.

But Father's Day was a wonderful day.

Our first Father's Day was in 1924, the third week in June, and I was home from school. Father got the car tuned up and Mamma packed a lunch. As soon as we got home from church, we put on our old clothes and started out. Timmie, the Irish setter, sat in back with me and the lunch and Father's geological hammers and some gunny sacks for rocks.

We drove to the lake shore where the blue waters of Winnebago rolled against the white sand, and Father built a real campfire like a woodsman while Mamma broke an egg in the big enamel coffeepot and measured the coffee. Timmie went off birding and Father and I walked along the shore just at the edge of the clear, frothy waves.

Father's eyes were keen and he saw every tiny shell, and he gathered them up and spread them in his strong brown palm and told me about the time when they were first developed. He found little fossils and described the great ocean that once covered our whole state. He said that little shells belong to living animals that were here long before there were even men at all.

Then we moved in to the cornfields where the farmers were trying to raise corn in the sandy soil. We walked carefully along the furrows with heads bent, Father always ahead, and me breathless behind him.

"Look what I've found!" he cried.

And he held up a smoothly shaped Indian ax head. Farther on, we found big gray arrowheads, which he said were for game, and little delicate quartz ones, which were for the small birds. There were also small colored heaps of clay bits that had been Indian cooking pots.

Father told me where the village had been, where the main council fires were built, and all about the great battle when the Fox Indians invaded the peaceful Winnebago lands.

Turning back, we walked slowly with our pockets and hands full. Father added a few scratched stones that had come all the way down from Canada with the great glacier, he said. And we climbed a ledge marked with the glacial scratches as if the ice sheet had signed its name as it went along.

Mamma had the fried chicken and the potato salad out and the coffee was done, and Timmie was eating his chopped meat on a paper plate by the time we came back to the picnic place. Timmie had a piece of Father's cake and got frosting all over his velvety nose.

The sun was setting over the little town in the valley as we drove home, and the sky was filled with soft fire. And as we turned into our own street, Father said, a little sheepishly, "I don't know who thought up this Father's Day business; there's really more sense to Mother's Day."

But Mamma and I knew better.

Papa Was a Riot

A. J. CIULLA

There was nothing out of the ordinary in the way Mrs. Rhees made the announcement. It was in the quiet, business-like monotone she always used. This one, however, gave me quick alarm. In my mind's eye I could see Papa's eyes gleaming, his portly body quivering in eager anticipation. He could no more resist this opportunity to show off than could a Hollywood ham. Actually there was no bigger ham in Hollywood or on the Broadway stage than was Papa, a shoemaker.

It wasn't that I didn't love Papa. You had to love him. He was kind and gentle and considerate, and everybody in the neighborhood had a good word for him.

"Students," Mrs. Rhees had announced, "our principal is sending out invitations to the parents of every pupil in school for our special program, and I am asking the fathers of all ninth graders to participate. I know most of the fathers will be working, and some will not feel like appearing on our program. But if I can get three or four who will agree to speak it will be sufficient."

I stole a glance at Spencer de Moss. He was smiling up at the teacher with that irritating smugness. His father was district attorney and a brilliant speaker. Madelaine Cotter's father was an alderman and wouldn't think of passing up a chance to pick up a stray vote here and there. But for the most part the teacher was going to get polite refusals.

Ordinarily Papa had no opportunity to come to the school functions. He worked every day. His shoe factory, however, was moving to larger quarters and Papa was enjoying a lengthy vacation. I couldn't picture Papa attending any affair without participating. I didn't want him attending this one because his English was so bad it was comedy.

It was Mr. Wright, our principal, who had thought of having a program for families with loved ones in the services. Most of the families in the neighborhood did. Carl, the oldest of our five boys, was in the thick of the fighting; Brother Victor would be called in two weeks. Mama was wearing a sick and worried look those days.

At the time I wasn't aware of what made Papa tick. Since then I have come to realize that his theatrics were the result of a naturally enthusiastic nature coupled with his training in Italian opera. As a youth Papa had sung baritone for a small opera company in Italy. Needless to say, he was very much in demand at social functions in our neighborhood, especially at wedding receptions.

These followed the same general pattern. When the festivities had reached a climax, the band would stop playing and the band leader would hold up his hands for silence.

"*Signore e signori,*" he would announce, "we have finally prevailed upon the good Signor Nicola Barone to sing a few songs for us. I give you Nicola Barone!"

Papa would swagger to the middle of the floor, the applause cascading all over the place. The mild-mannered Signor Domenico would seat himself at a piano and strike a few chords of introduction. Then Papa would proceed to rattle every window in the place with that big baritone voice of his. No matter what he sang, the crowd was wildly enthusiastic.

"Bravo, bravo!" they would cry. "Please, please, Signor Nicola, another one." Papa would smile majestically, nod to Signor Domenico, and launch into another inferno of sound.

When Papa thought he had sung enough, he'd hold up his hands for complete silence. It was the high point in his performance coming up, a flowery talk by Papa praising the virtues of the groom and the beauty of the bride. His talk would produce a riot of laughter. What I didn't want was a riot at school.

I was home the night Papa read the letter from Mrs. Rhees. His eyes grew wide. "*Grazia,*" he said in exitement, "see how my reputation as a speaker has reached the school!"

"You are the vain one," Mama sighed. "Has it not occurred to you, Nicola, that perhaps all fathers have received similar letters?"

"That is of no importance. I have been invited to speak, and I will accept. Yes, I will astound them with my oratory. I will add new glory to the name of Barone."

Mama laughed good-naturedly. Papa went into his absurd jig step that was designed to amuse Mama. Soon both Papa and Mama were laughing heartily. To voice an objection to Papa's speaking would have been no use at all. . . .

Two days later in history class Mrs. Rhees made an announcement. "In regard to our program," she said, "I have received four acceptances to my invitations to your fathers. The four who have agreed to speak are—Mr. Jacob de Moss, Mr. Arnold Cotter, Mr. Robert Furness, and—" there was a slight hesitation—"Mr. Nicola Barone. Will you thank these men for me?

That night I went into Sotile's Grocery Store to do some shopping for Mama. The bell over the door tinkled and Joe Sotile, Mr. Sotile's only son, looked up and waved good-naturedly. Joe was fullback on the football team. He was a hero to me.

"So your old man is gonna make a speech Friday! Boy, is he a character! He'll have them in stitches!"

"Silence, you!" roared Mr. Sotile, who was in the act of breaking up some spaghetti on wrapping paper for Signora Concetta.

"Do not criticize a fine man like Signor Nicola," said Signora Concetta. "I did not know he was going to speak Friday. My Tony did not tell me. I am surely going now. With Signor Nicola on the program, it will be a lively affair."

"Baloney!" answered Joe, startling me with his complete lack of respect for his elders. "Do you think it's a smart thing for Mr. Barone to embarrass the poor kid in front of all those people? He can't even speak English right."

Mr. Sotile gave Joe a dirty look. "It is my fault," he apologized to Signora Concetta. "My son's bad manners reflect the looseness of my training of him. You know the old saying, 'An unweeded garden produces a poor crop.' "

"Nuts," said Joe.

When I went home wih the groceries, I was in a disturbed state of mind.

"Ricco," Mama called, "come here. You have not been yourself lately. Is something wrong?"

"It's nothing, Mama," I answered. How could I tell her that I was ashamed of my father?

"Come with me, my son," she commanded. She sat me on the sofa next to her. "Now," she said, "tell me what this is all about."

Maybe after all I could make Mama see how absurd it was for Papa to speak at the school. "Mama," I began, "you know how kids are. If they get anything on you, they make life miserable for you."

Mama nodded.

"If someone in the family does something foolish, everybody in the family feels the shame of it. You understand, don't you, Mama?"

Again Mama nodded. Her voice was cold as she said, "You are trying to tell me something about your father speaking Friday, are you not, Ricco?"

"I will die of shame Friday if Papa speaks!"

"You," asked Mama with great suddenness, "ashamed of your father? I would never believe it. Go to bed, you ingrate. Your father has been too good to you. You do not deserve a father like that."

I went to bed feeling more discouraged than ever. Mama gave me the silent treatment for the rest of the week. But the affair on Friday wasn't bothering Papa in the least. If he had been asked to advise the President, I believe he would have done so without blinking an eye.

Friday finally came around. That afternoon in the assembly hall I was amazed at the response of the parents. The hall was jammed. Good-naturedly, many consented to stand. Papa was going to put on his act before a standing-room-only crowd.

Looking around, I spotted Mama sitting down front. Several rows back Signora Concetta was sitting with Mr. Sotile. It seemed the whole neighborhood was there.

The Murphy Post Band was entertaining with some old favorites and stirring marches. The program started with the pledge of allegiance to the flag. Then the band played "The Star-Spangled Banner" while we all sang. Our ninth grade certainly did itself proud. A barbershop quartet sang patriotic songs with nice effects, and we topped all efforts with a play on a historical theme. It went off smoothly, and Mrs. Rhees was grinning from ear to ear.

While the stagehands were clearing the stage, the Murphy Post Band entertained with more music. Then Mr. Wright went to the center of the stage and introduced Mr. Robert Furness.

Mr. Furness was a building contractor whose boy Jimmy was in our grade. He made a good speech filled with sage advice. Next, Mr. Wright introduced Madelaine Cotter's father. Mr. Arnold Cotter was fat and bald, with the eloquence of a practical politician. His speech certainly did his political cause no harm that day.

When Mr. Jacob de Moss strode to the center of the stage, I took a long and careful look. He was handsome and he was dignified. The mood created by him and by the other fine speakers was deadly serious. Papa was going to shatter that mood with a resounding crash.

Now Mr. Wright was introducing Papa, and Papa was striding toward the stage. I grew cold all over and slid down in my seat. I closed my eyes. Hearing him was bad enough, but to see the violent gestures would be too much. I prayed hard that it would soon be over. Here it comes, I thought, Papa the comedian. He'll have them rolling in the aisles.

Papa's voice came to me, and with a shock; it wasn't quite what I expected. His voice was no whisper by any means, but it was restrained and rather gentle. The accent was there. It was so thick you could slice it, but Papa was giving it a surprising charm. I sat up and opened my eyes. I felt myself thaw out. I looked Papa over as if seeing him for the first time. He was all dignity and sincerity. It came to me—Papa's been around!

Then I gave attention to what he was saying. I won't attempt to quote him verbatim; that would be impossible. He was saying in effect: "I regret that my limited knowledge of the English language forbids my saying to you the things my heart wishes to say. There are so many mutual anxieties I would like to share with you, so many hopes. Fortunately, the very capable speakers before me have said these things in grand style. There are, however, two languages that are universal—the language of music and the language of prayer.

When these two are combined, a thing of beauty is created. With your permission, I would like to sing for you a prayer set to music. We all realize the urgent need for spiritual guidance in these troubled times and we are all familiar with 'The Lord's Prayer.' I sing for you 'The Lord's Prayer.' "

Signor Domenico was climbing the steps to the stage. He went to the piano and struck a few chords. I thought, Papa's going to blast them out of their seats! But again I was wrong.

Papa caressed the lyrics of that yearning, pleading song with all the care of a diamond cutter. He had his voice well in check. There was beauty in it beyond belief. As he mouthed each note, making a gem of it, it came to me that he was truly a great singer. And he was my father! There was a tightness in my throat that I recognized as pride.

Many things were clear then. I recognized the Papa who in my selfishness had been a stranger—the Papa who paced the floor nights when he could not sleep, thinking of Carl overseas—where he might be, what he was doing, if he was well, and if he was alive. Then I thought of Papa's visits to our bedroom when he thought we were all asleep, staring at us one at a time. As I listened to Papa singing, I felt thoroughly humble. Mama was right! I didn't deserve such a father.

Papa let his voice out just a trifle, sending golden note after golden note. It sent a shiver down my spine. He drew the closing notes out tenderly; they came like angels treading on cobwebs. His *Amen* was beautiful.

Though I couldn't see, I could hear, and what I heard was absolute silence. They don't like him, I thought; they're sitting on their hands! I was growing angry and I wanted to stand up and tell the crowd what I thought of them. But slowly the applause came. It rose to thunder. Everybody was standing up and clapping furiously.

I felt a hand on my shoulder. When I turned to look back, there was Mrs. Rhees.

"Ricco," she managed to say—her voice had an odd catch—"what a great man your father is. You must be very proud."

I could only nod. Speech was impossible for me. And it was just as well, for what I wished to say could not be put in words.

Independence Day

(July 4)

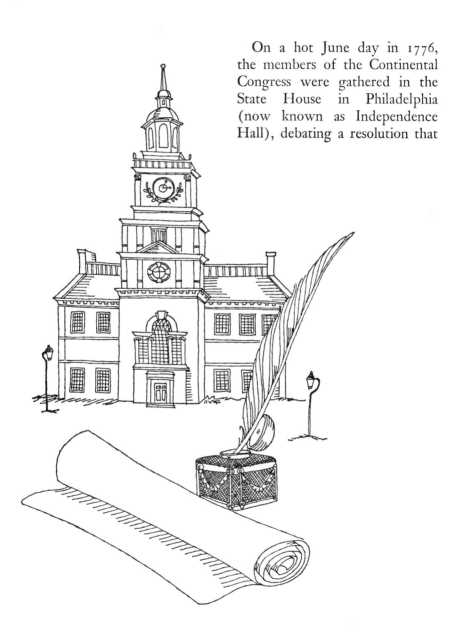

On a hot June day in 1776, the members of the Continental Congress were gathered in the State House in Philadelphia (now known as Independence Hall), debating a resolution that had been presented by one of the delegates:

Resolved, that these united colonies are and of right ought to be free and independent states.

Fourteen months had passed since the colonies had revolted. They would never be able to obtain the rights for which they were fighting, some of the members insisted, as long as they belonged to England. Other delegates argued that to try to cut all ties with the powerful mother country was too radical a step; the leaders in such a movement would doubtless be hanged as traitors if the revolution failed.

Finally, it was decided to delay a vote, since some of the delegates wanted to return home and discuss the matter with the citizens in their own communities. In the meantime, a committee was appointed to prepare a statement setting forth the reasons the colonies should separate from England. Then later, if the resolution passed, the Declaration of Independence would be ready.

One member of the committee, John Adams, suggested that the actual writing be left to Thomas Jefferson, who, at thirty-three, was already well known for his skill with words. Jefferson reluctantly agreed and returned to his Philadelphia lodging house, where he spent the next eighteen days close to his room. As he worked on the statement that was destined to become one of the great documents in history, he consulted no books or papers. But he remembered what other great thinkers, whose writings he had studied, had said about the rights of man. Although the ideas he presented were not new, he clothed them in ringing words that were to inspire men everywhere who yearned for freedom.

Events moved swiftly when the Continental Congress met again. On the first of July the delegates voted to declare the colonies independent. On the fourth, Thomas Jefferson's Declaration of Independence came up for a vote, and after a few changes had been made it was adopted. Now, after nearly two hundred years, Americans still celebrate the Fourth of July as Independence Day. The first celebration, though, did not take place until July 8, as you will read in the following true story.

The Birthday of a Nation

FRANCES ROGERS AND ALICE BEARD

"The big bell will ring at noon."

The word passed from one to another until everyone in Philadelphia knew, but the people did not wait until twelve o'clock. Well before that hour men, women and children in holiday attire were heading toward the open field behind the State House.

"Best to go early if you want to get close enough to hear—there's bound to be a most uncommon crowd of folk on hand." So said the wise ones.

Fortunately, the day was bright and gay, not a rain cloud in the blue sky. Perhaps the sun was a trifle too hot, but better that than no sunshine. For it would be a sad omen if joy in the first Independence Day were to be dampened by a downpour.

As it was, the celebration was four days late, for this was the eighth of July. But even if late, there must be a celebration, and this was the day appointed by Congress. In fact, under the circumstances, the eighth was the first possible date. The Declaration had been accepted too late on Thursday, the fourth, to permit plans for celebration on Saturday. Sunday, of course, was out of the question. So Monday the eighth it must be. There would be a parade; then the new Declaration would be read, from a special stage in the Yard, to the assembled citizens.

State House Yard, in 1776, was far different from Independence Square of today. The Yard was like a rough country field, without a single tree. And the "stage" from which Colonel Nixon was to read the Declaration was a high wooden platform built around the first observatory that had ever been erected in America. The platform, in honor of today's occasion, was gaily decked with flags, and from nearby windows of the State House fluttered more flags.

By high noon the Yard was packed with thousands of spectators, while overhead the great bell in the tower above the State House

184

boomed its message of freedom. Then all the bells of the city joined in chorus, and while the bells were in full cry the procession appeared. First came the Committee of Safety and the Committee of Inspection accompanied by several important gentlemen of the city. Then came the tall, dignified Colonel Nixon, carrying one of the newly printed copies of the Declaration of Independence. Above the lusty cheering that greeted him could be heard the voice of the Liberty Bell. Nor did it cease its noisy ringing until Colonel Nixon appeared on the high platform. With him were many members of Congress and high Army officers.

Then silence. A hush to be broken only by the voice of Colonel Nixon:

"A Declaration by the Representatives of the United States of America in General Congress assembled . . ."

And so on to the closing words of the great document:

And for the support of this Declaration, with a firm reliance on the protection of divine Providence, we mutually pledge to each other our lives, our fortunes and our sacred honor.

The reading had come to an end. And now it was the people's turn. "God bless the Free States of North America!" the crowd shouted.

Most of the townspeople, who had crowded the Yard to hear the official reading, already knew the content of the Declaration. The text had been printed in full in the Saturday newspapers, and there had been no lack of broadsides for handing about. The latter had been printed late Friday night, the printers having worked unceasingly to have them ready by Saturday. Then they were given to express riders, to drivers of mail coaches, and even to private travelers who might be going to assigned places. Copies had to reach the various assemblies and conventions, in order that the Declaration could be "proclaimed in each of the United States in such a Mode, as the People may be universally informed of it." General Washington himself would proclaim it at the head of the army.

So, the text of the Declaration began traveling from one colony to another, and the news was celebrated throughout the length and breadth of the country. In many of the celebrations, the King of Great Britain (though not by royal intention) played a leading role.

For example, in Baltimore, "an effigy of our late King was carted through the Town and Committed to the flames amidst the acclamation of many hundreds—the just reward of a tyrant."

In New York, the King took a leading part as villain of the piece. An equestrian statue of King George had been erected on Bowling Green, and New Yorkers watched with delight as a band of sturdy patriots hauled the rampant metal steed down from its high pedestal. In Boston Abigail Adams wrote her husband John, a delegate to the Continental Congress, about the multitude that had gathered in King Street "to hear the Proclamation for Independence read and proclaimed." A Colonel Crafts, standing on the balcony of the State House, read the proclamation aloud.

"Great attention was given to every word," said Abigail. "As soon as he ended, the cry from the balcony was 'God save our American States,' and then three cheers rent the air. The bells rang, the privateers fired, the forts and batteries, the cannon were joyful . . . Thus ends royal authority in this State. And all the people shall say Amen."

Jefferson's draft of the Declaration of Independence was written on paper. A piece of paper that is reasonably good in quality will last a long time if carefully protected. But in the case of a document intended to be timeproof (if that were possible), we revert to the ancient custom of writing on parchment.

Therefore on July 19 an order was given by Congress that the Declaration of Independence be engrossed on parchment. On August 2 came the formal signing of the document by all the members present at the time. President John Hancock signed first, in a large firm hand. As the story goes, he purposely "wrote large: so that," as he remarked, "George III may read without his spectacles." Then the delegates signed their names. Some signatures were bold and written with a flourish, others were very small and neat.

There may well have been an air of uneasy tension during that period when, one by one, the gentlemen stepped up to the President's table, picked up the quill, dipped it in ink, and wrote the signatures that might bring them to the "high gallows."

The signing of that document, as viewed from across the ocean by King George and his friends, was of course an act of high treason. In the summer of 1776 no man could know how the war with Great Britain would end. At the moment things looked black for the

Americans. Yet, regardless of the outcome, the United States chose to wave the flag of defiance and formally to declare for independence. The men who signed America's Declaration of Independence were risking their personal fortunes, their lives, the safety of their families—and the fate of a nation.

No member of the Continental Congress had worked harder than had John Adams to bring about the adoption of the Declaration of Independence. In a letter to his wife, he said: "I am well aware of the toil, and blood and treasure, that it will cost us to maintain this declaration, and support and defend these States. Yet through all the gloom I can see the rays of ravishing light and glory. I can see that the end is worth more than all the means, and that posterity will triumph in that day's transaction. . . ."

As the Fourth of July, 1826, was approaching, the citizens of Quincy, Massachusetts, where John Adams had returned to live in his old age, began planning an impressive celebration. In the opinion of the committee in charge, nothing could be more fitting for the occasion than a public speech by the oldest surviving signer of the Declaration of Independence.

But John Adams assured the committee that he had no desire to make "a last public appearance." He would, however, suggest a toast that could be presented as coming from him.

"I will give you," said he, 'Independence Forever.' "

While John Adams was dealing with the committee in Quincy, Thomas Jefferson lay ill in his bed at his home at Monticello in Virginia. He was too ill to be asked to take any part in the coming celebration of the national holiday. Nevertheless, the thought of that great day was in his heart.

He would leave one deathless word for the new nation—one word, sealed with his signature. For the last time in his life, he took up his pen and wrote:

Freedom, Thomas Jefferson.

When the sun rose on the Fourth of July, 1926, it found America joyously celebrating its fiftieth birthday. Before the sun went down on that same day, it looked upon joy turned to sorrow. But deeper than sorrow lay great wonder, for the day was woven of coincidence so strange that all the history of the world can scarcely offer a parallel.

On the Fourth of July, exactly half a century from the day on which the Declaration of Independence was adopted, the man who wrote it and the man who so ardently backed it—Thomas Jefferson and John Adams—both died, almost within the hour.

Both died, each leaving to the new nation a last message, which, the two being combined, reads:

Freedom and Independence Forever.

(This selection is condensed from the book by the same title *The Birthday of a Nation.*)

Soldier of the Revolution

DOROTHY CANFIELD FISHER

Ever since the Revolution, the Fourth of July had always been a great day in the little town of Sunmore up in the Vermont mountains. Every year since the old Liberty Bell in Philadelphia had first rung out in joy over the signing of the Declaration of Independence, the town had celebrated the Fourth with fireworks and a meeting at the Town Hall where people made speeches and everybody sang patriotic songs. After that, a picnic lunch was held out on the village green. If it rained, the lunch was eaten inside the Town Hall. And then, rain or shine, the procession formed to go out to the cemetery to put flags on the graves of the Sunmore men who had been soldiers in the Revolution. Nearly everybody in town marched in this procession, carrying flags and flowers and keeping step with music of the town drum-and-fife corps.

"Whee-ee-ee-ee-deedle-dee-ee!" went the high thin voices of the fifes; and "Boom! boom! boom!" went the deep voices of the drums. Tramp! tramp! tramp! went the feet of the Sunmore men and women and children—especially boys.

The boys looked forward to this celebration from one year to the next. Not only because of the fireworks and celebration, but because on that day they were allowed to fire off the little old cannon that stood on the Common in front of the Town Hall. The cannon was said to have been in the Battle of Bennington in 1777. But this was not sure. As the years went by, twenty, forty, fifty and finally by the time of this story, seventy years, fewer and fewer people could remember that battle. The only ones were the few old Sunmore men who had been Revolutionary soldiers.

They had walked at the head of the procession each year till their joints grew too stiff. After that, they rode in Dr. White's chaise, behind the doctor's slow, old roan horse, Dick. Dick was rather stiff in his joints, too, and was glad to walk as slowly as the rest of the procession.

The old soldiers always sat on the platform of the Town Hall, while the singing and speechmaking went on, their rifles across their knees, their soldiers' leather belts strapped on over their Sunday coats. Of course, what uniforms they had had seventy years before had gone all to pieces. After the speeches they had again ridden in Dr. White's chaise, heading the procession to the cemetery, where people handed up bouquets of flowers for them to lay on the graves of the Revolutionary soldiers who had been their comrades in the fight.

Dr. White knew more about medicine, of course, than anyone else in the community. But he also knew more about history. On the shelves of his library, all mixed up with his medical books, stood more histories of Vermont than the rest of the Sunmore people had all put together. When anyone wanted to find out something about what had happened in the past, Dr. White was always asked. He always knew the answer. In a way, he knew more about the Battle of Bennington than the aged veterans who had been there.

When May and June of the year 1848 came in, people began to plan for the Fourth of July celebration. But there were no old soldiers left. For four or five years there had been only two. Both of them were very old, of course, for the year 1848 was seventy-one years after the Battle of Bennington. One old soldier had been ninety, and the other eighty-six. Now both were gone. The older one had died recently. The family of the other one had moved away, so the old man went with them.

One of the boys in town, Andrew Bostwick, heard his family

saying, over and over, that the celebration would not seem right without any old soldier to make people remember what the Fourth of July was really about. Andrew was ten years old, a big, strong boy for his age. He not only knew all the paths and back roads in the mountains and valleys around Sunmore, but he also knew something about the Battle of Bennington and the Revolutionary War because he went to the district school and read about it in the Fourth Reader.

He thought it was hard luck for him that, just as he was big enough to help fire off the cannon and march in the Fourth of July procession, the last old soldier should have gone.

One day in June, when Andrew was out looking for a cow that hadn't come back to the barn from the high mountain pasture the night before, he met a schoolmate, Will Hunter. Will's mother had sent him out to see if the wild strawberries up on "that sloping field" were ripe yet. The two boys sat down on a stone to have a talk, and before long Andrew said something about the Fourth of July celebration with no old soldier left.

Will said, "There's an old man that lives with a family 'way up the Hollow from our house. He's their great-grandfather, I think. Maybe *he* was a soldier in the Revolutionary War. He's old enough to be. They say he's nearly ninety."

"But that house isn't in Sunmore," said Andrew, "it's in Canbury."

"No, it's not," said Will. "The people in that house don't come to Sunmore to buy things, because it's easier to go out the other end to Canbury than to follow the steep road up over Westward Mountain. But the way the town lines run, their house stands in Sunmore. People don't know much about them because they always go to Canbury. But they belong to Sunmore, all right. The man votes here, Town Meeting time."

The two boys looked at each other a long time. They had forgotten about looking for the cow, or ripe strawberries. "Let's go and see!"

So there *was* to be a Revolutionary soldier after all for the Fourth of July celebration! Everybody was talking about the old man, eighty-nine years or maybe ninety, or maybe more, back up on the far side of Westward Mountain, who had been remembered just in time. Andrew and Will had found him, and when they told their fathers about him two of the Selectmen of the town had gone over the mountain to see him. They said his back was bent with rheumatism and he was almost stone-deaf with age. He hobbled along with two canes to steady him, but he still had his old rifle and his cracked leather soldier's belt, just as the others had had. They reported that when, shouting loudly in his ear, they had asked him if he had fought in the Revolutionary War, he had nodded his head. Then they asked had it been in the Battle of Bennington. When he finally heard what they were asking he nodded his head and told them, "Yes, yes *sir*, it certainly was."

They said the people up there, for all he was so old, thought a great deal of him. It was his great-grandson's family he was living with—young people they were, who had been married only five or six years. They didn't know much about history, but they had always seen the old gun on the pegs over the fireplace, and the old belt there, too.

Wasn't it remarkable, Sunmore people said, that just that year when the last of the old heroes had gone, this other old Revolutionary soldier had been found? And who had found him? Why Andrew Bostwick and William Hunter. They were bright boys and patriotic, too. It was arranged that they were to stand on the platform during the meeting, on each side of the old soldier, and to march in the procession just in front of Dr. White's chaise, each one carrying an American flag. They were to be called the "Young Guard of Honor." You don't need anyone to tell you that the boys could hardly wait for the Fourth of July to come.

On the morning of the Fourth, Andrew's father got up early and drove their farm wagon all the way around the mountain and up into the Hollow to bring the old man back. It was ten o'clock when the wagon came into Sunmore Street. A crowd was waiting in front of the Town Hall. They began to clap their hands and cheer when Mr. Bostwick helped lift the bent old man out of the wagon and led him into the Hall. Andrew and Will, the Young Guard of Honor, went ahead of him, carrying his ancient gun for him. His rusty old belt was strapped on over his coat. When he was seated on the platform, Andrew put his gun across his knees and he gave such a pleasant smile of thanks that anyone could see why his great-grandchildren thought so much of him. He was a very nice-looking old man, with quiet gentle eyes; and although he hadn't a tooth left, his mouth still looked as though he liked jokes and laughing.

By now the Town Hall was filled. The meeting was about ready to begin when Dr. White, who always sat on the platform with the Selectmen and the speaker, called out to Andrew, "Here! Let me look at that gun! Pass it over to me."

Andrew was surprised. He put his hand on the gun, and leaning down to the old man, said as loudly as he could, "Dr. White wants to see your gun."

The doctor took one sharp look at it and motioned to the singers in the chorus who were ready to begin the first patriotic song. "Wait a minute!" he told them.

Then he put on his glasses, and looked carefully at a certain place near the trigger of the gun. Everybody kept still, wondering what was in his mind.

When he looked up, his face was all astonishment. "Why," he said, so loudly that everybody could hear him, "this is a Hessian gun! The old man must have been one of the Hessians who fought against the Americans."

There was such a silence in the Town Hall you could hear a wasp buzzing at one of the windows.

He was a Hessian! He had fought on the other side. People's mouths dropped open, they were so taken aback.

The old man hadn't heard a word of any of this because he was so deaf. He sat there, between the two little boys, looking quietly around at the people in the Hall with his gentle old eyes. For a minute, nobody said a word. Nobody could think of any words to say. Here they were celebrating the Fourth of July and the guest of honor they were so proud of turned out to be one of the enemy. Before they could collect their thoughts, Andrew ran out to the front of the platform and began to talk very fast, pleading for his old soldier.

"Listen," he said, "that was most a hundred years ago. Well, more than seventy years, anyhow. No matter how mad you are at somebody, you don't keep it up *forever*. The Bible says not to. He's lived right here close to us all that time, and farmed like anybody, and had his family and taken care of his children and paid his taxes. He's so old, he's like a little boy again. It would be too mean of us to——"

Now Andrew had never even spoken a piece in school before, and when he had time to think what he was doing, he felt very shy. He stopped talking and went back and put one hand on the old man's shoulder. The wrinkled, kind old face was lifted to smile at him, and Andrew smiled back. But he was so afraid of what might happen that his face felt dry and hot.

As soon as Andrew stopped talking the people had begun to whisper to each other. But when they saw that Dr. White wanted to say something, they were still again.

"I remember now, when I first came to Sunmore to practice medicine, and began to be interested in our local history, I did hear some very old people talk about a young Hessian soldier—hardly more than a boy—who had been wounded in the Battle of Bennington and was picked up unconscious in the woods the day afterwards. In one of the old Vermont history books in my library it is said that he was carried to a farmhouse and taken care of there till he was well enough to get around. By that time—this was many months afterwards—there were no more soldiers or armies left in Vermont, so nobody knew what to do with a prisoner. He was only nineteen then, and he had come to love Vermont and our ways of living. He didn't want anything but to be an American and live here.

"The history book didn't say anything more about him. But the old people here who talked to me about the story said they'd heard he married an American girl and lived on a back farm somewhere and that people came to like him because he was so cheerful and friendly. He said he'd been an orphan, seventeen years old, when he had been picked up off the street in the town he lived in and forced into the army. He had never liked soldiering. He had never understood what the fighting was about, because he never knew any English until he learned it from the farmer's family who took care of him after he was wounded."

The doctor was still holding the old rifle in his hands as he spoke. Then he turned around and laid it back on the old man's knees. "I think Andrew Bostwick is right," he said. "Seventy years is too long to go on being mad at somebody. We wanted an old American soldier for our celebration. Well, we have an old soldier who's been a good American for seventy years. I think our celebration had better go on."

When he sat down, the Moderator of the Town stood up. (The Moderator is the man elected to run the town meetings.) He said, "I think we ought to take a vote on this."

The minister called out, "That's a good idea, Mr. Moderator. It's something for everybody to decide. But before we do, I think we ought to sit perfectly quiet for a minute or two, and think this over. There's a great deal in it to think about. What we are deciding is whether we can live in peace when war has passed and long ago gone by."

The deaf ears of the old soldier, of course, had not heard a word. He followed all this activity with his bright, old eyes, thinking the meeting was going fine. His back was bent over with rheumatism, his hands lay thin and knotted on the arms of his chair, but his pleasant, clean, old face was smiling as he looked from one person to another, down in the audience. He had been friendly to everyone for so many years that he did not dream anyone might not be friendly to him.

Meanwhile Andrew was so afraid of what the vote might be that a big lump came into his throat. Everybody in the audience was looking at the old soldier. What were they thinking?

At last a man stood up. "Mr. Moderator, I move that our celebration proceed," he said.

Several people called, "I second the motion."

The vote was taken; everybody voted "Yes."

So that afternoon, after the speaking and the singing, and the picnic lunch, the procession formed as usual to march out to the cemetery. The old soldier—he looked very tired by this time, but he was still smiling—was helped up into Dr. White's chaise. The Young Guard of Honor stood by the cannon.

The bandleader lifted his head. "All ready."

The marchers held up their flags.

"Get up there, Dick," said Dr. White, slapping his reins over his horse's back. Men and women fell in behind the old shay, four by four.

Little girls in white dresses trotted alongside the carriage, carrying wreaths of garden flowers, roses and lilies and carnation pinks for the old soldier to lay on the graves of those who had once hated him.

"Whee-deedle-dee," went the fife. "Rat-a-tat-a-tat," went the drums, and "Boom," went the cannon as the Young Guard of Honor fired the usual salute to those who had fought for America—an America where the bitterest war and the bitterest hate could end in peace.

Labor Day

(First Monday in September)

"America was built by labor," Benjamin Franklin once said, and he believed that the future prosperity of the American people depended on their industry.

However, the time came when the laboring people of the United States, though they worked hard enough, no longer received their fair share of America's abundance. The people employed in factories and mines and on canals and railroads often received very small wages for laboring twelve or fourteen hours a day. To obtain their rights they formed labor unions, demanding better wages and working conditions and shorter hours.

By 1882, conditions had begun to improve, though much remained to be done. That year Peter McGuire, founder of the carpenters' union, suggested that a special holiday be set aside in honor of labor. There already were holidays for observing religious, civil and military events, but none, as he said later, "representative of the industrial spirit— the great vital force of every nation."

The idea was so appealing that the Central Labor Union of New York City arranged a parade for September 5. The marchers carried signs that read:

8 HOURS CONSTITUTE
A DAY'S WORK

LABOR CREATES ALL
WEALTH

ALL MEN ARE BORN
EQUAL

Similar parades were held in other cities and towns during the

196

following years, and in 1894 Congress set aside the first Monday in September as an annual holiday for the entire nation. Labor Day is still celebrated with parades and picnics, and millions of Americans join in the good times. The popularity of the holiday has undoubtedly helped labor unions to win widespread support for many of their demands.

One of the first great labor leaders was Samuel Gompers, of whom you may read in the following true story.

The Grand Old Man of Labor

The Story of Samuel Gompers

JOSEPH COTTLER

He heard the cry first in the street where he lived in the East End of London, and for the rest of his life the cry kept ringing in his ears. He was a small boy then with his nose flat against the windowpane. The tramping on the cobbles outside drew him often to the window, and he watched men—the fathers and older brothers of his playmates—moving aimlessly about. The cry of one of them penetrated the shut window and lodged in his brain:

"God, I've no work to do. My wife, my kids want bread, and I've no work to do."

When Sam was only ten years old, his father took him out of the free school for Jewish boys and apprenticed him to a shoemaker. The father was by trade a cigarmaker. Often after supper he rose from the table saying he was off to a meeting of the Cigarmakers' Society.

"I would rather be a cigarmaker than a shoemaker," remarked Sam.

"And why?" asked Father Gompers.

"Because shoemakers have no society," replied Sam.

With that, the Society of Cigarmakers enrolled a new apprentice boy. Sam took his place at a long worktable. In the daily company of men, his raw open mind was molded as tightly as the rich brown velvety leaves of tobacco he molded between his fingers. The men talked of hard times, of low wages and starvation in England. Some spoke of a land to the west, where wages were higher and they sang:

> To the West, to the West, to the land of the free
> Where mighty Missouri rolls down to the sea;
> Where a man is a man if he's willing to toil,
> And the humblest may gather the fruits of the soil.

Yet even there a civil war had broken out over the freedom of certain workers. Their champion, Abraham Lincoln, had no more loyal admirer in the whole world than the thirteen-year-old boy Sam Gompers. When his father one day announced that to save themselves from starvation they would have to leave England for America, Sam was thrilled to think that he would be closer to Abraham Lincoln.

But after his arrival in America he soon learned that the East End of London and the East Side of New York were much alike. The struggle to pay the landlord and the grocer was unchanged. The shop where he worked was his only university. All day long he took the soft tobacco leaves, one by one, off the pile. He examined each leaf and shaved off the frayed edge to a hair's breadth. Then he wrapped it around the sausage of tobacco, deftly shaping the cigar. Once his fingers had become expert, his mind was left free, and he enjoyed the work. Cigarmakers could cultivate one another's society during working hours.

"Read to us, Sam," they coaxed. Sam had a strong, mellow voice and there was always a book or magazine in his pocket.

Or they talked of themselves. A tool had been invented for molding cigars, and the craftsmen feared the time when their skill would no longer be needed. "Either we destroy the machine, or it will destroy us," declared some of Samuel Gompers' less-thoughtful shopmates.

"But to destroy the machine is to stop the wheels of progress," objected Sam.

Then the "sweatshop" menaced the cigarmakers. Some merchants had bought up a block of tenements. There they installed families of immigrants, whom they put to work making cigars. The immigrant family paid rent to the merchant and was forced to buy raw tobacco and tools from him, and even food. The cigar merchant paid these people very little for their labor. Naturally, he was able to sell his cigars at extremely low prices.

But at whose expense? Samuel Gompers visited sweatshops. He found that merely to keep alive every member of the sweatshop family had to work early and late, seven days a week. The low price of the sweatshop cigar dragged down the price of the factory cigar, and that in turn beat down the wages of all craftsmen like Samuel Gompers. They found themselves unable any longer to provide their families with decent food or living quarters. The workers were desperate.

Then in 1873 there was a depression in the country. Through the blizzards of the winter Samuel Gompers saw lines of men outside the free-soup kitchens. Again the cry rang in his ears:

"God, I've no work to do. My wife and my kids want bread, and I've no work to do."

Was there no answer to this cry?

Sam Gompers knew of no cure-all for the ills of the working-man; he knew only his distress. And he pitied him and stood ready to risk his own welfare to help him. His shopmates often told what he once risked for "Conchy."

Conchy, as he was nicknamed, was a middle-aged sick man with very weak eyes. Sam Gompers and he worked at a bench near the windows of the dim factory. One morning when Sam came to work, he found Conchy sitting at a bench in the dimmest part of the factory.

Sam went to him. "What's the matter?" he asked.

"They put me back here and gave that new young fellow my seat near the window," Conchy said plaintively.

"What for?"

"They just put him there, that's all. I don't know why."

Sam went back to his seat and sent a callboy to Mr. Smith, the new foreman. The boy came back with word that Mr. Smith was busy.

"Tell him, please, it's important," insisted Sam.

Mr. Smith arrived. "Well, what do you want?" he demanded.

"Why did you put Conchy away back in the dark and the young fellow down here in the light?" asked Sam. He pointed out that Conchy was an old employee, whose sight had failed in the work.

"That's my business," said the foreman.

"You mean to say you're going to let the new fellow keep Conchy's seat?"

"Yes, I am. What are you going to do about it?"

Sam rose. He gathered up his tools. "Not much," he said, "except that he can have this seat, too."

There was a second of silence. Then another voice broke out, "Yes, and he can have this seat, too."

Another man rose. "And this seat."

Fifty men pushed back their chairs. "And this seat."

The men had struck.

Five minutes later the strike was settled. The factory was working as usual, with Conchy back in his old seat.

"We must always act together," Sam Gompers told his shopmates. That was his answer to the cry in the streets, the cry he could never forget since his childhood in London.

"Let us act together," was not a new appeal in America. In the past workingmen had formed unions to try to improve working conditions. In such unions the shoemakers and printers protested against low wages, the hatters and other factory hands against their fourteen hours of daily toil. But these unions were temporary. When indignation welled up in a trade, the workers rushed together; but later they drifted apart.

Sam Gompers believed that the workers in many different trades must unite, and he labored for years to bring this about. He looked forward to the time when employer and worker would sit at the same table and talk frankly and freely of each other's needs and problems. Then, he felt, there would be no more misery among the toiling citizens of America.

At last, in December of 1886, came the moment Sam Gompers had worked for. The American Federation of Labor, the union of all labor unions, was organized. For many years after that he served as its president. In the ripeness of time he became a mighty champion who, by urging workers to act together, improved the conditions of working people not only in the United States but in other countries, too.

"Mr. Gompers," a certain government official once said, "I regard you as the spokesman for the underdog of the world."

The Smithy

P. V. RAMASWAMI RAJU

Adapted from a Hindu fable and arranged
BY FRANCES JENKINS OLCOTT

Once words ran high in a smithy.

The furnace said: "If I cease to burn, the smithy must close."

The bellows said: "If I cease to blow, no fire, no smithy."

The hammer and anvil, also, each claimed the sole credit for keeping up the smithy.

The ploughshare that had been shaped by the furnace, the bellows, the hammer and the anvil, cried: "It is not each of you alone, that keeps up the smithy, but *all together*."

Citizenship Day

(September 17)

This holiday is celebrated on the anniversary of the signing of the United States Constitution. Replacing "I Am an American Day," once celebrated on the third Sunday in May to welcome new citizens from other countries, this holiday is set aside to honor new citizens of foreign birth and also native-born Americans who have reached the age of twenty-one. This is an important day in their lives, since they are now old enough to vote, and, through their votes, to help elect the government officials who will make and enforce the laws.

To be granted citizenship, a person of foreign birth must have lived in the country for five years. He must be able to read and write in the English language; he must understand the fundamentals of American government; he must know about the main events in American history; and he must be of good moral character. Two native Americans who know him personally must testify as to his qualifications.

In a mass ceremony presided over by a Federal judge, new citizens take the following oath of allegiance to the United States:

I hereby declare, on oath, that I absolutely and entirely renounce and adjure all allegiance and fidelity to any foreign prince, potentate, state, or sovereignty of who or which I have heretofore been a subject or citizen; that I will support and defend the Constitution and laws of the United States of America against all enemies, foreign and domestic; that I will bear true faith and allegiance to the same; and that I take this obligation freely and without any mental reservation or purpose of evasion; so help me God. In acknowledgment whereof I have hereunto affixed my signature.

The following selections, a story about new citizens and an excerpt from a famous speech by the late Dr. Martin Luther King, emphasize the importance of citizenship as an individual experience.

Vasil Discovers America

LESLIE G. CAMERON

From the first day, Vasil liked grade 4B. There were red and silver fish in a bowl near the window, flowers on the window sills, gay crayon pictures on the blackboards; and pinned around the walls were silhouettes made by a former class. Miss Hester wasn't young and goldy like Miss Maribell in 3A. She was fat, and her face screwed into wrinkles when she laughed, which was often; but somehow Vasil knew she loved boys and girls.

Vasil liked the boy in the seat opposite his. His name was Nikola Novan, but everyone called him Nicky. Nicky had come from Albania. He had lived in America three years, and had an all-American baby sister born in Ohio. Vasil had an all-American baby brother, Peter; but it was only two years since his family had left Albania. Vasil was glad that Nicky was his marching partner.

At noon Vasil rushed home to tell his mother about the new room, about Miss Hester, and, most of all, about Nikola, who had come from a village across the mountain from Pogdanoc. To his dismay he found her sitting in the kitchen, her head on the table—crying! In all his ten years Vasil had never before seen his mother cry. Always she was quiet, strong, working for father, little Peter or Vasil, and always there was a smile in her eyes and near the corners of her mouth. And now she was crying!

"Mamma," he cried, "are you sick? What hurts you? Is it Peter?" But rosy Peter was sleeping in the crib.

Vasil caught her arm. "Shall I run for my father?" He pressed close to her. "Oh, Mamma, don't cry."

"Vasil," she said brokenly, "what can we do? Ljuba Novan has moved into this street."

"Ljuba Novan?" He stared at her wonderingly.

Tears slid down her cheeks again. "It is the feud, Vasil, the feud of Pogdanoc!"

"Feud?"

"Yes. Have you forgotten? Your father's uncle killed Ljuba's

206

uncle, and the uncle's brother killed your father's cousin, and your father is the only man on his side of the family. You know we do not remember the feud in our country when women are present, and for a year Ljuba Novan stirred nowhere without his wife; then they all came to America. Oh, I hoped we had lost them forever. Why did they have to come to this city and this very street?"

"But, Mamma, has Ljuba Novan a boy like me—Nicky?"

His mother did not know. Neighbors, formerly Albanians, had been in to tell her that the Novan family had just moved into the street, three houses down, two flights up.

When the noon hour was over, Vasil put his arms around his mother. "We will talk to my father," he said. "We will beg him not to carry on the feud."

She held him close. "My son, never once has your father spoken to any of us except in kindness. Every day he works hard, and now every little while he gets more money in the pay envelope. But here in America they do not understand Albanian customs. A brave man lives according to the ways of his country."

Back at school that afternoon, Vasil did not seem to see Nicky, who came over to him in the yard at recess.

"We are going back to Ohio," he said. "My father came home this noon and said we must move back. Someone in our street has a feud with us. But we have to stay here a month because the rent is paid."

Vasil's heart fell. So much could happen in a month.

Next day Nicky kept aloof from Vasil. But two or three days later they met at the drinking fountain, and Nicky said, "It's your father has a feud with mine."

"I know it," responded Vasil unhappily.

Nicky took a long drink. "That makes a feud between us, too, doesn't it?"

Vasil nodded thoughtfully. "I suppose it does," he said. After that, he and Nicky met only at marching time.

The month was almost over. Vasil's mother showed strain and anxiety. Peter was sick, and his father was moody and stern. Vasil carried a weight of dread.

One morning Miss Hester began to talk of a program for Columbus Day. She told her forty-eight bright-eyed immigrant pupils the old, old story of the brave adventurer who would not turn back even when his sailors mutinied. As soon as she had finished, forty-eight waving hands shot up.

"Oh, please, Miss Hester, can I speak a piece?" "My mother wants always I should sing alone." "My father likes I should play the violin." "Oh, Miss Hester, Antonio you just gave the piece to, he don't speak no good English. I'm American. I could speak it better." "So could I, Miss Hester. I was born in New York." "Oh, Miss Hester, I'm American. I was born in Chicago." "You was not!" "I was so!" "I'm American, Miss Hester; my father's got his first papers." "My father's got his second ones, teacher. I want a piece!"

Voices ceased when Miss Hester called Vasil and Nikola. On Columbus Day Vasil was to stand in the front of the room and lead the singing, so he must know very well indeed the words of *The Star Spangled Banner* and *America, the Beautiful.* Nikola had a wonderful piece to speak that began:

> *Breathes there the man, with soul so dead,*
> *Who never to himself hath said,*
> *This is my own, my native land!*

Then from the back of the room came a question that struck 4B speechless. "What is papers?" asked Carlo Depella, who had come from Porto Rico five months before. Everyone wanted to tell him, but Miss Hester hushed them all and explained. Carlo from Porto Rico was already an American, so he would never need naturalization papers. But people from other countries who wanted to become citizens wrote their names in an office and received papers.

Milan Neditch jumped to his feet. "You take papers. You forget your country. You say, 'Bah, my country dirty, dumb place. I 'shamed to be born there.' But I say and my father say, 'Never! Never! America, rich, clean land, but I always love my Montenegro!'"

Miss Hester understood. "That is right, Milan. You must always love your country. She is like your mother. You would never forget or stop loving your mother."

"Miss Hester, please," said little Wu Long, "we forget only hard days in old country. Days, no rice, baby sick, much hungry. But lotus flower on water we not forget, temple we not forget, and honored ancestors we never forget."

"Yes, Wu Long," agreed Miss Hester. "All the good we are proud and glad to remember."

Patrick Mulligan, eldest son of a city policeman, spoke. "My father says we come to this country because it's the land of the brave and the rich and the free, and we got good schools and public baths and a police force to look after us, and it ain't good to be taking everything and giving nothing back, not even a 'thank you,' and he's been American ever since he was twenty-one, and all us seven kids is American."

Vasil besought Miss Hester's attention. "But dead cousins, Miss Hester, cousins that was shot, do we say, 'Oiya—let it go!' Is it like that?"

Miss Hester was puzzled. Nikola eagerly explained. "He means feuds, Miss Hester. Do we forget feuds?"

A glimmer of understanding came to Miss Hester. "Yes, Nikola, you do not bring your feuds to America. They are left behind with the kind of clothes you used to wear and the kind of lessons you used to learn."

A great hope made Vasil's heart beat quickly, and when they all settled again to their lessons he found it hard to keep his mind on his work. Perhaps that is why he did not look carefully before he crossed the street on his way home that night. Suddenly, he looked up. A huge truck was bearing down upon him with terrible speed. Fright paralyzed Vasil. His schoolmates on the sidewalk screamed, but before a policeman could reach the spot, there sounded high above the children's shrieks and the clang of traffic a wild, shrill, ringing call that Vasil recognized. It was the call of the Albanian mountaineer to his friends, the greeting he had often heard echoing from peak to peak in the land of his birth. He turned. Nikola was standing on the sidewalk, his hands over his ears as Albanians hold theirs to keep the eardrums from bursting when they call in the thin atmosphere of the mountains. Vasil darted back out of danger just as the great truck swept on.

"Nikola made you turn around; Nikola saved you!" the children said, crowding about Vasil.

"I know it," responded Vasil, still pale from the vision of the great truck wheels steering directly for him. "Tonight I shall tell my father."

"When you get papers," explained Vasil that evening to his

father, "we forget the feud. We remember only that Nikola gave the Albanian call and it made me run."

Vasil's mother spoke, "Marosh, must our sons grow up with this feud hanging over their heads?"

Marosh Tsilta was a man of few words, and he made no reply to his wife or to Vasil. Then one evening he spoke. "Elena, call Vasil. We will take Peter and go to the house of Ljuba Novan."

Vasil's mother turned white, but she put on Peter's things, and Vasil silently found his cap. The news ran quickly from door to door. Neighbors watched them cross the street. Some even followed them up two flights of stairs and waited while Marosh knocked at Ljuba's apartment.

There was no response until one of the followers called shrilly, "Have no fear, Ljuba. Elena, his wife, is here, too." A bolt slid back; the door opened a crack.

Marosh Tsilta touched his heart and his forehead. "Peace to this house," he said.

The door space widened. They went in, and the bolt was shoved back again to keep out the inquisitive neighbors.

"Ljuba Novan," said Marosh, "I come in peace today because I am no more Albanian except in love for my fatherland. Today I have first papers! Soon I shall have second and last. I have said in writing that America is my country. And now, as my Vasil's teacher said, I leave in Pogdanoc the feud between your family and mine."

Joy overran the rugged face of Ljuba Novan. "And I, my friend and brother—only yesterday took my first papers and as soon as may be will come the second; then we will all be Americans." Ljuba's wife tried to speak, but suddenly she and Elena were in each other's arms crying together.

Nicky and Vasil edged toward each other.

"I never knew the uncle who carried on feud in your family," said Ljuba.

"It was my father's cousin's son who was killed, and never had I set eyes on him," explained Marosh.

So they drank cups of thick, syrupy Turkish coffee, crying to each other the Albanian greeting, *Pacim sa malit!* (We have seen you as the mountains.) And Marosh thanked Nikola for sounding the mountain call that had saved Vasil.

On Columbus Day the parents of Vasil and Nikola sat side by

side listening to the program of 4B. Marosh Tsilta nodded appreciatively when Vasil's clear voice soared above the others:

America, America, God mend thine every flaw,
Confirm thy soul in self-control,
Thy liberty in law.

I Have a Dream

MARTIN LUTHER KING JR.

> The Fourteenth Amendment to the U.S. Constitution granted citizenship to Negro men born in the United States, and the Fifteenth Amendment stated that no citizen should be denied the right to vote because of race or color. In actual practice, though, many Negro citizens were denied this right because of local laws in some of the states. Their great leader, Dr. Martin Luther King, was convinced that only by exercising their legal right to vote could they eventually change the laws and vote out of office those officials who stood in the way of their enjoying the rights guaranteed by the Constitution. In 1963, the Centennial of the Emancipation Proclamation, 200,000 Negroes and white friends joined in an impressive March on Washington, which helped speed the passage of a new civil rights bill. The following excerpts are taken from the eloquent speech Dr. King made on that day.

Now is the time to make real the promise of democracy. . . . Now is the time to make justice a reality for all of God's children. There will be neither rest nor tranquility in America until the Negro is granted his citizenship rights. The whirlwinds of revolt will continue to shake the foundations of our nation until the bright day of justice emerges.

And that is something I must say to my people who stand on the threshold which leads to the palace of justice. In the process of gaining our rightful place we must not be guilty of wrongful deeds.

Again and again we must ride to the majestic heights of meeting physical force with soul force. The marvelous new militancy that has engulfed the Negro community must not lead us to a distrust of all white people, for many of our white brothers—as evidenced by their presence here today—have come to realize that their destiny is tied up with our destiny. . . .

There are those who are asking the devotees of civil rights, "When will you be satisfied?" We can never be satisfied . . . until justice rolls down like water and righteousness like a mighty stream. . . . Though we face the difficulties of today and tomorrow, I still have a dream. It is a dream deeply rooted in the American dream. I have a dream that one day this nation will rise up and live out the true meaning of its creed: "We hold these truths to be self-evident, that all men are created equal."

I have a dream that one day on the red hills of Georgia the sons of former slaves and the daughters of former slave-owners will be able to sit down together at the table of brotherhood . . . I have a dream that my four little children will one day live in a nation where they will not be judged by the color of their skin, but by the content of their character.

This is our hope . . . the faith we will be able to hew out of the mountain of despair a stone of hope.

(For another story about citizenship, read "The Tomahawk Family" in the following section on "American Indian Day.")

American Indian Day

(Fourth Friday in September in most states)

In 1914 Red Fox James, a Blackfoot Indian, rode horseback across the continent, calling on state governors to endorse a suggestion that a special day be set aside to honor the first Americans. When he reached Washington, the lone rider presented the endorsements to President Woodrow Wilson. His dramatic ride helped to arouse interest in the plight of the red men, most of whom could not vote. They had been denied citizenship in a land that had been theirs for thousands of years before white settlers arrived.

In the beginning, many of those earlier Americans had been friendly. They had taught the Pilgrims, among others, how to fish and hunt and plant corn and how to survive in the wilderness. But with the coming of more and more settlers, the Indians had often been cheated. They had fought back desperately when the white men demanded more land—always more land—and drove them westward. By the early nineteen hundreds most Indians were living on reservations that the Government had set aside for their use. They were wretchedly poor, but most white people did not realize this, or did not care.

The year after Red Fox's ride more than a thousand members of the American Indian Association met in Lawrence, Kansas, and issued a proclamation, reading in part: "Now that the glory and the shadows of the past have become a part of the historic record . . . we are not to forget the present and the future of our people that we may henceforth live in greater fullness."

In 1917, New York State observed the first American Indian Day, and now most states celebrate it with special programs and exhibits. Many more white Americans have come to appreciate the Indians' love of beauty, as expressed in their crafts and dances and ceremonials; their kinship with nature; and their love of freedom, too often thwarted in the past. Since 1924 Indians have been allowed to vote and—though much remains to be accomplished—the government has taken many steps to help our first Americans to take rightful place in the life of the nation.

The Creation of Man

A Folktale from the Pacific Coast
Retold by
KATHERINE CHANDLER

> In the old days, when California still belonged to Spain, the children on a ranch across the bay from San Francisco liked to listen to stories told by the Indian servants. Wantasson the blacksmith told them about Coyote, who was so clever that he had made the world and all the other animals. Coyote had even made Man, according to Wantasson. The children, who had studied their catechism, said the stories were not true but all the same they were wonderful to hear.

Coyote looked around the earth, but there was nothing to do. All the animals were warm and fat, and living without fear of anything. "They don't need any help," sighed Coyote, "but I must do something. I think I'll make a man."

He went down to the creek and began to model a figure out of the clay. As he worked, he became dissatisfied with the figure. I wish I could make it better, he thought to himself. I think I will ask the other animals for their opinions. Perhaps they can give me some good ideas.

He called all the animals of the world to meet together on the hilltop. The fishes wobbled up from the sea, the birds swept down from the heavens, and the other animals came hurrying from all the corners of the earth. They sat round in a circle—Cougar, Grizzly, Antelope, Mountain Sheep, Deer, and so on, down to little Mouse, who was on the left of Cougar. In the center sat Coyote.

He said: "It is time for us to make man. Tell me how we shall make him."

"O-ho!" burst out Cougar. "That's easy. Give him a mighty voice to frighten all the animals, and long hair, and strong talons with

216

terrible fangs at the end of them. Then he will be master of the world. O-ho!" and Cougar chuckled, as poor little Mouse shrunk away from him.

"Gru-u-u!" rumbled Grizzly. "It's perfectly ridiculous to have such a great voice. Half the time it frightens the prey so that it can hide. Give him a big enough voice, of course, but give him sense enough to use it seldom. Let him move quietly and swiftly. And let him have great strength to hold his capture."

"Huh!" wheezed Deer. "Strength to hold is good enough, but he would look foolish without antlers to fight with. I think, with Grizzly, that it is perfectly absurd to give him a roaring voice. I should pay less attention to his voice and more to his ears and eyes. Have his ears as sensitive as the spider's web, and his eyes like coals of fire. Then he can detect any approaching danger."

"Baa-aa!" bellowed Mountain Sheep. "Antlers are only a bother They always catch in the brush. You would do better to roll up the antlers into little horns on either side of the forehead. That will give his head weight and enable him to butt harder."

"Oh, you animals have no brains," interrupted Coyote. "You each want man to be just like yourself. You might as well take one of your own children and call it *man*. Now you know that I am wiser than any of you, and yet I want man to be better than I am. Of course I wish him to have four legs like myself, and five toes. But Grizzly's toes spread out straight so that he can stand on two feet. That is a good thing. I want man's toes to be spread out like Grizzly's.

"Then, too, he'd better have no tail, like Grizzly, for tails are only good for fleas to ride on. He may have a voice like Cougar's, but he need not roar all the time. But as to giving him thick hair, that would be a burden. Look at Fish. He is naked, and he is comfortable under the hottest sun. So I want man's skin to be like the skin of Fish. As to claws, they should be like Eagle's, so that he can carry things. Deer's eyes and ears are good, and his throat, too. So I'd make man with ears and eyes and throat like Deer's. His brains should be like mine, so that he can rule the whole world."

"Nonsense! nonsense!" Beaver had been gurgling for some time. "No tail! no tail! Why, he could not live without a good broad tail. How would he haul his mud and build his house without a tail?"

"And no wings?" hooted Owl. "No wings, indeed! You are perfectly senseless not to think of giving him wings."

"Pu-u-u!" sniffed Mole. "It's senseless to have wings. They only bump you against the sky. And eyes are useless, too. The sun only burns them. It would be better to give him a soft fur and let him cuddle down in the moist, cool earth."

"Living in the earth is the worst nonsense of all," exclaimed Mouse. "He will need to creep into the sunshine to get warm. And he needs eyes to see what he is eating."

"O reech-o!" began Screech Owl, when Coyote ordered: "Stop your screeching. You may all go home. I'll make man myself."

Each animal echoed, "I'll make man myself," and they all rushed, quarreling and snapping, to the clay bank. Each began to model a figure.

At sundown they stopped to sleep—all but Coyote. He went on working. When he heard snores from every bush, he went among the models of the other animals and destroyed every single one. Then he returned to his own figure and worked steadily. As the morning star mounted in the heavens, the figure of man was finished.

"Shine bright on him, O Morning Star!" whispered Coyote. "Give him life from the heavens, for he is to be superior to us all."

The morning star flashed five rays on the figure. Man straightened himself up. His eyes brightened. He stretched out his arms. Coyote took his hand and said: "You were partly made in the light, so you will always love the sunshine. You were partly made in the night, so you will never fear the darkness. Your mind will be active under sun or stars. You must gather cunning from all times, for henceforth you are to be the ruler of the world."

The Tomahawk Family

NATALIE SAVAGE CARLSON

Frankie and Alice, a Sioux brother and sister, attended the Little Axe school on the Indian reservation in South Dakota, where they lived with their Grandmother Tomahawk. Grandmother clung to her old-fashioned ways and was not much interested in the children's education or in the school's PTA. Perhaps one reason was that the president was Mrs. Two Bears, a much younger woman who had been elected to the Indians' tribal council—an honor which Grandma felt rightfully belonged to her. Alice and Frankie were dismayed one day when she wanted them to stop school.

Trouble shadowed Tomahawk cabin when Frankie reached home. Alice's eyes were red from weeping. But Grandma looked happy as a rabbit in May.

"Iron Shells [trains] come by here," she announced. "They take you and Alice Nebraska to pick potatoes. You and Alice make potato money."

Alice burst into fresh tears. "I don't want to pick potatoes in Nebraska," she howled. "I don't want to be an old potato picker all my life. I'll miss out at school. Money isn't everything. I want to go to college like teacher and get educated."

Frankie agreed with her. "We can't leave school to go potato picking," he said. "The Iron Shells will be gone for weeks."

Grandma crossed her hands over her breast and stared at him. The children could see it was no use to argue. Perhaps there was some other way to change her mind. If they could get Grandma

Tomahawk to the PTA supper at school, she might learn how important it was for children to go to school.

Miss Anna Hansen, their teacher, told the children that they were to write invitations to take home to their parents. She wrote a form on the blackboard.

"Dear Mother and Father," she wrote:
"We are going to have a PTA supper at school next Thursday night at six o'clock. We invite you to come. We want you.

Your son (or daughter),

Name"

The children were given pieces of snow-white paper for the invitations. They were told to use their best penmanship.

Frankie ruined two pieces of the paper before he was able to write all the way through without a mistake. "Dear Grandma," he began. As he wrote the third copy, a sudden inspiration came to him. He didn't sign the note "Frankie." He boldly signed it, "Miss Anna Hansen, fourth-grade teacher."

If Grandma Tomahawk thought that teacher had written the invitation herself, she might come. She might feel that she had to come. . . .

As he had expected, Grandma Tomahawk was very impressed.

"Teacher write everybody parents?" she asked.

Frankie shook his head. "No, indeed," he said. "You're the only one with an invitation to the PTA signed Miss Anna Hansen."

That was the truth anyway.

"Why teacher send invite only me?" asked Grandma suspiciously. Her eyes had read and reread the piece of paper. Even if Grandma couldn't speak good English, she could read it.

"It's because her parents are coming too." said Alice. "They're probably old so she wants you to be their hostess. That means you're to talk to them all evening and make them welcome."

"Me welcome Teacher parents?" asked Grandma in awe. "Not Pauline Two Bears?"

"Mrs. Two Bears isn't old enough," said Alice.

Grandma read the invitation over and over. No white person had ever invited her to anything on a piece of white paper.

"Teacher not write good," said Grandma critically. "Look like bird tracks."

Frankie flushed. He should have let Alice write the invitation because she had such a neat hand. "But she real polite," admitted the old woman. "Call me grandma." It was lucky for Frankie that "grandma" was a title of respect given by the Sioux to old women.

Grandma carried the paper inside. She tacked it to the wall next to a newspaper picture of an Indian tribal dance.

"Me go PTA supper," she announced.

Frankie and Alice were overjoyed but Alice's happiness did not last long.

"Me wear Indian dress to PTA," said Grandma. "Fancy dress me weared to Black Hills pageant."

Alice was horrified. "You can't wear Indian clothes to the supper," she cried. "The PTA is real civilized. Nobody wears Indian clothes."

But Grandma's mind was made up. "White people at pageant like my Indian clothes. Teacher parents white."

"They won't be in Indian clothes," insisted Alice. "Nobody'll be in uncivilized clothes but you. Everybody will think our grandmother looks like an old Indian."

Frankie didn't see why Alice was so upset about what Grandma wore. The important thing was to get her there. "Grandma can look like an old Indian if she wants," he defended.

But Alice thought that Grandma's appearance at the PTA supper in doeskin, quills and beads would disgrace the Tomahawk family.

She even told Miss Hansen, the teacher, about it, "My grandmother's going to wear her Indian clothes to the supper," said Alice, shame reddening her face. "No matter what I say, she's still going to wear all those beads and feathers. Everybody will laugh at her."

Miss Hansen looked at Alice intently. "Oh, I'm sure that won't happen." She patted Alice's shoulder. "I promise you that I won't let it happen."

Alice didn't see how teacher could keep the PTA from laughing at Grandma Tomahawk, but she knew that Miss Hansen wouldn't laugh anyway. She wanted to tell her about the potato-picking problem, but she couldn't. Potato picking in Nebraska was an even more painful subject than Indian clothes at a PTA meeting.

The Tomahawks were ready for the PTA supper. Alice had washed her extra blouse and socks. She had shined her old rundown shoes and had sponged her worn serge skirt. Her black hair hung in waves because she had put it up in rags again. Frankie was clean too. His hair was wet and shining from all the water and brushing.

But Grandma Tomahawk made the most striking picture. Her white doeskin dress, embroidered with beads, hung in long fringes. An apron of dyed quills covered it from the breast to the knees. Her braids were lengthened by yellow eagle feathers hung on the ends. Alice shuddered every time she looked at her.

When Grandma's friends, the White Eagles, came banging up to the cabin, even Mrs. White Eagle couldn't help exclaiming at Grandma's appearance. "I bet you could get on TV," she said, and that was the best compliment Mrs. White Eagle could give anyone.

Grandma settled herself stiffly in the back seat. She didn't trust automobiles. She was sure that someday Mr. White Eagle's car was going to explode, but she was brave.

Other automobiles and trucks were driving the roads toward the school. Some families who didn't live too far away were on foot.

Soon they could see the Little Axe School through the cloud of dust. The school looked like a ranch with its windmill and small outbuildings that needed paint, a teacher's cottage and the principal's house enclosed by a barbed-wire fence. On the other side of the school buildings was the mess hall and behind that the log community cabin where the parents met.

The White Eagles and the Tomahawks followed the crowd. The cabin had inherited the old discarded school furniture. There were crooked benches and broken desks along the wall. All were occupied, and some men and children were sitting on the floor.

Mr. and Mrs. Spooner, the principal and his wife, and the two teachers were standing near the door to greet the arrivals. Mrs. Two Bears in a new blue silk dress that covered her like a tepee stood with them.

Alice made the introductions. "This is my grandmother I told you about," she said to Miss Hansen.

Miss Hansen greeted Grandma Tomahawk warmly. "It was

wonderful of you to come," she beamed. "You have made your grandchildren so happy."

Grandma smiled graciously and shook hands. Then she looked all around. "Your papa and mama," she asked. "Where?"

"They haven't arrived yet," said Miss Hansen. "They have such a long drive. But I'm sure they will be here soon."

A young woman got up from a bench to make a seat for Grandma Tomahawk. Grandma sat down majestically between Mrs. Tall Cow and Mrs. Her Many Horses.

"Are you going to dance, Grandma?" asked Mrs. Her Many Horses, looking her up and down.

"No," said Grandma Tomahawk.

"Going to sing?" asked Mrs. Tall Cow.

"No," said Grandma. "Going to chaw."

Alice hung around long enough to satisfy herself that nobody was going to laugh at her grandmother. Then she went to the dining cottage to help make the hamburgers.

Frankie had made up his mind to stay as far away from that cottage as possible. He squatted on the floor with some of the men.

He was there when Miss Hansen's parents arrived. There were excited voices at the door. Miss Hansen went outside to meet them. She proudly led her parents into the cabin.

A stunned silence fell over the assembly.

Miss Hansen's parents didn't look civilized. The mother wore a black velvet dress with a bright red vest. A long white apron with inserts of crocheted lace was tied around her waist. A bib of heavy silver ornaments hung across her breast and a starched white linen bonnet stood out in wings over her ears.

Mr. Hansen was in black knee pants with a red vest decorated with bright silver buttons.

"These are my parents," Miss Hansen announced proudly. "Mr. and Mrs. Olaf Hansen."

Surprise couldn't make Grandma Tomahawk forget why she was there. She rose quickly and went over to be hostess to Teacher's parents. Mrs. Two Bears had moved toward them, but Grandma pushed herself right in front of the PTA president.

"This is Mrs. Tomahawk," Miss Hansen told her parents. "She is the grandmother of two of my best pupils."

"How!" greeted Grandma, politely putting out her hand.

"Pleased to meet you," said Mrs. Hansen, taking the thin, gnarled hand in a warm grip. Mr. Hansen shook hands as if he were pumping water from a well.

"I heard that you were wearing your beautiful Indian costume tonight," said Miss Hansen to Grandma, "so I asked my parents to wear their Norwegian dress. They didn't come to this country until after they were married, you know."

Mrs. Hansen nodded her swanlike bonnet. "Ya! Ve come from the old country," she said.

"There are many Norwegian-Americans in my home town," explained Miss Hansen. "Once a year they have a big festival and wear their native clothes.

"Ya," put in Mr. Hansen. "Have a big vedding and dance polkas. Ve are Americans now but it is good to remember the past."

Grandma was too much of an Indian to show her surprise at the Hansens. The parents of Teacher had even broken their English. But she couldn't hide her curiosity about Mrs. Hansen's clothes. She lifted the apron and looked at the crocheted lace. She fondled the silver ornaments.

"Real?" she asked.

"Ya," said Mrs. Hansen. "I vore them at my vedding and my mother vore them at her vedding. Old family silver. All the way from Hardanger."

Grandma patted her own breast. "My mother wore," she said. "Real quills. Real eagle feathers. Real doeskin."

"Yee whizz," said Mr. Hansen with admiration. "Real old-time Indian duds."

Frankie was drinking in everything with his eyes and ears. Alice had come back and stood in the doorway with her eyes as big as sunflower centers.

Miss Hansen took her parents around the room to meet everyone and Grandma Tomahawk followed. She was not going to let the Hansens be separated from her for a minute. Every time Mrs. Two Bears would try to talk to the visitors, Grandma would step in front of her and interrupt. Pauline Two Bears hadn't been invited to be their hostess.

The supper bell clanged impatiently from the dining cottage. All of the Indians swarmed toward it. Grandma Tomahawk lingered behind with the Hansens, and so did Mrs. Two Bears.

Mr. Hansen went to his car to get a big basket of apples that he had brought from his farm. Grandma followed Mrs. Hansen and her daughter into the dining cottage.

It was as nicely furnished inside as the schoolrooms. The walls had been painted gray and yellow and there were new brown-topped tables and brown-trimmed chairs, and Miss Hansen showed her parents where to sit. Grandma pushed Mrs. Two Bears aside and seated herself beside Mrs. Hansen. In a huff, the PTA president went to sit beside her husband at another table.

Mr. Hansen seemed to realize that the president was insulted. He turned to his table companions. "I go sit vith the Four Bears," he said in a loud voice, with a twinkle in his blue eyes. His daughter frowned at him as if he were a naughty pupil, but all the Indians laughed. They liked jokes. Mrs. Two Bears laughed good-naturedly too.

Alice passed the hamburgers at Miss Hansen's table. She was so busy looking at Mrs. Hansen that she dropped two of them on the floor. Many of the men and boys had taken their plates outside since there wasn't enough room at the tables. But Frankie ate his food standing behind Grandma's chair. He didn't want to miss anything. Grandma could hardly "chaw" for looking at Mrs. Hansen.

"You American citizen?" she asked.

"Oh, ya," replied the Norwegian lady enthusiastically. "Ve come from Norvay because ve vanted to be American citizens. Ve studied it and took the examination. Now ve got our papers."

"Me citizen too," boasted Grandma. "Government make me citizen. Big paper in Washington. Why you leave Norvay?"

Grandma supposed that Norvay was some town east of the Missouri River.

"Olaf and me vanted to live in such fine free land for our children," said Mrs. Hansen. "Here everyone has equal chance. Think of it. Ve come here with nothing. Ve vork hard and now ve got fine farm with big red barn and apple orchards. It could not happen in Norvay ven ve vere young."

"Where Norvay?" asked Grandma. "In South Dakota?"

"Oh, no," replied Mrs. Hansen. "It's vay across the ocean."

"You educated?" asked Grandma Tomahawk.

"No," said Mrs. Hansen regretfully. "Ve didn't get that chance when ve grew up in old country."

"Old-time Indian school no good too," said Grandma. "Learn

English and wash hands. Government give Indian good school now. White man more civilized nowdays."

"But our Anna's got a good education," put in Mrs. Hansen. "That is vy this is such a vonderful country. Here our Anna graduated from college. And you know vat she said to me the day she graduated? So pretty she vas in her cap and gown and diploma tied with ribbon. She said, 'Mama, it is a vonderful thing to be a teacher. Perhaps some boy I teach vill be President of the United States.' That's vat our Anna said."

"You mean Indian boy in this school?" asked Grandma in amazement.

"Vy not?" demanded Mrs. Hansen. "In this country it is possible."

Grandma turned in her chair and looked at Frankie. There was an expression in his eyes as if he were seeing an Indian boy's vision. He was seeing where the white man's road could lead him.

"My Frankie President of United States?" asked Grandma in awe.

"Vy not?" demanded Mrs. Hansen again. "Our Anna is good teacher."

Grandma was speechless for the rest of the meal. She ate her cake and drank her coffee with a faraway look in her eyes. Mr. Hansen's apples from the fine farm with the big red barn were passed around and Grandma cut hers into slices so that she could chew it. But she had little to say.

The meal finished, all of the company trooped back to the community cabin for the PTA meeting. Grandma followed in Mrs. Hansen's steps. She sat beside her on a bench.

Then Mrs. Two Bears called the meeting to order. She began to write names on the shaky blackboard while her husband and Mr. Hansen held it steady.

"As you know," she told the audience, "this meeting is to elect officers for the coming year. It should have been held before school was out last year, but the attendance dwindled so." She looked over the names. "Are there any nominations from the floor?"

There was no comment; then Mrs. Hansen quickly stood up. "Vy don't you nominate Mrs. Tomahawk?" she said. "She is the only grandmother here and she has a great interest in education. Ve have been talking about it during supper."

Everyone was surprised and the buzzing of voices disagreed at first, then began to murmur more softly. Yes, Mrs. Hansen's mother was right. Grandma Tomahawk had the wisdom of age. Once the Indians had greatly respected age. They still did. Why hadn't someone thought of Grandma Tomahawk before?

So votes were cast and Ester Tomahawk was elected the new president of the PTA. "And now we're going to discuss plans for getting the school buildings painted and the doors repaired before winter," said Mrs. Two Bears because she was in no hurry to give up her authority.

The men began shuffling restlessly. One of them rose to go out for a smoke. A couple of others started to follow. PTA was really women's business, remarked one of them.

But Grandma Tomahawk rose imperiously.

"You men sit down," she commanded. "PTA everybody's business."

Then realizing the great dignity of the speech which she was about to make, she used the Sioux language. She spoke eloquently with many gestures, like the true daughter of a chief.

Alice, her duties in the dining cottage ended, sat on the floor with her eyes on Grandma. She was so proud of her. Grandma was like teacher's parents. She wore the clothing of her people and spoke broken English, but she was a real American citizen. She could lead people when the need arose.

Suddenly Grandma Tomahawk realized that some of her listeners could not understand the Indian language. She grinned at them mischievously. "Me say everybody fix school," she explained. "No fit for President of United States with broken doors and no paint. Saturday everybody meet and paint. Big chaw after."

The meeting finally broke up and the Tomahawks headed home in the White Eagle car. Frankie still didn't know what would happen about the potato picking in Nebraska. He finally mustered up courage to ask.

"Do we have to go to Nebraska with the Iron Shells, Grandma?" he asked.

The old woman snorted. "Potato picking. Me make big joke. Course you stay in school. Peoples come all way from Norway across the ocean to go our school."

Frankie was satisfied.

Grandma was quiet for a long time; then she began chuckling to herself. "Me Great White Father of PTA," she giggled.

Alice hurried into the cabin and lighted the kerosene lamp. The flame lit Grandma's face as she stood in the doorway. Her hawk eyes looked all around, pouncing on one defect after another.

"This house need fixing too," she declared. "Need whitewash and new curtains. Not fit for president of PTA."

She and Alice went to sleep in the bed. Frankie curled up on a pallet on the floor. Tomorrow he would confess to Miss Hansen about how he had tricked Grandma into going to the PTA supper. Teacher would understand.

(This story is from the book of the same title.)

(For two other stories about Indians, see the Thanksgiving Day section.)

High Holy Days—
Rosh Hashanah and
Yom Kippur

(Continue for ten days through the Hebrew month Tishri)

In their everyday life Americans of the Jewish faith use the same calendar other Americans use, but they also have a special Hebrew calendar for religious observances. According to Hebrew reckoning, this ancient calendar began with the Creation, 3,760 years before the Christian era, and therefore the year 1980 would be called 5740. Rosh Hashanah, the Hebrew New Year, is celebrated in autumn, during the Hebrew month Tishri.

Rosh Hashanah, observed by services in Jewish synagogues, is believed to be the day on which God passes judgment on mankind. The service may open with

230

the blowing of the shofar, a trumpet made from the horn of a ram or an ox. The congregation prays, and during the next ten days the members ask forgiveness for any wrongs they may have done to others. From sundown of the ninth day until the following evening is a time for fasting, and the tenth day is observed as Yom Kippur, or the Day of Atonement. On this, the most holy of all Jewish holidays, pious Jews gather again in their synagogues for an impressive service. For those who have sought forgiveness it is a time of great release and joy—a time to look ahead to a new year of happiness and peace.

Simon and the High Holy Days

DOROTHY F. ZELIGS

The congregation stood in hushed silence as the stirring call of the shofar sounded through the house of worship.

It was a solemn moment in the service of Rosh Hashanah, one of the most holy days of the Jewish year. As the notes died away, the voices of the worshipers rose in prayer.

To Simon Levy, who was sitting in one of the front rows, it was a new experience. He had arrived in the city just a few days ago, from a small town in the West where there were only a few families. In all his eleven years he had never been in such a large and stately synagogue.

After the services, a hubbub of greetings arose. "Happy New Year! Happy New Year!" A number gave the greeting in Hebrew, according to the old custom. "*L'shonoh Tovoh Tikosevu*," they said, which means, "May you be inscribed for a good year."

Simon walked out with his uncle and aunt, Dr. and Mrs. Jonathon, and his two cousins, thirteen-year-old Maury, and blue-eyed, freckled Ruthie, who was ten. It seemed as if everyone stopped and greeted them. "I want you to meet Simon, my nephew," his Uncle Phil was saying. "He is going to be with us a whole year. His parents went to South America and so they loaned him to us."

The September air was brisk. "You like it here with us, don't you, Simon?" Ruthie looked up at him with a gay smile.

"He doesn't like to be bothered with girls all the time, remember that," Maury told her with a superior air.

"Why—why," Ruthie sputtered, but Simon squeezed her hand and said shyly, "Ruthie's okay, Maury." And the rest of the way he kept hold of her hand.

When they reached home, they gathered around the attractive table, set with the best dishes and decorated with flowers in honor of Rosh Hashanah. Dr. Jonathan recited the holiday Kiddush over the

232

silver goblet of wine. After saying the prayer in Hebrew, he repeated part of it in English. "Blessed art Thou, O Lord our God, King of the Universe, who createst the fruit of the vine. Blessed art Thou, O Lord our God, King of the Universe, who hast kept us in life, and hast taken care of us, and enabled us to reach this season."

Over the two loaves of white bread twists that lay at the head of the table, Dr. Jonathon chanted, "Blessed art Thou, O Lord our God, King of the Universe, who bringest forth bread from the earth."

On the table stood a dish of honey surrounded by slices of apple. Each one took a piece of apple, dipped it in the honey and ate it, reciting the Hebrew blessing, "Blessed art Thou, O Lord our God, King of the Universe, who createst the fruit of the tree."

"It is an old custom," Uncle Phil explained, "to eat something sweet on Rosh Hashanah as a symbol for a sweet New Year."

"What's the matter, Simon?" asked Aunt Elsa. "You look a little bewildered."

"I guess I am," the boy admitted. "At home, we didn't celebrate the Jewish holidays very much. Even on Rosh Hashanah, we didn't have all these interesting ceremonies. Last night, when the holiday began and you lit candles on the table and everything, it seemed sort of strange. But I liked it very much."

There was little conversation for a while as all settled down to the pleasant task of enjoying the holiday meal. "What do those words *Rosh Hashanah* mean, Uncle Phil?" he asked.

His uncle smiled at him. "The words are Hebrew and mean *Head of the Year.* Rosh Hashanah and the holiday that comes ten days later, Yom Kippur, are known as the High Holy Days, because they are the most solemn occasions of the Jewish year. Most of the time we are too busy to think much about how we are behaving to our family and friends—to the whole world, in fact. But on the High Holy Days we put everything else aside and spend the time in thought and prayer. We ask forgiveness for past sins and resolve to lead better lives in the future."

"I like to hear the blowing of the shofar in the synagogue," Maury said. "It's sort of exciting—like calling the people to arms or something."

"It is an important part of the Rosh Hashanah service," his father replied. "The shofar is made of a ram's horn, and it's a very interesting musical instrument. The Bible mentions it many times. As

Maury suggested, it was used as a call to arms, in times of war. But it had many other uses. The shofar summoned the people together for an assembly in times of crisis. It was used to announce events of national importance, such as the crowning of a new king. But the call of the shofar was familiar to the people even in their ordinary lives. On late Friday afternoons, the sound of the shofar, blown from the housetops of the city, proclaimed the arrival of the Sabbath. And, of course, the New Year was greeted with the blowing of the ram's horn."

"I guess that's why we heard it today," put in Ruthie.

"The shofar call also makes us think of certain important events in the history of our people," Dr. Jonathon continued. "It reminds us of the thrilling time at Mount Sinai when the Israelites received the Ten Commandments while the loud blasts of the trumpet sounded through the desert air."

"On Rosh Hashanah the call of the shofar might be regarded as a call to conscience," Aunt Elsa added. "It says, 'What ho, there! Stop rushing around so much and think more about where you are going. Are you on the right road? Are you making the most of your life?' It is a warning signal to 'Stop, Look, and Listen' to the voice of conscience."

"Very well said," Dr. Jonathon nodded.

"Ruth," Aunt Elsa interrupted, "what are you doing? You've eaten every bit of that big dishful of honey. I hope it doesn't make you ill."

"It's good," Ruth replied calmly, as she daintily wiped her sticky fingers on a napkin. "Now I'll be sure to have a sweet year."

After dinner, the family wandered into the living room. "The High Holy Days always bring me back to the period of my boyhood," Dr. Jonathon remarked as he relaxed in an armchair.

"Tell us about it," Ruthie demanded.

"They were events of the greatest importance in our little village in Lithuania," her father began. "For a whole month before the holidays arrived, there was an atmosphere of solemn expectancy. People said their prayers more earnestly and watched their behavior more carefully. In all the little wooden cottages with their thatched roofs, preparations went on for days ahead of time. Floors were freshly scrubbed, the huge tiled stoves were made ready for the winter, the brass samovars where the steaming tea was brewed shone with cleanliness, and the silver candlesticks were polished until they gleamed.

"But far more important than these things was the preparation of one's soul. For it was believed that on Rosh Hashanah God judges one and decides his fate for the coming year. On Yom Kippur the decree is made final and the judgment is sealed."

"Go on, Daddy," Ruth begged, although she had heard his stories many times before. "Tell Simon about the Tashlich."

"It is a special ceremony," Dr. Jonathon explained, "observed on the afternoon of Rosh Hashanah. Tashlich is a prayer recited on the banks of a river or some other body of fresh water. Flowing water is the symbol of purity, and this prayer asks for forgiveness and purification. This ceremony represents man's desire to repent of his wrongdoing and his resolve to start the new year with a clear record. Tashlich is the Hebrew word for 'Thou wilt cast.' "

"Of course," Aunt Elsa put in, "we mustn't think that just going through the ceremony of Tashlich will free us of the responsibility of our acts. It is only a symbol of what should go on within our hearts on Rosh Hashanah."

Simon was thoughtful. "I'm glad Yom Kippur comes so soon."

"Yes, in just ten days," his uncle said.

Late in the afternoon of the Day of Atonement, Simon, Maury, and Ruth entered the synagogue and took their places. As the concluding service began, the cantor's voice took on a deeper note. The choir sang with greater feeling. Earnestly, the rabbi prayed, "The day is fading, the sun is setting; the silence and peace of night descend upon the earth. Grant rest, O God, unto our disquieted hearts; lift up the soul that is cast down. Turn, in Thine all-forgiving love, to Thy children who yearn for Thy mercy. Let this hour bring the assurance that Thou hast forgiven . . ." the earnest voice went on.

As the dusk began to fall, the notes of the shofar rose triumphantly on the air. The people of Israel had made their peace with God. With light hearts and merry greetings, the congregation moved slowly out, the rabbi's benediction upon them. "The Lord bless thy going out and thy coming in, from this time forth, even for ever. Amen."

The Most Precious Thing
A Tale for Yom Kippur Eve

DOROTHY F. ZELIGS

Once upon a time, there was an angel who disobeyed God. The angel was summoned to appear before the Throne of Judgment to answer for his misdeed. He pleaded for mercy and begged God to forgive him. God looked down upon the angel kindly, and said, "I shall not punish you, but you must atone for your wrongdoing. I will give you a task to perform. Go down to earth and bring to Me the most precious thing in the world."

The angel sped down to earth, happy to have a chance to win God's forgiveness. Over many countries he roamed, for many years, looking for the most precious thing in the world. One day, he came upon a great battlefield. He saw a young soldier lying there badly wounded. This young man had fought bravely in defense of his country and was now dying. The angel caught up the last drop of blood from the soldier's wound and hastened back to heaven with it.

"This is indeed a precious thing that you have brought back," God said to the angel. "A soldier who gives his life for his country is very dear to Me. But return, and search once more."

So the angel returned to earth and continued his quest. For many years he roamed through cities, woods, and plains. Then, one day, he saw a nurse in a great hospital. She was dying of a dread disease. She had nursed others through this disease, working so hard that she had worn down her own strength and so caught the illness herself. She lay pale and gasping upon her cot. As she was dying, the angel caught up her last breath and hastened to heaven with it.

"Surely, God," said the angel, "the last breath of this unselfish nurse is the most precious thing in the world."

"It is a very precious thing that you have brought to Me," God replied. "One who gives his life for another is indeed worthy in My sight. But return, and search again."

Then the angel returned to earth again to search once more. Far and wide he roamed for many years. One night, he saw a villainous-looking man on horseback riding through a dark forest. The man was armed with a sword and a spear. The angel guessed on what wicked errand this man was bound. He was going to avenge himself on the keeper of the forest, who would not permit him to poach on the king's game. The man came to the small hut where the forester and his family lived. Light streamed from the window. Getting down from his horse, the villain peered through the window. He saw the wife of the forester putting her little son to bed. He heard her teaching him how to say his evening prayers. Something within his hard heart seemed to melt. Did the scene bring back memories of his own faraway childhood and his own mother, who had also taught him to pray? Tears filled the man's eyes, and he turned away from his evil deed and repented of his ways. The angel caught up one of his tears and flew back to heaven with it.

"This," said God, "is the most precious thing in the world, for it is the tear of a repentant sinner. And repentance opens the gates of heaven."

Columbus Day

(October 12)

The first celebration of this holiday on a national scale, in 1892, marked the four hundredth anniversary of Christopher Columbus's first landing in the Americas. In commemoration of that event, the World's Columbian Exposition was held in Chicago the following year. One state after another set aside October 12, the date of his landing on San Salvador Island, as a day to honor him, and since 1937 it has been a national holiday. The day is celebrated also in many places in Italy, where he was born; in Spain, under whose banner he sailed for the New World; in Canada; and in Latin America. The man who changed history by opening up two new continents for settlement after years of discouragement is a hero that all of these countries have in common.

In addition to the following true story of Columbus, you may read about a modern celebration of Columbus Day in "Vasil Discovers America" in the section on Citizenship Day.

239

Sailing West to Find the East

RUTH CROMER WEIR

"Good-bye! Good-bye! God be with you!"

It was an exciting moment when the sails swelled in the morning breeze at the port of Palos, Spain, on August 3, 1492. Columbus looked over the three vessels which had been furnished him by the king and queen of Spain. The ships seemed almost as anxious as Columbus to be off.

The largest of the three ships, the *Santa Maria*, was commanded by Columbus. Next in size was the *Pinta*, commanded by Captain Martin Pinzon. The third ship, the smallest of all, was named *Nina*, which means "child." It was commanded by another Pinzon brother, Vincente.

Proudly, Columbus looked up at the clean new sails and at the Spanish flag waving in the breeze. "How beautiful is the green-and-white flag of their Majesties for this expedition!" he thought. He was glad that the flag had a large cross, for he hoped to carry the Christian religion to the lands he visited. Never had any sailors set off on such a great adventure into the unknown.

The sound of weeping broke in on his thoughts. The wives and children of some of the sailors had come to see them off. Some of the women cried loudly that their husbands would never return. It had been hard to get ninety men to join the crews of the three small ships. To many, Columbus's adventure into the mysterious sea of darkness was as foolish as a trip to the moon seemed at that time. But "gold" and "treasures" were magic words. Men would risk their lives for them.

Columbus stood on the forecastle, the deck at the head of the ship. He stood there until the city of Palos disappeared. He stood there until the great hill behind the city and the outline of La Rabida on top disappeared. He stood there until there was no land in sight and the ships headed into what might be a world of sea.

Then he went below deck. He picked up his pen and began a journal of his voyage: "Besides describing every night the occur-

240

rences of the day, and every day those of the preceding night, I intend to draw up a nautical chart, which shall contain the several parts of the ocean and land in their proper situations."

What Columbus "described" and "drew up" turned out to be the most exciting journal of a trip ever written. This journal has been copied again and again in many languages.

The vessels steered south and southwest toward the Canary Islands off the coast of Africa. After three days out, the *Pinta* had a broken rudder. Could some of the men on board have broken it, hoping that the trip would be called off?

In spite of the broken rudder, the ships reached the Canary Islands safely. There they lay at anchor for three long weeks while the *Pinta* was being repaired. For three weeks Columbus grew more and more impatient. But at last the ships sailed on September 6.

"Sailed due west," "West," "West," Columbus wrote in his journal. According to his maps, Japan lay straight west.

At first everything went well. The weather was fair, but as time passed the crews became restless. Columbus began to make two records of the trip so that the crews would not know that the ships were getting so far away from home. "Sailed sixty leagues (about one hundred eighty miles) at the rate of ten miles an hour," Columbus wrote in his journal. "Reckoned only forty-eight leagues that the men might not be terrified if they should be long upon their voyage."

As the days stretched into weeks, the men became not only restless but frightened. Some told stories of sea monsters that swallowed ships. Others told of boiling waters where no ship could safely sail. It was not these stories that bothered the men so much—although plenty of them were told. It was the strong trade wind, which was blowing from the east and was carrying them along swiftly, farther and farther away from home.

The sailors shook their heads and huddled together.

"Does our captain take us for fools?" they muttered. "In spite of his reckoning, we know how far and how fast we are going. These tubs we're riding in can never get back home bucking that strong east wind."

Then, almost as though in defense of Columbus, the winds changed. Some days there would be good signs. The sight of birds gave the men hope that land was near. But when they saw great patches of floating seaweed, they became frightened again. They were afraid that the ship would get caught in the seaweed and not be able to sail on. Columbus tried to calm their fears. He told them again and again of the great wealth that they would find when they reached the Indies.

One evening several sailors thought that they saw palaces of a great city in the distance. "Land ho!" they cried excitedly, but when morning came, there was nothing but water in sight. Perhaps they had seen a cloud or a rough spot of water. Perhaps they were so anxious to see land that they imagined they saw it.

Day after day the sailors on the three ships grew more tired and homesick. At last, on October 10, what Columbus had feared happened. The sailors decided that they would go home. They openly rebelled.

"This time you will not talk us out of it," somebody yelled hotly. The story is told that some of the sailors even threatened to throw Columbus overboard. They were determined to turn back.

Columbus had said that he had set out to sail to the Indies and "with the Lord's help" he would sail there, but he saw that he had pushed the men as far as he could. He offered to turn back if land was not sighted in three days.

The next day the sailors saw land birds flying and a green branch floating beside the ship. That evening Columbus declared that he saw a flickering light. Everyone on board was excited. No one slept. Sailor after sailor climbed the rigging and strained his eyes to see the west. Each one wanted to be the first to sight land. What new sights would daylight bring? Again, would there be nothing but water all around them?

It was two o'clock in the morning, October 12, when there was a shout from the *Pinta:* "Land ho! Land ho!"

As the sky began to lighten, the men cried out in joy. It was true. Here was real land at last—green trees and a smooth, sandy beach.

Landing boats were lowered over the sides of the ships. Columbus and Captain Martin Pinzon were among the first to reach the shore. There they knelt and gave thanks to God. Then they raised the Spanish flag and claimed for Spain the land they had discovered.

Columbus believed that he had landed on one of the islands of the Indies. When he saw the friendly natives, the people who lived there, he called them "Indians." These natives were "of fine shapes, very handsome," he wrote in his journal. "I presented them with some red caps and strings of beads to wear upon the neck and many other trifles of small value. They were delighted and became wonderfully attached to us. Afterwards they came swimming to the boats, bringing parrots, balls of cotton thread, and many other things."

The friendly Indians called the explorers "men from heaven," and generously offered them anything they wanted.

This place where Christopher Columbus first landed was one of a group of islands which we call the Bahamas, off the coast of what is now Florida. Columbus named the island San Salvador, which means Holy Savior. He was excited with the beauty of the place, but he was also anxious to sail on and to try to find China and Japan.

A few days after leaving San Salvador, Columbus discovered another beautiful island now called Cuba, and later he also found the island known as Hispaniola. Here the *Santa Maria* went aground on rocks, but the crews with the help of friendly natives were able to save almost everything—even the lumber of the wrecked ship.

By that time Columbus had formed a plan. He had his men begin to build a fort of lumber from the wreck. Many of the sailors begged to stay and look for gold while Columbus returned to Spain. He chose forty men to stay and left food and guns with them; then he sailed for home as commander of the little *Nina*. Soon he and his sailors saw the *Pinta*, also homeward bound.

"Home! Spain!" Columbus thought happily. He believed that he had reached the Indies. He had not found as much gold as he had expected, but he did have some gold, which he was taking with him. He had some trees and fruits and parrots. And he also had some Indians to show his king and queen. . . . Finally on March 15, 1493, the *Nina* sailed into the harbor at Palos, Spain. The *Pinta* reached Palos later the same day.

Cheers and shouts greeted the arrival of the *Nina*, and the news of Columbus's success spread rapidly. It was the most exciting news those people of the Old World had ever heard. "Columbus! Columbus!" they cried. "He has found the way to the riches of the Indies."

The king and queen invited Columbus to come to Barcelona,

where they were holding court. All the nobles and important people of the city were present. As Columbus approached the thrones, the king and queen arose.

"Your Highnesses," he said as he knelt before them.

The king and queen had tears of gratitude in their eyes. They told him to rise and take a seat of honor beside them. Then Columbus told the court about the wonders of the lands he had discovered for Spain.

There were many parties in honor of the famous "Admiral of the Ocean Sea" and "Viceroy of the Indies," as Columbus was called, but there were some people who were jealous of him. At one party one of the nobles said, "If you had not found the Indies, someone else would soon do so."

Columbus did not answer at first. Then he took a hard-cooked egg still in its shell from a bowl on the table.

"Gentlemen, you make this egg stand on end as I, the first to discover the Indies, will do."

One by one, the dinner guests tried to make the egg stand on end, but each of them failed. At last, the egg was returned to Columbus. He placed it on the table, crushing the shell at the end as he did so. There the egg stood firmly. In this way the great Admiral of the Ocean Sea reminded the guests that it is easy to know how to do something after someone else has done it.

Nevertheless, Columbus was not a man to sit back and take it easy at court just because he had become famous.

"I will start colonies on the islands I have discovered for Spain," he promised the king and queen. "I will find the mainland of China and meet the emperor. I will find gold mines. And I will take priests to begin the work of teaching the Indians our religious faith."

Already he was planning a second trip.

> EDITOR'S NOTE: Columbus made not only a second but a third and a fourth voyage, but he never found the gold and other riches he had expected. Discredited by his enemies, he finally died sad and disillusioned. But his son Ferdinand—who as a fourteen-year-old boy had sailed on the final voyage—always cherished the memory of his father, and when he grew up he wrote a "Historie" based on the Admiral's journals. The son knew how much his father had accomplished, and now the world knows, too.

United Nations Day

(October 24)

This special day is observed in more than a hundred countries, and in some places U.N. programs are continued throughout United Nations Week. As specified at the time of its adoption in San Francisco, the United Nations Charter went into effect after it was approved by the governments of forty-six countries. The last representative signed on October 24, 1945, and that date, therefore, was chosen to be the official U.N. birthday.

The U.N. Charter begins with the words "We the people of the United Nations" and states that the purpose of the organization is "to save future generations from the scourge of war." The name and the idea both originated with President Franklin D. Roosevelt, although he did not live to attend the San Francisco Conference. Since that time the number of member nations has more than doubled.

The main U.N. headquarters is an impressive group of buildings overlooking the East River, in New York City. The work of the United Nations is carried on by five principal departments: the General Assembly, the Security Council, the Economic and Social Council, the Trusteeship Council, the International Court of Justice, and the Secretariat, as well as by a number of specialized agencies. Successful in settling some disputes among nations by peaceful means, the organization unfortunately has not been invested with the power to make all war impossible. Yet world leaders, realizing that nations must learn to work together if there ever is to be real peace, continue to place their faith in the United Nations as the most practical way of reaching this goal.

Young people especially have a big stake in the United Nations, in the opinion of Dag Hammarskjöld, the Swede who served as Secretary General for several years. He told the world's youth, "What the United Nations does and does not do will determine the kind of world you take over in the days to come."

Danny Kaye, UNICEF Ambassador

KURT SINGER

Dag Hammarskjöld, Secretary General of the United Nations, had decided to give a party for his hard-working crew at headquarters, and invited an impressive list of entertainers to donate their talents. Among the notables were Ezio Pinza, Marian Anderson, and Danny Kaye.

When the evening was over, Danny was thanked by Dag Hammarskjöld for his generous performance, to which Danny replied:

"It was wonderful to be here. The work you are doing is inspiring, and if I can ever do anything for you again, please call on me."

At one o'clock the next day, Dag Hammarskjöld and his co-worker, Maurice Pate, called Danny and asked for a conference.

"Aren't you going to South Africa?" inquired Mr. Pate, when Danny arrived.

"Yes," replied Danny. "I have some promotional theater appearances to do there."

"We have little money and few people we can call on," continued Pate. "While you are in that area, would you be willing to visit our UNICEF installations and photograph the work being done?"

"What is UNICEF?" Danny inquired.

"That array of initials stands for United Nations International Children's Emergency Fund," explained Mr. Hammarskjöld.

"Gee, that sounds like a fine idea," exclaimed Danny. "If I can help kids, I'm all for it."

Twenty-four hours later the modest request that Danny take some pictures in the South African area had grown into a gigantic round-the-world project. For Danny, upon returning to his hotel, began to mull over the idea. Two hours later he had called the Paramount Studios in Hollywood and lined up a camera crew of two, complete with the latest in camera equipment. He convinced the

248

studios that this was their contribution to the kids of the world. Two cameramen, Prager and Dukoff, agreed to join the expedition. But South Africa seemed too small a district for their activities. Danny's next step was to suggest that he and his entourage return to Hollywood via Asia—at Danny's expense.

Pate was overwhelmed, Hammarskjöld delighted, and plans began to take final shape. For Danny, they were new and exciting. He had spent years with kids who had the money to visit him in theaters, kids who understood his language. Now he was to meet the dirty children, the helpless ones, the urchins, the children in the shadows of disease and starvation.

During his first briefing session, Danny was shocked to learn that two-thirds of the world's nine hundred million children lack adequate food, shelter and protection from disease. The result is a high mortality rate.

"You, Mr. Kaye," said Maurice Pate, "can directly or indirectly help to vaccinate some fifty million children. You can also help to cure a few million cases of yaws (boils). I need to warn you that your trip will not be easy. You will be in areas of the earth that no tourist has ever seen. You will be uncomfortable. You will miss your warm shower and good food. You yourself will not always be safe against disease. Think it over again, but know this: Yours would be a tremendous contribution."

Danny did not think long. It was exactly what he wanted to do.

"I confess," he recollected, "I didn't quite appreciate the seriousness of the assignment, until I received my 'orders': *The United Nations Children's Fund has the honor to appoint you its Ambassador-at-Large, charged with making known the needs of children throughout the world.*

"My first reaction to this can be summed up in two words: *Who, me?*"

The result? In the weeks that followed, Danny, the man of many emotions, experienced the emotional heights of his life while bringing light into the huts of darkness and silence, suffering and poverty. His work began when he reached Asia.

"My UNICEF work started in India with a visit to a tiny village many miles inland," he said. "This was a village selected as a typical example of the UNICEF tuberculosis vaccination program at work.

Days before we arrived, teams of UNICEF workers had circulated leaflets telling about the program. All mothers were invited to bring their children to the village square for the vaccination.

"My job primarily was to film the work being done, but once in the midst of such exciting work it was impossible to remain a disinterested observer. As soon as a small crowd assembled in the square I began to do what I could to entertain them. No one there had ever heard of a guy named Danny Kaye. I don't think anyone there had ever seen a movie. They didn't speak my language. I didn't speak theirs.

"But I jigged through a couple of dances, shouted a couple of songs, and got the children clapping their hands to accompaniment. Pretty soon the crowd doubled, redoubled and redoubled again. Kids came flocking from all over the village to find out what all the commotion was about. They stayed to receive a lifesaving injection of TB vaccine, courtesy of UNICEF.

"The long lines at the vaccination center are probably the most rewarding tribute I have ever received for my peculiar ability to make funny faces.

"But, after all, what's the use of being a comic if you can't amuse children? It didn't make any difference that the kids had never heard of me. I made funny faces. I clowned through the villages, trying desperately to play a new kind of Pied Piper. And the children laughed and followed. Nobody fears a clown."

In New Delhi, the capital of India, UNICEF's program was to test approximately one million people for tuberculosis. Danny accompanied the UNICEF doctors and regional health officers to the crowded, fly-ridden city districts, into the outskirts of town and to the neighboring villages. The methods of the UNICEF team were not unlike those of a traveling circus. There was a band with its drummer to attract the crowds, followed by a jeep with a loudspeaker system that explained the medical program. The people were told about the T.B. tests, and those who were found to be infected were urged to return at once for vaccination. Unorthodox tools of medicine, but they worked. Everywhere the UNICEF team went, there were swarms of people, both children and adults.

Later, the team was split into five units of twenty-five persons each. Danny divided his time among them, as he traveled through India and most of the other Asiatic countries. Each unit tested approximately thirty-two thousand people. In New Delhi alone, eleven doctors examined sixteen thousand children in one day, and followed up the next day with vaccinations. It was a massive program—a race against disease and death.

Danny traveled through twenty-seven countries for UNICEF and could report for hours on his experiences—the people he met, the conditions he found. A new world opened its doors to him, a world which before had had little meaning. Few people have the imagination or the bravery to visualize so much human suffering.

"You cannot bring health and happiness to a million children by talking about it, signing a paper or waving a wand," he said. "It has to be child by child. It has to be done personally and with love. And that's the way UNICEF works."

> EDITOR'S NOTE: *The Danny Kaye Story*, the book from which the above selection was condensed, relates many other amazing experiences of the well-loved comedian. A short documentary film, *Assignment Children,* made from the pictures taken on his trip, was shown throughout the world.

The U.N.'s Marian Anderson

ESTHER M. DOUTY

She stepped hesitantly into the airport at Saigon, Vietnam, a tall, proudly straight, brown-skinned woman, ten thousand miles away from her Philadelphia home. For a moment she felt lost. Then the children came to welcome her—two rows of them, with lustrous, dark eyes and moon-pale faces. In strange-sounding English their voices sang, shrill and sweet, "Getting to Know You," from the American opera *The King and I.*

Marian Anderson's generous mouth broke into a radiant smile.

She could have hugged them all, especially the little ones in front, whose huge straw hats served as music stands for the larger children behind.

"Getting to Know You." The words of the song were indeed fitting, the world-famous American contralto must have thought, for that was exactly why, in 1957, the United States State Department was sending her as a goodwill ambassador to the Far East. By getting to know Marian Anderson personally, the American government hoped that the Asian people would also get to know something of the America that had produced her.

But who really was Marian Anderson? As with any human being she was several persons in one. To millions of her fellow countrymen she was the illustrious singer whose magnificent voice was described by the great conductor Toscanini as "one heard once in a hundred years." To others she was a symbol of what America stood for—the land of opportunity and freedom for all its people. Marian had been a fatherless child from a Negro family so poor that the widowed mother had taken in washing. But Marian had talent and courage, and by hard work and determination she had won the place in the nation to which she was entitled. It was true that she had battled prejudice, stupidity and hate, but in her climb toward fame she had had the help of white friends as well as black—something she always remembered when she spoke of her country to foreign friends.

To Marian Anderson herself she was mostly a woman who loved to sing, whose singing made her feel close to people of every kind and to God, who had made them all. When she sang, this understanding and sympathy came through to her listeners, and they were moved and drawn to the singer. Her voice spoke in every language.

As a goodwill ambassador from the United States, Marian Anderson traveled 35,000 miles and visited twelve Asian countries. She arrived by helicopter in the Korean hills to sing for the United Nations troops gathered there. Soldiers from Turkey, Britain, France, Greece, Thailand and Korea, as well as those from her own America, responded to the deep feeling in her voice as she sang the great Negro spiritual "He's Got the Whole World in His Hands."

In Seoul, capital of the Korean Republic, Marian accepted with simple dignity an honorary degree from Ewha Women's University. "Your success against great odds has encouraged others in their struggle for justice and human rights," the University president told her. "You stand as an example of Christian service to mankind."

In Bangkok, capital of Thailand, where the King had risen from his throne to greet a foreign dignitary only a few times in his life, Marian Anderson was surprised and touched that he stood up for her. In the Bangkok schools she sang for the children and told them about the poor boy who was born in a log cabin and rose to become one of the greatest American presidents—Abraham Lincoln.

She enchanted vast audiences in Singapore and Taiwan, in Hong Kong, Burma and Ceylon. In the brand-new nation of Malaysia, where Chinese, Indians, Malayans and Eurasians lived peacefully together, she sang at a boys' school on the very day their country's flag was first raised at the United Nations. "There is no doubt in my mind," she told them, "that some of you who sit here today will have the destiny of this new country in your hands. It is so very important that you not let little things like hate and fear destroy you, restrict you from being the kind of big person you could be."

In India, Marian Anderson was the first foreigner ever invited to speak at the shrine of India's saint, Mahatma Gandhi, who during his lifetime had sent many inspiring messages to the Negroes of America.

It was not her singing, great as it was, that brought her this honor, for there have been other great singers. It was rather that she had a remarkable power of communicating with others as she sang. While she gave of her understanding and sympathy to her Asian listeners, Marian Anderson also told them many things about America. She realized that many of the people to whom she sang had had false impressions of her country.

When President Eisenhower heard of Marian's success as goodwill ambassador, his thoughts went to certain words in the preamble to the United Nations Charter—"to reaffirm faith in the fundamental human rights, in the dignity and worth of the human person." It was plain, he thought, that in her travels and in her life Marian Anderson had clearly demonstrated that she lived by this belief. He decided, in 1958, to appoint her one of the ten United States delegates to the United Nations. She was to serve on the Trusteeship Council, a special group concerned with the well-being of peoples under U.N. trusteeship.

The appointment pleased the singer. "Any group dedicated," she said, "to doing the best it can to bring about understanding among people—dedicated to humanity—must be a great force in the world."

In the opinion of her fellow delegates, the singer represented her country with unusual honor and distinction. Marian Anderson herself had an explanation for this. "When I was a member of the United States delegation at the U.N.," she said later, "I understood better, I think, than others serving with me a great many things that motivated the hopes and pleas and demands of the little nations, particularly those whose people are dark-skinned. How much my people could contribute to our government's understanding of these other nations! But at the same time my government is learning more about my people, because it's concerned now with the world. So this is good—good for my country, and my people. I believe this."

She might have added that it was good for the United Nations, too.

Halloween

(October 31)

Halloween means the eve of All Hallows, or All Saints Day, which is a religious holiday in many churches. When Europeans, especially the Irish, came to America to live, they brought with them the idea of celebrating Halloween. Some of the customs are decidedly not religious, and some go back to pagan times. Dressing up as ghosts and witches, bobbing for apples and playing Trick or Treat—all of these things are great fun, but why do we celebrate this way? Why, for instance, do we have bonfires and jack-o'-lanterns?

The Druids, pagan priests of long ago, lighted autumn bonfires to show gratitude to their sun god for a good harvest. There was also an old superstition that witches, ghosts and evil spirits wandered the earth on Halloween. Since these beings were supposed to be afraid of bright light, many people built bonfires or carried torches to frighten them away. Why should a witch want to bring along a cat? Some people said it was because cats had once been human beings who were being punished for their wicked deeds in life. Probably no one who liked cats ever believed that story.

As for the jack-o'-lantern, the story goes that once upon a time a man named Jack was too wicked to enter heaven. But Jack had played a trick on the devil, who refused to let him into hell. Poor, wicked Jack was condemned to spend eternity wandering about with a lantern. But nobody on earth wanted him, either; so people used to carve a scary-looking face on a pumpkin and place a candle inside. When Jack saw the jack-o'-lantern glaring at him from a window, he would be afraid to enter the house.

The eating of nuts and apples —or the drinking of cider made from apples—at Halloween parties can be traced to an ancient Roman harvest festival honoring Pomona, the goddess of fruit trees.

Probably the most fun of all on Halloween is ringing doorbells and, when the doors are opened, crying out, "Trick or treat!" This custom goes back to the time when Irish farmers went from door to door in a village and begged food for a Halloween party. If they were refused, they threatened vengeance, a threat not made in fun as it usually is today.

Most of our Halloween customs come from old superstitions, but it is no superstition that the United Nations Children's Fund needs money to help the children of the world. Now when the young people ring the doorbell and shout "Trick or treat!" the person who opens the door may give them not only candy but also a contribution for UNICEF. A great deal of money has been raised in this way, and how it is used you may read in the story of Danny Kaye, in the section for United Nations Day.

Horace the Happy Ghost

ELIZABETH IRELAND

Horace was a happy ghost. He lived with his father and mother in a big old house with lots of creaking stairs and windows that rattled. It was just right for ghosts.

Of course, people lived there too—a whole family of people—but they all got along very well together. The ghosts didn't mind the noise the people made daytimes, and the people didn't mind the noise the ghosts made at night.

There was only one trouble.

Horace!

Horace was a well-behaved little ghost in some ways. He had learned his vanishing lessons perfectly. One moment he was there and then—whisk!—he wasn't. Sometimes he vanished for his family's visitors at after-midnight tea, and they all said they had never seen finer vanishing. Besides, he could creak doors, and he rattled windows as well as a grown-up ghost.

But he couldn't moan, and he couldn't groan, and when he tried to clank his chain, it jingled!

"What is wrong, Horace?" his father and mother asked him often. "It's perfectly silly for a bright little ghost like you not to moan and groan. What is that horrible noise you make?"

"People call it laughing," Horace said. "I'm sorry. I just can't moan and groan. I'm too happy! I haven't anything to moan and groan about!"

His father and mother would groan softly, and float upstairs to talk things over.

Horace wandered around, creaking a stair or two and rattling at the second-biggest window just for practice.

Once he laughed. When he did, the people upstairs woke up suddenly and sat up in their beds and said, "What was that?"

"Oh, dear!" Horace said to himself. And he put one hand over his mouth and kept it there till daylight to make sure he wouldn't laugh again.

258

"Horace," his mother said when he went upstairs to go to bed that morning, "today you must stay up at least till noon. Maybe that will teach you to moan and groan."

"All right, Mother," Horace said cheerfully. He felt a little queer inside, though. He had never been up after sunrise in his whole life.

He floated downstairs very slowly and started to haunt the breakfast room. He felt ever so jiggly as he peeped inside for the first time. How bright it was!

And it was positively full of people laughing and talking and drinking milk and orange juice and eating breakfast food.

Horace took a deep breath, stepped out beside the kitchen cabinet, and vanished.

The littlest boy at the breakfast table saw him. He gurgled and waved his spoon. Horace vanished again beside the refrigerator.

"Funny thing," the father said, and rubbed his eyes. "I could swear the refrigerator door was open just a minute ago. But it isn't."

Horace vanished again behind a window curtain.

"Mother, there's a ghost behind the curtain," the next-to-littlest boy said.

"Finish your cereal, Tommy, and stop trying to fool me," the mother laughed.

And after that nobody paid any attention to Horace! Even when he laughed, somebody else laughed too, and nobody noticed him. Finally he perched on top of the refrigerator and watched the family finish breakfast.

Then he went outside. It was queer and scary in the bright sunlight with no nice comfortable dark, no big hoot owls and whippoorwills singing songs that Horace loved, and no dogs howling far over the hills. But pretty soon he found out he was getting used to the daytime and the songs of the other birds and all the queer daytime sounds. There wasn't a single thing scary about them, once you knew what made them.

He wandered around having a fine time, though he did get a bit sleepy. As the big grandfather clock struck noon, he whisked upstairs and woke up his mother.

She looked at him anxiously. "Did you learn to moan and groan, Horace?"

Horace shook his head. "No, I found out that daylight is just as nice and friendly as dark!"

"Oh, dear!" his mother groaned. "Well, go to bed, Horace. But whatever you do, don't laugh! Mother needs her sleep. I've tossed and turned all day."

Horace went to his own room, yawning. He didn't laugh, but he couldn't keep from chuckling a little bit.

That night his mother and father had a ghost visitor to after-midnight tea.

When she heard Horace laugh, she shrieked. "Dear me! What a horrible child! Really he takes the curl right out of my hair. Why don't you do something about that laughing?"

"What can we do?" Horace's mother moaned.

"Shut him in a lighted room with lots of people," the visiting ghost snapped. "If that does not teach him to moan and groan, I don't know what will!"

"It sounds cruel," Horace's father said, "but I think we had better try it."

A week later, sure enough, Horace's mother marched him downstairs and opened the big living room door a tiny crack.

"There!! Inside with you! And mind you stay at least an hour!"

Horace didn't come back upstairs for three whole hours!

His mother was walking up and down, wringing her hands, when he appeared.

"Oh, darling, I shouldn't have done it! Forgive me, Horace! Was it so terrible?"

"I had a wonderful time, Mother!" Horace said. "It was a Halloween party. Everybody was dressed up. There were three other ghosts like me, only I think they were real people. We played games. I won a prize, too. A horn!"

"Ooooh!" his father groaned. "Where it is? Did you learn to play it?"

Horace shook his head. "No, I gave it to another little ghost who couldn't vanish the way I did when we played hide-and-seek."

Horace's father and mother looked at each other and sighed.

"All right, Horace, go rattle your chain for a while," his mother said, "and remember, *do* try not to jingle."

"Yes, Mother," Horace said happily and floated off.

"At least he didn't bring the horn home," his father said. "That's one thing to be thankful for."

Loud jingling sounded from the next room, Horace's father and mother groaned, clapped their hands over their ears and vanished.

But the very next evening something happened. Horace and his family woke up just at sundown and smelled something perfectly delicious.

"What is that *wonderful* smell?" Horace asked.

His mother and father exchanged a mysterious smile. "It's ghosts' favorite food—and that's all I will tell you now," his father said.

And his mother said, "Hurry and put on a clean sheet. It looks as if we're going to have a party tonight!"

They floated downstairs in a great hurry, and out the hall to the kitchen. They stopped by the door.

In the kitchen Tommy was saying to his mother, "But what happens to the middle of the doughnuts, Mother?"

His mother laughed. "Why, doughnut middles are the favorite food of ghosts, Tommy. See that big bowl that looks empty? It's full to the top with doughnut middles!"

Horace jiggled up and down excitedly. He had often heard about doughnut middles, but he'd never eaten one. He could hardly wait to try them.

As soon as the people had taken their doughnuts to the dining room, the ghosts swished into the kitchen and began eating doughnut middles.

Horace's mother ate only two dozen, because she was on a diet.

Horace's father ate four dozen.

But a little later, when his mother and father looked for Horace, they couldn't find him anywhere. He wasn't in the cellar or the attic or the garden or downstairs. At last they found him, curled up in bed in his own room.

"Oooh," he said, "I have a pain!"

"Horace!" His parents both hugged him. "You moaned, too!"

"Yes," Horace said, "because I have a pain in my middle. How about some spirits of peppermint or something? OOOH. OOOO-ooooOOO!"

And ever since, Horace has been able to moan and groan beautifully. Even if he's happy, all he has to do is think about the time he ate too many doughnut middles. It always works.

But he still can't clank his chain!

The Jack-o'-Lantern Witch

CAROLYN SHERWIN BAILEY

The grim iron doors of the prison clanged shut and the turnkey fastened them. Desire touched the homespun sleeve of the little boy with whom she was walking home from market down the narrow street of the musty old town of Salem.

"Did you hear that sound of the locking of the doors, Jonathan? It means that they've caught and imprisoned another witch."

The boy—a quaint figure in his long trousers, short jacket, and ruffed shirt—looked wide-eyed at the little girl. Quite as strangely dressed a child as Jonathan was Desire, the only daughter of Elder Baxter, who was high in authority in old Salem in those faraway days. Although she was not quite twelve, her gray frock with its short waist and long skirt nearly trailed the gray cobblestones of the street. Her soft brown hair was braided close to her head and pulled back tightly in front from her white brow and tucked out of sight beneath her stiff cap. A white kerchief was folded closely about her primly held shoulders, and over her frock she wore a long, dark cape.

Jonathan set down the rush basket of food supplies that he was carrying, and he touched the iron paling that shut in the prison.

"Do you know who the witch is?" he asked, his voice low with awe.

"No," Desire answered, "but they do say that she had been

brewing her spells for six months before the elders caught her. I heard my father and mother talking about it only this morning. They said that before the day was over the witch that was the cause of all our recent troubles in Salem would be caught and safely imprisoned."

"What troubles?" Jonathan asked.

"Have you not heard, Jonathan?" Desire lowered her voice and looked up and down the street to see that no one was listening.

"Abigail Williams was ill of the whooping cough and she had three fits which, as everyone knows, is a sign that a witch had cast a spell over her. And Mercy Talcott's teakettle boiled over and nearly scalded Mercy's mother. On the way to the doctor's for some ointment to put on her mother's hand, Mercy saw the witch herself flying over the tops of the trees on Gallows Hill." Desire's voice was a whisper now. "And she was riding on a broomstick."

"How did Mercy know that it was a witch, and how could she be riding on a broomstick?" asked the practical Jonathan.

Desire tossed her head. "I can't explain that to you, Jonathan. It was toward evening, and Mercy says that she saw a long, dark form in the trees and she heard the dry leaves rustle."

"Crows!" said Jonathan.

"For shame, Jonathan," said Desire. "Do you not know that the eyes of Mercy Talcott are keen for seeing witches? She is to be at the trial tomorrow, and identify the evil creature."

Desire repeated the words which her elders often used in those faraway Colonial days of ignorance and superstition. "When shall we rid ourselves of this pest of witchcraft in Salem?" she said.

Jonathan swung the basket upon his shoulder and led the way along the street again. "There'll probably be one less witch tomorrow. She won't have a chance to escape if that tale-bearing Mercy Talcott is at the trial. Let us go on by the side street and see if Jack is safe at Granny Hewitt's."

The two children hastened their steps and passed the scattering of little brown houses of old Salem. Their quaintly gabled roofs made them look like dolls' cottages. The windows with their tiny diamond-shaped panes were neatly curtained with white. At one house, a little larger than the others and having no garden, they caught their breaths.

"The Witches' House," said Desire.

It was here that so many of these unfortunate creatures of the dark days of Salem had been kept in confinement before they met their punishment in prison, on the ducking stool, or on Gallows Hill. A little farther along the children passed a great white meetinghouse where a gilded weathercock pointed bravely to the sky and high, white pillars stood at either side of the doorway.

"The witch will be tried here in the morning," Jonathan said.

The two children walked a little faster toward a pleasanter stopping place, Governor Endicott's big white house, set in the midst of his fair English garden. Even now, when the wind blew cold from the waterfront, the Governor's garden was a pleasant place to see. Bright little marigolds, defying the frost, lifted their orange blossoms along the path. Great beds of scarlet dahlias and purple asters made a mass of color. The late sun marked for itself a long, golden shaft across the sundial, and at the back of the house could be seen a patch of winter squashes and pumpkins mellowing in a sunny spot.

"Was not the Governor kind to give us the pumpkin?" said Jonathan.

"And wasn't Granny kind to show us how to make it a hobgoblin like our Jack?" added Desire. "She said that almost no other granny in Salem was old enough to remember about carving a pumpkin into a face as they did long ago in England. She told me that we must keep it a secret until All Hallow E'en. Then we shall take the pumpkin with a tallow drip shining inside him, lighting his funny face, down through the street to show the other children."

"I lighted it last night," Jonathan confessed. "I went to Granny's house with a cheese ball that was a gift from my mother to Granny."

"How did the pumpkin look?" asked Desire eagerly.

"Fearsome!" said Jonathan. "We put it in the window and I went outside in the dark to look at it. It had the appearance of a grinning monster." The boy laughed at his memory of the Jack-o'-Lantern.

By this time the children had reached a tumbledown cottage at the end of a tiny lane. Granny Hewitt lived there alone, a little wrinkled crone with a face like a brown walnut and eyes that shone like two stars when she smiled. Having no kin of her own, Granny Hewitt loved the boys and girls who passed her cottage on their way to and from school. She made molasses cookies and vinegar taffy for them. She put balm on their scratches and covered their primers and spellers with pieces of bright calico. No wonder Desire and Jonathan wanted to stop a moment at Granny Hewitt's house. They went up the white gravel path with its neat border of clam shells. Desire lifted the big brass knocker on the door, letting it drop with a clang.

There was no sound inside.

"She has gone to market," Jonathan said.

"Well, good-by, Jonathan," Desire said, taking her basket from the boy's hands. "I probably shall not see you tomorrow. It may be that my father will let me sit in our pew in the meetinghouse during the witch's trial."

Jonathan's eyes almost popped out of his head in surprise. "Could I go, too?" he asked.

"I'll see if I can get you in," Desire promised as the two friends parted.

The morning of the witch's trial was as bright and peaceful as the fall sun lighting fields and dingy streets and roofs could make it. Although the trial was not to begin until ten, by half past seven the green common that surrounded the Second Meetinghouse was a moving black and gray mass of gray-gowned women and stern men in their dark capes, buckled shoes, and tall hats.

Inside the meetinghouse every pew was filled. The platform was lined with the black-gowned elders, and the Governor himself, a dignified figure in his flowing cloak and powdered wig, occupied the pulpit. Desire sat, prim and quiet beside her mother, her head not much above the high back of the pew. On the other side sat Jonathan.

It was rumored that the witch who was about to be tried was of some repute in the practice of magic, and that she was to be made an example for any followers whom she might have.

Jonathan nudged Desire's elbow. "Where is she?" he asked.

"*Ssh.*" The little girl put a warning finger to her lips. "They'll bring her out in a minute." As she finished her whispered warning, her father, Elder Baxter, rose and began to speak.

"We are met together to pass judgment upon a woman of Salem town who has wrought her magic arts to the undoing of its citizens. She has cast her spell over a child and thrown it into dire sickness. She has bewitched the kitchen of our neighbor, Elder Talcott. A child of twelve years and well versed in the art of discovering witchcraft saw this same witch after she had practiced her arts. Mercy Talcott will please come to the platform. Bring in the witch."

Desire and Jonathan craned their necks to see better as the black row of the elders parted to let in a bent, trembling little old lady. Two jailers guarded her, one on each side. She still wore her tidy white apron with its knitting pocket, and her white cap was tied under her chin. She was shaking from head to foot with fright. Her head was bent low so that no one could see her face. She held her Bible clasped closely to her heart.

At the same time Mercy Talcott—a little girl dressed like Desire but with a less winning face—stepped up, also, to the platform. It was the custom of those strange days to believe that certain children could identify witches, and Mercy was one of these children.

The elder spoke again. "I have not made one most important charge of all, as I wish to make it in the presence of the prisoner herself. She has a creature of some other kind than human with which she consults on matters of witchery. It has been seen at night looking out of her window with glaring eyes and wide-open mouth set in a huge head.

"Look up, witch. Mercy Talcott, is this the witch that you saw leaving your house the day that your mother was burned?"

Slowly, and in terror the little old lady lifted her head. At the same time and in the same sobbing breaths, Jonathan and Desire said, "It is Granny Hewitt!"

Mercy saw, too, who it was. She remembered the little rag doll that Granny had made her when she was a very little girl. It wore a gay pink calico dress, and its cheeks were stained red with pokeberry juice. Mercy caught her breath and hesitated. She knew that it was only in fancy that she had seen the broomstick and its wild rider. As she waited, Desire pulled Jonathan from his seat. Before her mother could question or stop them, the two children were at the front of the pulpit, facing the Governor.

Desire clasped her hands and raised them in pleading toward the great man who bent down toward her in surprise. The whole meetinghouse was still as Desire spoke in her sweet, high voice.

"Your Excellency, I beg your mercy for our dear Granny. She is not a witch, but a kind friend to all the children of Salem. It is I who should be punished in her place. If your Excellency will but think back to the last tithing day, you will remember that you gave two children, Jonathan and me, a pumpkin for our play. We took it to Granny Hewitt's house and she helped us to make it into a Jack whose tallow drip, lighted, in Granny's window someone saw and spoke of to you. My father did not know that it was my fault, else he would not have accused Granny."

Jonathan, made courageous by Desire's bravery, had gone to Mercy's side. "It was crows you saw on Gallows Hill," he said in her ear. "You never, never saw Granny Hewitt riding on a broomstick. Say so."

Mercy looked into Granny's tearstained face. Then, with a rush of love, she threw herself into her arms. "I never saw Granny riding on a broomstick. She isn't a witch," Mercy declared.

The white doors of the meetinghouse opened wide. The people waited with heads bowed, half in shame and half in joy, as Granny, surrounded by the children, passed into the sunshine and the freedom outside. Then they followed, making a kind of triumphal procession to the cottage at the end of the street. Kind hands led Granny all the way and kind hearts made her forget all about her experiences. In her window there still stood the grinning Jack-o'-Lantern, and at sight of it bursts of laughter took away all thought of fears. One of the elders set it upon one of Granny's fence posts and then held Desire up beside it.

"Hurrah for the Jack-o'-Lantern witch," someone said, and the crowd shouted their happiness and relief.

The Giant Ghost

ELIZABETH HOUGH SECHRIST

It happened on Halloween. It was one of those nights that ghosts are fond of, with great floating clouds in the sky and a chill wind. The wind swept the clouds before the moon and made them look like the heavy folds of a witch's cloak maliciously hiding the moon from the earth. Now and then the moon peered out from behind the clouds to look upon the village below. She could see the wind furiously at work, pushing its way through the dry cornstalks in the fields, then rushing through the village streets. She saw the dry leaves that had fallen from the trees scurrying along the ground like frightened squirrels. She saw the wind, with evil groans and whisperings, catching at old men's hats and young girls' skirts, and tearing at clotheslines until the clothes and pins were sent flying. Shutters on the houses of the village clattered and banged, and banged and creaked until the folks within felt sure the witches were at their mischief.

But in spite of the autumn wind there were brave souls out that night. Most of them were boys and girls who were making their way from house to house as they always did on Halloween, wearing their Halloween costumes. There were witches and ghosts aplenty among them, but it was plain to see that they were not real ones. The eeriness of the night and the wildness of the wind made them huddle together as they struggled against the wind, for who knew what might lurk behind the deep moving shadows?

Just in front of the church Burying Ground old Jake was on his way home. He was late for supper and very hungry, and the wind seemed intent on holding him back from the hot meal that was waiting. Head down and pushing against the evil breeze, the ghost was almost upon him before he saw it. Almost as big as his own whitewashed cottage, it came toward him with terrific, pounding speed, an apparition of whiteness that had neither shape nor body nor head!

Jake gave a yell and jumped out of the way. He had just time enough to spring over the fence into the Burying Ground. A graveyard was the last place he would have asked for as a retreat at such a time as this, but Jake had no choice.

But the ghostly giant sped up the road past the Burying Ground without so much as a sidewise glance, and it was plain to Jake that the ghost was not looking for him! As he leaned weakly against the fence for support, he could see the white, flowing garments of the gigantic figure just disappearing around the bend in the road. Then it was gone. It was so utterly gone that Jake drew his shaking hand before his eyes to make sure he had not been dreaming or imagining things. He wasn't quite sure. It was all very strange. He looked once more down the road, where all was blackness except for a few lights of houses. Jake wanted to know the truth: Had he seen a giant ghost or hadn't he? He climbed the fence of the Burying Ground and followed in the direction in which the apparition had vanished.

Meanwhile, six boys were making their way along the same road, coming from the opposite direction. All of them were dressed in long flowing sheets. They were on their way to a ghost party in the village. As they walked, they practiced waving their arms in ghost-like ways and making strange, hollow sounds.

"I am the Ghost of Hamlet! Beware!" said one of the boys.

"And I am the Ghost of Groans!" another wailed, proceeding to do some horrible groaning.

"Shucks!" exclaimed a third one. "I can scare 'em worse than anybody with these good old bones." And he rattled the bones that he had been collecting for this very occasion.

"That does sound spooky, doesn't it?" asked the fourth boy, who was rather timid.

"What would you do if you saw a ghost?" asked the fifth boy.

"Look!" The last boy suddenly stood still, clutching at the arm of one of his companions with one hand and pointing with the other. "Look there! There *is* a ghost!"

They all stood stock-still and stared. Coming toward them was a sight that struck them dumb: An enormous creature clothed in white had emerged from the black bushes with a rush and a roar, and was coming straight toward where they stood in the road.

As the ghost came closer, one of the boys found his voice. "Run!" he shouted.

The voice roused the others from their temporary stupor, and they turned on their heels and ran with all the speed they could muster.

At this moment two hired men were coming from the Inn of the Red Lion, where they had been working. They were having an argument.

"Don't tell me you believe in ghosts!" one of them was saying scornfully. "Brother, there ain't no ghosts!"

"I dunno about that," and the other shook his head doubtfully. "My old mother has seen plenty of ghosts!"

"I say there ain't no ghosts, and I don't believe in sech things as spirits and—holy cow!"

The speaker stopped short, the words frozen on his lips. His companion looked up to see what had shocked him into silence. They both looked, their eyes bulging and their mouths hanging open. Before their very eyes they saw, coming along the road, a whole host of small ghostly figures whose white robes flew in all directions as they covered the ground with tremendous speed; and behind these apparitions—more terrifying still—a giant ghost that bellowed and roared and tore at the air with gestures wild and terrible!

The men wasted no time. They ran!

A hundred yards they ran, two men and six ghostly figures all pursued by the giant ghost. They would be running still if Farmer Brown had not been, at that moment, walking through the village.

Farmer Brown was a sensible man. He wasn't even thinking of ghosts. He was thinking of his lost cow, Violet. She was a prize cow and he meant to find her if it took him all night. He had started his search by going from house to house in the village asking whether Violet, by any chance, had strayed into the wrong shed or stable.

Now, as the strange procession came tearing down the street, the farmer stopped, calling out, "Ho! What's this?" Then he recognized the two hired men as they came nearer.

"What's up, Sam?" He held one of the men by the arm by sheer force, for Sam was unwilling to stop.

"It's ghosts!" Sam panted.

"Run!" shrieked six breathless boys in one word. "It's a ghost!"

The farmer took in the situation at a glance. As the great giant ghost in its flowing folds of white pounded down upon them, he jumped in front of it, and managed, somehow, to stop it.

"Well, I swan!" he ejaculated, tearing a large bedsheet from a frightened animal. "Ef it ain't our Violet!"

Everybody stopped running. Everybody looked. Sure enough, the ghost was none other than Farmer Brown's cow. From somebody's clothesline, she had got one end of a large white sheet fastened to her horns and had become terrified as she ran and the large, white, billowy folds had blown back over her body.

While the two men and the six party-ghosts stood gaping at the cow and feeling a bit shaken and a little foolish, another person put in an appearance. It was Jake.

"Pshaw, now!" he said disappointedly, as he saw the cow. "I thought she was a giant ghost. This is Halloween, isn't it?"

Veterans' Day

November 11 is the day on which the American people pay special honor to members of the armed forces who have given their lives for their country. Armistice Day, as it was originally called, was the anniversary of the Armistice, or truce, signed November 11, 1918, between Germany and the Allies, marking the end of World War I. Americans were convinced that the war had been fought to bring an end to war forever. Yet in 1941 the United States was drawn into an even more terrible conflict.

It was in memory of the men and women who had taken part in World War II, as well as in the Korean War, which broke out a few years later, that the name of Armistice Day was changed (1954) to Veterans' Day. Of the many celebrations held on that day none is more solemn than the annual rites at the Tomb of the Unknowns in Arlington National Cemetery, just across the river from Washington, D.C. This beautiful cemetery in Virginia was once the estate of the great Confederate general, Robert E. Lee. Ever since the Civil War it has served as a military burying place. During World War I so many soldiers had been killed who could not be identified that it was decided to honor all of them by honoring one.

On Armistice Day, 1921, the body of an unidentified soldier was brought from France and buried in a magnificent white marble tomb, on which were inscribed these words:

HERE RESTS IN HONORED
GLORY
AN AMERICAN SOLDIER
KNOWN BUT TO GOD

This epitaph now honors not one soldier but three. On Memorial Day, 1958, the bodies of two other unknown servicemen—one from World War II and one from the Korean War—were brought to Arlington. Armed sentries are on duty twenty-four hours a day guarding the monument that has become a symbol of the nation's gratitude to its honored dead.

Another tomb in Arlington National Cemetery, to which thousands of visitors, from every state and from many foreign countries, have come to pay homage, is that of President John Fitzgerald Kennedy, a veteran of World War II. His courage as a PT-boat commander was one of the stirring examples of heroism in recent times.

Jack Kennedy, Navy Veteran

FRANCES CAVANAH

Jack Kennedy wanted to join the Navy but was turned down. He then tried the Army and was turned down again. The doctors who examined him said that his weak back, which he had hurt in playing football while attending Harvard University, could not stand the strain of combat.

But Jack refused to give up. For five months he took special exercises to strengthen his back muscles and was finally able to pass the Navy fitness test. Late in 1942, nearly a year after the United States had entered World War II, he was assigned to a Motor Torpedo Boat squadron, made up of small Patrol Torpedo boats— PT boats, they were called. It was an ideal assignment for a young man who had been handling small boats since he was a child.

And those PT boats were really something to handle. Made of plywood, they offered little protection to their crews in time of battle. But a PT boat was fast. It could dodge through heavy gunfire from a warship, and fire its own torpedoes at close range. Then it could escape—if the crew was lucky. "Fire—dash—pray!" was a popular saying among the sailors who rode the small, dangerous craft.

After weeks of intensive training, Jack shipped out of San Francisco for the Solomon Islands in the South Pacific, and in April, 1943, he was given command of his own boat, the PT-109. He was now a lieutenant, junior grade, and on the night of August 1 he was on patrol duty with a crew of twelve. As he stood at the wheel peering through the black night, it must have been a source of satisfaction to him to know that he had a part in the vast combination air-sea-ground counterattack against the enemy in the Pacific.

On that night the PT-109 was one of a squadron of PT boats patrolling the stretch of water known as Blackett Strait. The engines were muffled as the boats passed close to the shores of islands still held by the Japanese, and the crews kept a sharp lookout for enemy destroyers. On Lieutenant Kennedy's boat, Ensign George Ross stood at the bow peering through a pair of binoculars.

Suddenly Ross turned and pointed toward a vague shape in the darkness. It was a Japanese destroyer—but even as Jack spun the wheel to prepare for an attack, there was a sound of splintering wood. The larger boat had rammed the smaller boat. The force of the impact threw Jack violently to the deck. He looked up to see the destroyer slicing through the PT-109, splitting it in half. With a blinding flash, the gasoline ignited, and part of the boat caught fire.

"So this is how it feels to be killed," thought Jack.

But he was not killed. At the moment, he hardly realized that his back had been hurt again. After the destroyer had dashed off into the darkness, everything was very quiet except for the low, hissing sound of burning gasoline. The gasoline had spread over the surface of the water, making it appear that the water was on fire. The part of the boat where the fire had broken out had sunk. The part to which Jack clung was half submerged.

The two ensigns and four of the crewmen also were clinging to the hull. What had happened to the others? Jack called out and was answered by several feeble shouts a hundred yards away. He and the two ensigns swam to the rescue.

Fortunately the crewmen who had been thrown into the water were wearing their life jackets—a Navy requirement for men in combat—and the life jackets kept them afloat. But the men had been stunned by the force of the ramming. Several were almost unconscious from inhaling the gasoline fumes. The engineman, Patrick McMahon, aged thirty-seven and called "Pop" by the younger men, had been badly burned. When Jack reached him, Pop protested.

"Go on, Skipper," he said. "I've had it."

Jack paid no attention. Fighting a strong current, he finally towed Pop back to what was left of the PT-109, then went to help other members of the crew. Finally ten of his men were accounted for. Two were missing. Jack called their names again and again but received no answer. He knew that they must have gone down at the time of the collision.

For the rest of that night the survivors tried to keep their balance on the slanting deck. The boat was slowly sinking, and daylight brought the danger of capture. The shipwrecked crew was in enemy territory, in plain view of several islands. There might be a Japanese base on one of the larger islands. Others seemed mere dots on the water, but beyond them was a green oval of land with tall trees. It looked big enough to shelter eleven men but too small—Lieutenant Kennedy hoped—to interest the Japanese. Anyway, the risk must be taken; his men could not stay where they were.

Two of the crew could not swim, but a plank was found in the wreckage. This plank would have to serve as a float. With four men on each side, and a ninth man at the end, they could hold on to the plank with one hand and paddle with the other. All of them could kick. Lieutenant Kennedy would take charge of Patrick McMahon. After easing the badly burned man into the water he grabbed a strap from Pop's life jacket. Holding the strap between his teeth, he towed the injured man through the water toward the island three and a half miles away.

It was a painful swim for both of them. Pop's body felt as though it were on fire. For Jack every stroke was torture. His fall on the deck had aggravated his old back injury, and for several hours the pain had been getting worse. None of his companions realized how badly he had been hurt, Pop least of all.

"Is it much farther, Mr. Kennedy?" he asked.

"Not much farther," Lieutenant Kennedy replied.

With the strap clenched between his teeth, it was impossible to keep his lips closed tight, and the salt water that he had to swallow made him ill. Occasionally Jack stopped to rest, and nearly four hours went by before he reached the island. There he lay on the beach, too tired to move, his feet still in the water.

But he and Pop did not dare to lie for long on the exposed beach; they would make easy targets for an enemy plane. After a few minutes they dragged themselves to the safety of some bushes. From there Jack saw his other shipmates swimming toward the island with their plank. He stood up and waved. In a short time they were all together again—eleven men, weary and ill, who had been without food or fresh water for fifteen hours. As they crouched under the bushes, no one spoke for several minutes. There was only the sound of their loud breathing.

And then they heard the hum of a motor. A boat was approaching the island. When the men looked out from their hiding place, they saw that it was a Japanese boat. Had the castaways been seen? Were they to be captured after all? But the motorboat did not stop. The sound of its engines grew fainter in the distance.

Jack's back was throbbing, but at least his men were safe—for a while. He had brought them through their first ordeal. He had brought Pop McMahon through.

The enemy was too close to risk a long stay on the island, and after a brief rest Jack started out on another long swim. With him he took a ship's lantern wrapped securely in a kapok life jacket and fastened to his belt. Perhaps he would be able to signal an American boat patrolling the waters in the darkness. The following night Ensign Ross tried the same plan. Neither he nor Jack had any success. Both returned to their companions exhausted and numb with cold after long hours in the water.

By the third day the situation was desperate. All of the men were ill, and they had to have food. The few coconuts found on the island were soon gone. The castaways swam to another island where they could see coconut palms growing. Again Jack towed Pop McMahon all the way. Pop's condition was pitiful to see, but he never complained.

Nor did the young lieutenant, although by now he was in constant pain. In the distance he could see Rendova Peak, rising high above the American PT base. It wasn't far—perhaps less than forty miles away—but the men had almost given up hope of being rescued.

And then, the next afternoon, they were found by two natives. The natives, whose names were Biuku and Erono, could speak very little English, but they seemed friendly. Jack husked a coconut, and with his knife scratched a message on a smooth part of the shell: *Eleven alive. Natives know position. Kennedy.*

He handed the shell to Biuku and Erono and pointed in the direction of the American base. "Rendova, Rendova," he said. The natives nodded, climbed into their dugout canoe, and pushed out into the water. But Jack could not be sure they had understood. He resolved to make one last effort to contact the Navy.

The natives had shown him where they had hidden a canoe, and as soon as darkness fell he and Ross paddled their way to Ferguson Passage. Although American PT's often patrolled this stretch of water, there was none to be seen that night. On the way back to the island, a sudden storm came up. As the two men tried to beach the canoe, the waves spun it around in a dizzy circle. Jack found himself lying in a little eddy near the shore. Ross landed on the sharp rocks of the coral reef, and his arms and feet were badly cut.

Jack glanced at his companion, who lay on the beach gasping for breath. He and McMahon, as well as several of the others, must have medical care soon. How long could they hold out? Had Biuku and Erono really gone for help?

As it turned out, they had. Jack's message finally reached Rendova, and a PT boat came to the rescue of the castaways. It was a bedraggled group of eleven half-starved men, their eyes bloodshot, their hair matted, who arrived back at the base on August 8, seven days after the ramming of their boat. They were warmly welcomed. The crews of the other PT boats in their squadron, after seeing the 109 catch fire, had not believed it possible that anyone could survive in that flaming sea.

Later, Lieutenant Jack Kennedy was awarded the Navy and Marine Corps Medal for his "courage, endurance and excellent leadership" which "contributed to the saving of several lives." Saying nothing about his injured back, he volunteered for another tour of duty, but the pain grew steadily worse. He also had malaria, and he was finally sent back to the United States. In the spring of 1944, he entered the Chelsea Naval Hospital, not far from the family summer home at Hyannis Port, Massachusetts. That was one of several long stays in the hospital for Lieutenant Kennedy. Twice he had spinal surgery, and the second operation was so critical, it did not seem he could possibly live.

"He fought his way out of it," his father said later. "Jack's always been a fighter."

Meanwhile, John Kennedy had entered politics, and again he proved that he could put up a good fight. Early in his first political campaign—when he ran for Congress—he decided that the way to win was to work harder than any of his rivals. Though it did not come easily at first, he visited voters in their homes, stores and offices. He even stopped strangers on the street and asked them to vote for him. And his efforts paid off. At the age of twenty-nine, he went to Washington to take his seat in Congress. Four years later he was elected to the United States Senate. In 1961 he was inaugurated

President of the United States—the youngest man ever to be elected to that office.

The afternoon before Inauguration, Washington was struck by a blinding snowstorm. Though snow blanketed the city, by noon on January 20, 1961, a mammoth crowd had gathered before the east front of the Capitol. The crowd shivered in the cold wind that whipped across the plaza but listened with rapt attention as the new President gave his inaugural address. Whether or not they had voted for John F. Kennedy, they knew they were listening to a great speech.

It was a speech not only to the American people but to the people of the world. He pledged friendship to American allies. To the people who were struggling to break the bonds of poverty in huts and villages of half the globe, he promised that Americans would try to help them help themselves. Of those nations that would make themselves enemies of the United States he made a request that "both sides begin anew the quest for peace." All that needed to be done, he pointed out, could not be accomplished in a few days, or perhaps even in the lifetime of those listening to his voice.

"But let us begin," he said.

The parade following the Inauguration took place on schedule, in spite of the freezing weather. Among the many floats that passed before the reviewing stand in front of the White House was a replica of a Navy PT boat. Mounted on a truck, it looked exactly like the PT-109 that young Lieutenant Kennedy had commanded the night when it had been rammed by a Japanese destroyer. Seven of the original crewmen were on board and they cheered and waved. The new President waved back with obvious enthusiasm.

There was a half smile on his face, a little sad, and not a little proud, as he watched it disappear down Pennsylvania Avenue.

(Adapted from *Meet the Presidents.*)

Thanksgiving Day

(Fourth Thursday in November)

The early settlers we call Pilgrims are usually credited with holding the first Thanksgiving in America in 1621. Actually, several thanksgiving celebrations—all religious—had been held farther south, in Virginia, before the Pilgrims landed in Massachusetts. The first thanksgiving service was held in 1607 when the Jamestown colonists disembarked on a sandy beach close by; the second came two years later, after the "starving time," when a ship from England brought supplies to the hungry and desperate colonists.

Early in December, 1619, thirty-nine settlers sailed up the James River to a place named Berkeley Hundred, where they knelt on the riverbank to give thanks for their safe arrival. The leaders of the expedition gave instructions that the day should be "yearly and perpetually keept holy as a day of thanksgiving to Almighty God."

That was the first time our Thanksgiving Day was actually called by that name. It was two years later that the Pilgrims had their celebration. Even though it was not the first one, it has become an important part of our Thanksgiving tradition. It was the Pilgrims' example that inspired other colonists to hold similar feasts.

After the United States won its independence, President George Washington proclaimed a national day of thanksgiving in gratitude for the adoption of the Constitution.

People continued to set aside a day in November for giving thanks, but there was no uniform date for every state. It was not until 1846 that Sarah Josepha Hale began promoting her plan to have Thanksgiving observed by every American on the same day. Mrs. Hale, editor of *Godey's Lady's Book*, a well-known magazine—also remembered as the author of "Mary Had a Little Lamb"—published editorials in her magazine and wrote letter after letter to several different Presidents. Her efforts finally met with success when President Abraham Lincoln, in 1863 and again in 1864, proclaimed the last Thursday in November as the national Thanksgiving Day.

The Pilgrims' Thanksgiving

GRACE HUMPHREY

It was in December of 1621 that Governor Bradford announced that first day of thanksgiving for the people, later called Pilgrims, in the little colony of Plymouth.

Not quite a year had passed since the *Mayflower* anchored in a harbor of that rocky coast. What a year it had been—a year of hardships in a new land, a year of hunger and cold, of fear and sickness! The supply of food grew less and less.

At one time all but seven persons in the colony were ill. For the sick there was not the right kind of food. Week by week Pilgrims had died, till six and forty graves were dug on the bluff overlooking the bay. But with the spring even the most discouraged among the Pilgrims took heart once more. Go back to England, three thousand miles away? Never! Here they could worship God in their own way. Here they were free men.

With steadfast faith, the fifty colonists began to sow their seed. Twenty acres of corn they put in, six of barley and six of peas. Without ceasing they cared for these fields. They watched the growth of their crops anxiously. Well they knew that their lives depended on a full harvest.

Spring and summer days flew by. The land was blessed with showers and sunshine. Autumn came and dressed the woods in gorgeous colors—gold and crimson and brown. Their crops stood ready for the gathering. They reaped the fruit of their labors and housed it carefully for the winter.

In December, Governor Bradford looked abroad on the little colony. Seven houses he counted, and four for community use. He gazed over the empty fields—the twenty acres whose golden shocks of corn had stood so close together, yielding a harvest such as old England never knew. The barley, too, had been a successful crop.

"Yes," said the Governor to himself, "after the 'starving time' we've lived through there's ample food on hand now for all of us. There's a peck of meal a week for each person, and since the harvest there's the same amount of Indian corn. We can face the winter and the future with lighter hearts. There'll be no second 'starving time'!"

If a man counted only hardships, Bradford's thought went on, this first year in Plymouth had a goodly number. If he counted only blessings there were many. How could he best bring this truth home to his people?

"We have fasted together," he said in suggesting his plan. "Now let us feast together. Let us have a special day to give thanks for all the goodness of God. He has remembered us. We will remember Him."

The date was set for the thirteenth of the month.

"Let us invite our friends the chief Massasoit and some of his braves," suggested Elder Brewster.

A runner went to Mount Hope to take the invitation to the Indians. Four men were sent fowling, and such good fortune attended their shooting that in one day they got wild turkeys, partridges and wood pigeons—enough to last the whole colony almost a week.

As soon as the plan for the feast day was announced the women set to work. Indeed, it was a big task for the five of them, with a few young girls to help. There were turkeys to be plucked and dressed and stuffed with beechnuts; fish from the bay to be cleaned and broiled; barley bread and corn bread to be made; and many another good thing to be prepared. Busy, busy were the women and girls of Plymouth for days beforehand.

Early in the morning of the thirteenth, shortly after Captain Standish had fired off the sunrise gun, there came a great shout from the woods. Another shout, a shriek, and a wild whoop! Through the trees came a long line of Indians—the chief Massasoit and ninety of his braves.

In their best dress they came, with flourish of tomahawks in honor of this feast day of their friends the palefaces. Some of them had wide bands of black paint on their faces. Some had feathers stuck in their long straight black hair. Some wore the furry coats of wildcats hanging from their shoulders. Some wore deerskins.

With the Governor, Captain Standish went to meet them. Were they surprised at the number? Were they dismayed at the thought of the food necessary for ninety visitors? Courteously, they received their Indian guests.

Presently the beat of a drum announced morning prayers. Every day began with this brief service—how much more important on this feast day! The red men looked on quietly, listening reverently while the grave Pilgrims prayed to the Great Spirit.

Then came breakfast—clam chowder with biscuit and hasty pudding served with butter and treacle, for milk they had none. At the north end of the little village colonists and visitors assembled.

"Military exercises under the direction of Captain Miles Standish," announced the Governor.

The trumpets sounded. From the fort came the roll of drums. Down the hill in soldierly array marched the regiment of Plymouth—a regiment of twenty men. Over them floated the flag of England.

March and countermarch, wheel and turn, right about face—through all the maneuvers Standish put his men that morning. Frequently they discharged their muskets. Once in answer there came a great roar from the four cannons of the fort.

The red men danced, acted out stories, and played games with the children. The colonists sang their songs. A target was set up and the soldiers fired at it. The Indians, standing in closer, shot at it with their bows and arrows. There was a friendly contest to see which side would make the larger score.

Meanwhile Mistress Brewster and Mistress Winslow with the three other women of the colony were hard at work. Remember Allerton and Mary Chilton, Priscilla and Desire and the younger girls helped as they could. Back and forth to the kitchen they went countless times, bearing pewter plates and heaping platters of good things to eat. At last dinner was announced.

What a meal that was, served at the long tables under the leafless trees! There were clams and scallops, wild turkey with Priscilla Mullins' famous dressing of beechnuts, dumplings made of barley flour, pigeon pasty, bowls of salad wreathed with autumn leaves, and baskets of wild grapes and plums.

Did the Indians surmise that their presence made extra work for the women of Plymouth? Did they wish to bring something of their own for the feast? The brother of Massasoit offered to lead a hunting party into the woods to look for deer. His braves knew well their favorite haunts. It would not take long.

"Yes, go," said Governor Bradford.

The next morning back came the red men with five deer. One they roasted whole. The others were cut up into steaks and smaller pieces for venison pie.

For two days more the feasting went on. Between English colonists and fierce Indians there was hearty fellowship and good will. Peace had been established on a firm foundation. Without such a peace the Pilgrims would never have won a footing on that bleak coast. Without it, Plymouth could never have survived.

It was these friendly savages who told the newcomers how to use shad to fertilize their fields, when to plant corn—"as soon as the oak leaves are as big as a mouse's ear"—and where to find wild fruits and berries. Much was owing to the red men, thrice welcome to the colony's feast day!

This is the story of that Pilgrim Thanksgiving in faraway 1621, but the reasons for giving thanks in 1621 have remained to this day, with many others added. It is a day when the people recognize all the blessings of God and His goodness to our land, a day to give thanks for bountiful, golden harvests, for peace and prosperity, for the general welfare—a day for prayer and rejoicing.

The Thanksgiving Stranger

RUTH GIPSON PLOWHEAD

Polly Prence learned to knit when she was five years old. By the time she was six, she had made a gay sunshine patchwork quilt. Now that she was eight, she was learning something much harder. She was learning to be a pioneer.

The past spring Polly and her family had left New York and journeyed along the Oregon Trail, settling in a cabin in far western Idaho. The change meant hard work, loneliness and sacrifices for all.

One November day Polly Prence was alone on the homestead. That is, she was alone save for Sammie, the shepherd dog, and Benjamin, the tortoise-shell cat, who had made the long journey across the continent with the family.

With her feet on the fender, Polly had settled down to her sewing. In another month it would be Christmas and there was the muslin apron to finish for Mother. Then there were the striped wristlets to knit for Father and the brothers. Polly was humming to herself snatches of a tune from the book of carols:

> *Mind ye the stranger who comes to your door;*
> *See that he's hungry and weary no more.*

Over and over she hummed the little strain. Perhaps it was because Mother had asked her to be ready to feed the hungry family when they returned. Now and then she glanced up from her sewing at the huge iron kettle of beans simmering over the fire.

Mother had not wanted to leave her alone, but about noon she had been summoned to go to the aid of a sick neighbor several miles down the valley. Father and the older brother, Jim, had left a week before for the trading station to get supplies. That morning the younger brother, Tom, and the hired man had cantered away on horseback to the grist mill, ten miles distant, with sacks of corn and wheat for grinding.

"Polly," Mother had said, "I can't refuse to go to a neighbor in trouble, and I can't take you with me. Tom and Will should be back by the middle of the afternoon, and Father planned to return today. If I am not home by five o'clock, I shall send someone to see that you are all right. Nobody travels this way very often, so you are safe. Watch the fires, and remember that you have your faithful Sammie and your Bible."

Polly Prence put the last stitches in the strings of the Christmas apron. She fixed the fires, and stirred the beans, all the time humming:

> *Mind ye the stranger who comes to your door;*
> *See that he's hungry and weary no more.*

"Kitty," she said to Benjamin, "doesn't the time pass slowly? I wonder why Father doesn't come."

For perhaps the dozenth time she went to the window and gazed down the trail. It was beginning to snow, and she thought what fun it would be to have a white Thanksgiving. She could make a snow man. Then suddenly her heart seemed to stop beating. A tall figure was coming across the sagebrush plains. No one ever came on foot that way. Had Father and Tom met trouble?

The figure came closer. Then Polly saw the gay blanket and long strands of black hair and realized that it was an Indian. What should she do? Where could she hide? Should she bar the door and have Sammie attack the intruder?

But something was wrong. The Indian walked slowly, staggering as though his strength was almost gone. Perhaps he was hungry or ill. She couldn't help feeling afraid, but could she shut the door on a man in trouble? Again the song she had been humming flashed through her mind:

> *Mind ye the stranger who comes to your door;*
> *See that he's hungry and weary no more.*

The Indian had now reached the house. Without waiting to knock, he turned the knob, and fell into a chair with his head on his breast. Sammie's fur bristled. He savagely bared his fangs, and crouched, ready to spring.

"Down, Sammie, down," whispered Polly. "Can't you see the poor man has hurt his arm? What shall I do?"

She did what she thought Mother would have done. With trembling hands, she drew cloth from the linen chest, and tore soft strips of muslin. She washed the arm in warm water, applied healing salve, and bound up the wound. She heated milk, and when the Indian opened his eyes, held the cup to his lips. With the last gulp the unwelcome guest slipped to the floor, and fell into a sleep that was so deep it was almost a stupor. Polly covered him with a buffalo robe, her heart full of pity.

Then calling Sammie to her side, she began a long, tiresome wait. She took up the wristlet and knitted rapidly, as though the work of her nimble fingers could still the beating of her heart. Finally, she laid her knitting down and placed her arms around Sammie's neck.

"Oh, Sammie, do you suppose there has been a fight with the Indians?" she sobbed softly.

Sammie licked her neck gently, and Benjamin rubbed against her legs, purring loudly.

Now it was growing dusk and time to think of supper. Polly stirred the beans, tended the fires, made a large pan of corn bread, and went out to feed the chickens. When she returned, the Indian was sitting up. He looked rested and years younger.

Pointing to himself, he said, "Flying Cloud. Flying Cloud." Then he pointed to his mouth and to the pot of beans saying, "Hungry. Hungry."

He had seen enough of white men, evidently, to learn a few English words. When he saw how frightened Polly was, he said, "No hurt. No hurt."

Polly Prence bustled about, glad of a chance to be busy. If an Indian could smile like that, perhaps he meant no harm. She heaped a tray with beans, thick chunks of corn bread, and slices cut from a cold roast of venison. Then slowly she went down into the dugout cellar. She lifted the lid of a crock and took out a cake of comb honey. They had only one hive of bees, and sweets were scarce. But Polly had been well trained in the law of Western hospitality. The best must be given to the guest.

When she placed the tray on the floor before the Indian, Polly was shocked by his lack of manners. He ate greedily and loudly. Then he made a sign that he wanted more bread and meat, which she gave him. When she saw him stuffing it into a pouch, she realized that he was probably going on a long journey and would need all the food that he could carry. She slipped into the pantry and came back with her own little dried-apple turnover which Mother had made for her supper. The red man gave a nod, which was probably meant for a grunt of thanks.

Polly returned it with a polite curtsy. "Good luck to you," she said, as the Indian disappeared into the darkness.

It was a relief to see him go, but afterwards she was lonelier than ever. She buried her face again in the big dog's fur. "Oh, Sammie, Sammie, why doesn't somebody come?"

The door slammed, and Father and Jim rushed in. They were wild with alarm. They had had a glimpse of the Indian slipping over the prairie.

"Polly," cried Father, "what has happened? Where are your mother and brother?"

Polly sobbed forth her story.

"Thank God you are safe!" said Father, holding her tightly in his arms. "You have done well. You have sheltered and fed the stranger within our gates. Nevertheless, it must be managed so you are never again left alone."

By evening the rest of the family had returned, and Polly Prence found herself quite a heroine.

A few days later Thanksgiving preparations were in full swing. On the night before the holiday, the family were singing songs and hymns of praise. When they sang:

> *Mind ye the stranger who comes to your door;*
> *See that he's hungry and weary no more,*

Polly thought of the tall strange guest who had glided like a shadow into the darkness. Had he a dark-skinned little daughter? Did he reach her safely? Would he tell her the story of his young hostess?

Thanksgiving Day arrived. The sky was like a huge turquoise, and the sun seemed to flood the white earth with diamonds. In the kitchen two wild fat geese were roasting over the fire. The little house was filled with rich, spicy odors. Polly sniffed them with delight as she helped her mother prepare dinner. Suddenly, the door opened and Tom burst into the house.

"Folks, there's a prairie schooner coming down the trail," he cried excitedly. "Jim is saddling our ponies, and we will ride to meet it. Who can it be? Wouldn't it be fun if we had company for dinner?"

Polly, just as curious as the boys, bundled into her hood and coat and ran outside to wait. She was dancing about impatiently in the snow when the wagon came close. To her surprise the boys beckoned and she ran to meet it. She was even more surprised when a tall young man jumped from the wagon and lifted her high in the air.

"Oh, Uncle Peter!" Polly cried. Here was her favorite uncle, whom she had thought was in New York, come to spend Thanksgiving with her. "How did you get here?"

"As near as I can figure, I am alive and here today because of you, small chicken," he replied. "But come, here are my two friends, and we are mighty hungry. How about something to eat?"

"Oh, goody, you can have Thanksgiving dinner with us," Polly replied as she was carried into the house on Uncle Peter's shoulders.

It was not until the bountiful Thanksgiving dinner had been eaten, and the family were gathered about the fireplace, that Uncle Peter told his story.

"It was in August," he said, "that I decided I could wait no longer to see Polly again. So I joined these friends of mine who were coming West. I did not write, as mail is so long in reaching you. If we did not arrive on time, I was afraid that you might worry.

"Well, all went well until a few days ago, when our wagon train was attacked by Indians. We in advance were surprised and taken prisoners, and hustled away so that we were not in the thick of the fight. However, we learned later that the Indian party was finally routed. Their leader was shot through the arm, his horse killed, and he himself chased for miles over the plains.

"Meanwhile our wagon had been driven to a temporary hiding place. Perhaps the Indians thought their chief had been captured and were saving us as hostages. At any rate, on the evening of the following day their wounded leader appeared in our midst. We wondered where he found the fine white linen with which his arm was bound."

"Why, Uncle Peter," Polly interrupted, "that must have been Flying Cloud. I fixed his arm with part of one of Mother's old sheets."

Uncle Peter nodded and went on with his story. "We had been searched, and among other things the Indians took was a little black case which I was carrying in my pocket. This Indian had a great time unfastening the clasp. When he finally got it open, guess what he saw, Polly?" Uncle Peter turned to smile at his niece. "He saw a picture of a smiling little girl with shining curls. She was wearing a plaid silk dress trimmed with crisscross velvet bands and——"

"It was I, Uncle Peter? Wasn't that my daguerreotype?" cried Polly Prence. "I wonder if the Indian knew me."

"Indeed he did, for he seemed very much excited. He passed the picture to Fred, who shook his head, then to Alex, asking, 'Him yours?' Fred also said no. But when the Indian passed the picture to me, I made a great fuss over it. I saw that something about it had excited him.

"He evidently thought that you were my daughter, Polly. From then on we were well treated. The next morning Flying Cloud took us to our wagons. He returned most of our possessions, but he kept the picture. Then he guided us a long way down the trail. We were all much puzzled at his change in manner."

"That was not so strange as it seemed," said Father. "You do not know what a brave little pioneer your niece has become. Polly shall tell you just why your life was spared."

So now it was Polly Prence's turn to tell a story. Everyone agreed that her kindness to the dark-skinned stranger who had come to her door had made this a never-to-be-forgotten Thanksgiving.

Hanukkah

(November or December, usually a short time before Christmas.)

This Jewish holiday, sometimes called the Feast of the Dedication, is also known as the Festival of Lights. It is a joyous festival that begins on the twenty-fifth of Kislev, the third month in the ancient Hebrew calendar, and lasts for eight days. On each of these days children usually re-

ceive a present. Each night a new
candle is lighted, until by the
eighth night eight candles are
blazing like diamonds of light in
the darkness.

This beautiful custom, of
which you will read in the following story, goes back more
than twenty-one hundred years.

Jerusalem had been captured by
enemies who tried to force a
pagan religion on the Jewish
people, but their great warrior
and patriot, Judas Maccabeus,
was finally triumphant. In 165
B.C. he dedicated a new altar in
the Holy Temple to the worship
of the God of Israel.

293

The Festival of Lights

GENEVIEVE FOSTER

Over the Temple and housetops of Jerusalem, over its smoking altar, and its Mount of Zion, a red winter sun was slowly sinking—much too slowly, it seemed to the two children who were watching it that December afternoon in 43 B. C. from the palace of their grandfather, the High Priest, Hyrcanus.

Mariamne, a very beautiful little girl of eleven or twelve, stood quietly leaning against the window frame, her long lashes and heavy dark curls turned to red bronze in the sunlight.

Aristobulus, who was nine and more impatient than his sister, kept turning in his hands a small unlighted torch, and wondering aloud if tomorrow was never going to come!

Half an hour or more the two royal children had been watching and waiting for the sun to disappear behind the dark edge of the city wall and let the new day begin. For each new day began, not at midnight, but at sundown in Jerusalem.

And tomorrow was a Festival! The beginning of Hanukkah! Always in December the Hanukkah, or Festival of Lights, was celebrated by the Jews.

At sundown, as soon as it was dusk, the first one of the eight lamps would be lighted in the Hanukkah lampstand. That was what Aristobulus was waiting for. The next evening, they would light two lamps instead of one. The next, three, and so on, until on the last day, all of the eight branches of the Hanukkah lampstand would be ablaze with light. Lights would be shining out from all the houses in Jerusalem.

The sacred gold lampstand in the Temple had only seven branches, like the seven days of the week or the seven planets in the sky. But the Hanukkah lampstand had eight lights, in memory of the miracle.

According to a legend, that Mariamne and Aristobulus never tired of hearing repeated, a miracle had taken place in the Temple in the days of one of their early ancestors, Judas Maccabeus. It had been

294

on a December day about one hundred years before, when the Greeks instead of the Romans had ruled over Palestine.

The Temple, after being long misused by the Greeks for the worship of one of their many gods, had just been won back again by the Jews and was about to be rededicated to Jahveh, the one and only God of Israel. Everything was ready. The altar had been cleansed and purified. New golden basins had been provided to catch the blood of the lambs, waiting to be sacrificed. The twelve loaves of unleavened bread had been laid on the table in the Holy Place. And there, too, once more, standing like the tree of life, was the great sacred lamp, or candlestick, with its seven branches. It had only to be filled and lighted.

Then, to the dismay of the priests, no pure lamp oil could be found! A frantic search unearthed but one small dusty jar, containing only enough sacred oil to last a single day, but with it the seven cups were filled and lighted. The next day, to the amazement of the priests, it was still burning, and the next. For eight days, it was said, the oil continued to burn. In joy, then, and thanksgiving, Judas Maccabeus had decreed that every year for eight days the miracle should be commemorated with a solemn festival of joy and thanksgiving.

For eight days, therefore, this year, as every year, while the Hanukkah lights were burning, the Temple walls would resound with singing of psalms, and their chorus of Hallel-u-Jah, or "Praise-to-Jahveh," God of Israel . . .

Mariamne and Aristobulus looked up. The sun had suddenly dropped below the western horizon, and it was tomorrow! It was Hanukkah. The first day of the Festival of Lights.

Hanukkah at Valley Forge

EMILY SOLIS-COHEN, JR.

Head down and deep in thought, Judah trudged the snowy path toward home. The icy wind tore at his scarf and tingled his face and fingers, but he was unconscious of the cold. For in two days the Hanukkah Festival would begin. And this was the third season without Father.

His mind flashed back to that morning in April when Father had burst in upon them in the kitchen. Word had just reached Philadelphia of the Battle of Lexington. Judah was only nine then. He wondered why his mother was crying. Father gathered his things hastily, held them both close to him for a long moment, snatched up his rifle and was gone. Mother explained that all the patriots were joining the Continental army to fight for liberty.

And now Father was among the soldiers at Valley Forge, such a short distance away. A furlough was out of the question because the Red Coats were all over Philadelphia.

What could he do? He kicked at the crusted snow. There would be some satisfaction in celebrating in the midst of the enemy. Almost like throwing defiance in their teeth—and King George's, too! Perhaps King George wasn't as wicked as Antiochus the Syrian, whose soldiers had captured the Temple and tried to force the Jewish people to worship heathen idols, but he was a tyrant just the same. As Patrick Henry had said, "He'd better profit by example."

Judah's chest swelled. If the war wasn't won soon, King George would have him to reckon with. His name wasn't Judah for nothing. He was indeed a Lion—and a Maccabee! If only he could be a drummer boy! But Mother wept when he mentioned it. He was all she had—her twelve-year-old man of the house.

He was almost home when the idea came. He would take the lamp to Father—then all the Jewish soldiers could enjoy Hanukkah. It would be a long day's walk to Valley Forge, but he could do it. What about the sentries? If he carried the lamp boldly, right out in full sight, they might think he was visiting somewhere. It was worth chancing. But this year Hanukkah fell on the same day as Christmas. It would rouse suspicion to reach camp then. He would wait until after the Sabbath and Sunday. If he left very early Monday morning he should get there at sundown, in time for the fifth light.

Here was his gate! He opened it, stamped off the snow as he walked up the steps, and lifting his chest, opened the door.

On Monday, December 26, 1777, at Valley Forge, a ragged sentry paced his post. Stooping to adjust the rags that bound one foot, he wondered what it would be like to be warm, really warm, again. The last rays of the sun had disappeared, and the still cold bit through to his very bones. The British soldiers were warm and snug in his town, only twenty miles away. He thought longingly of home. A single star came out. "Tonight they will be lighting the fifth candle, Esther and the boy," he said to himself. "These lights we light because of the miracles, mighty deeds——"

Miracles and mighty deeds! They had won that first great fight of the Jews for religious freedom almost two thousand years ago. How this struggling new nation needed them now! It was hard for men to feel heroic when their stomachs were empty and their bodies cold.

Suddenly he was alert. Shadows were coming near, and he could hear feet crunching through the snow.

"Halt! Who goes there?"

The spokesman was one of their own men. He carried a large bundle wrapped in his own torn coat.

"It's a boy, sentry. We found him in a snowdrift. We're taking him to the nearest cabin."

As they turned to go, the bundle stirred. "The lamp. Where is the lamp?" a weak voice cried.

The sentry's heart skipped a beat. Judah's voice? His son? What had happened? He pulled back the ragged coat that covered the figure.

The boy's eyes opened. "Father? Oh, Father! The lamp—where is it?"

Strength came back to Judah, and he struggled to his feet as his father clasped him roughly. "My son, oh my son!"

In the excitement that followed, the father explained to the soldiers that the boy had brought him the lamp for the special Hanukkah service.

One of the soldiers volunteered to see if the officer of the day would allow an exchange of sentries. At any rate they would keep the boy safe until his father was free. The group moved on again with the boy.

Halt! Officers! General Washington himself was making the rounds.

They explained to him what had happened.

The General listened quietly. "Let the boy come with me. I will order the exchange of sentries. The officer will understand. Tell the father to come to my quarters." He turned to Judah. "So it's come—the feast of the Maccabees?"

Judah nodded weakly as he followed the General inside.

Before long his father came in carrying the lamp. It had been found, one branch thrusting out of the snowdrift where Judah had fallen.

The boy forgot his twelve years and threw his arms about his father. The story poured out in a heap of words. "It has been so long, Father. And I thought all the Jews in camp could celebrate Hanukkah with you, so I brought the lamp!"

The father looked at General Washington. This was unheard-of behavior. But the General recognized boys with spirit. "It's all right, man. He's a son to be proud of. We are all Maccabees here. This boy, too."

Judah looked at the General with wonder in his eyes. "Do you know about it, sir? How Judas drove the tyrant from the land and cleansed the temple? And how the Maccabees threw down the idol?"

Washington nodded, "Yes, Judah. And we have a Temple to cleanse today—the Temple of Liberty. It is that for which we are fighting. Please God we shall soon rekindle its lamp—the light of Freedom. Do go with your father. We must be about our duty."

The father saluted his chief, and father and son went out together.

It was eleven years later. The war had been won; independence was gained; the Temple of Liberty had been cleansed; and the Thirteen States had built a New Roof. That's what folks were calling the Constitution. General Washington had refused a crown, but he had been elected our first President.

His Excellency the President was in Philadelphia receiving a delegation from the Hebrew Congregation. They had come to present him with an address on behalf of the Congregations in the Republic.

Manuel Josephson began to read:

> "Sir:
>
> The wonders which the Lord of Hosts hath worked in the days of our forefathers have taught us to observe the greatness of His wisdom and His might throughout the events of the late glorious revolution. While we humble ourselves at His footstool in thanksgiving and praise for the blessing of His deliverance, we acknowledge you, the leader of the American Armies, as His chosen and beloved servant. But not to your sword alone is our present happiness to be ascribed. That indeed opened the way to the reign of Freedom, but never was it perfectly secure until you helped to give us the Federal Constitution. You renounced the joys of retirement to seal by your administration in peace, what you had achieved in war . . ."

Something stirred in Washington's memory. He glanced at the tall youth standing at attention beside the reader, caught his eye, and looked long again. Now he remembered. Valley Forge! He smiled at the young man. Judah smiled back.

Christmas

(December 25)

The birthday of Jesus is the most joyous holiday in the Christian calendar. We remember the angels' song of peace on earth, good will toward men—a message that was to bring new hope and set a new goal for much of mankind. Christmas was not always observed at the same time, since there was no record of the actual date of Jesus' birth. It was not until 325 A.D. that December 25 was chosen by the Church for the celebration of the Nativity. "A.D." stood for *Anno Domini*, the Latin words for "the Year of Our Lord." Each year in the Christian calendar dates from the year in which Jesus was then believed to have been born.

In America Christmas is not only a religious festival but a time for fun—a time for attending parties, for acting in plays, for singing carols and gay Christmas songs, and for listening to stories about Santa Claus. Christians exchange gifts, in memory of the ones the Wise Men brought the Baby Jesus, though in some countries children must wait until the New Year for their presents.

Since the United States was made up of people who came from other lands, many Christmas customs were brought from far-off places. Some date back to ancient times, long before there was a Christian Church.

Burning a huge log, known as the Yule Log, was a picturesque custom long observed in England. The Druids—Celtic priests of long ago—kept sacred fires going during the darkest season of the year, and they believed that holly and mistletoe were sacred plants. "Yule" was an old Anglo-Saxon word meaning a winter month, and after the coming of Christianity the name was often applied to Christmas. We still decorate our houses with holly and mistletoe and other greens during the "Yuletide" season.

And why do we sing carols? At one time the word "carol" meant "to dance in a ring" to the accompaniment of song, but with the coming of Christianity the songs took on new significance. Songs telling of Jesus' birth and hymns of praise were sung in churches throughout France and Italy. In England, carolers went from house to house on Christmas Eve singing hymns and carols.

Santa Claus has been called by various names—Father Christmas in England, le Père Noël in France, and Kris Kringle in Germany. The Dutch children who came with their parents to New Amsterdam (now New York) more than three hundred years ago talked a great deal about San Nicolaas. That was the Dutch name for St. Nicholas, who had been bishop of Myra, in Asia Minor, in the Fourth century. He was considered the patron saint of children and was believed to bring them presents in December. Boys and girls who had come to the colonies from England listened eagerly to the story but found the Dutch name hard to pronounce, so they changed it to Santa Claus.

Christmas trees are a heritage from Germany. One story tells how Martin Luther, leader of the Protestant Reformation, looked up on his way home from church one starlit Christmas Eve, saw the stars gleaming through the branches of an evergreen tree, and was inspired to light such a tree indoors with candles for his children. Whether or not that is the true explanation, it is certain that Christmas trees have long been a part of the German celebration—a custom that gradually spread to other countries.

The Fir Tree

Retold from
HANS CHRISTIAN ANDERSEN

Once upon a time there was a pretty, green little Fir Tree. The sun shone on him; he had plenty of fresh air; and around him grew many large comrades, pines as well as firs. But the little Fir was not satisfied. He did not think of the sun and the fresh air. He wanted to be a big tree like the others.

Sometimes the little children living in the cottages nearby came into the woods looking for wild strawberries. They ran about, laughing and talking, and often they brought a whole pitcher full of berries, or a long row of them threaded on a straw, and sat down near the young Tree. "Oh, what a nice little Fir!" they said. But the Tree did not like to hear them talk that way. He did not like to be called "little."

By the time he was a year old he had grown a good deal. Another year passed and he was another long bit taller. With a fir tree one can tell by the number of shoots it has how old it is. "Oh, if I were only as tall as the other trees," he thought. "Then I could spread out my branches and look out into the wide world. The birds would build nests in my branches, and when there was a breeze I could bend with a stately bow like the others."

The Tree sighed, taking no pleasure in the sunbeams and the birds and the red clouds which morning and evening sailed above him.

In the wintertime, when the snow lay white and glittering on the ground, a hare would often come leaping along. Sometimes he jumped over the little Tree, and that made him very angry. But by the third winter the Tree had grown so large the hare had to go around it. That made the Tree feel better. "The most delightful thing in the world," he thought, "is to grow and grow and be tall and old."

In autumn the woodcutters came and cut down some of the largest trees. This happened every year and the little Fir Tree, which

304

was not so little any more, was frightened. How he trembled as the magnificent trees fell to the earth with a great noise and crackling. After the branches had been lopped off, the trees looked so long and bare that it was hard to recognize them. Then they were laid in carts, and the horses dragged them out of the woods.

"What becomes of them?" the Fir Tree wondered.

In spring, when the Swallows and the Storks came, the Tree said to them, "Do you know where they have been taken?"

The Swallows did not know anything about it, but one of the Storks nodded his head thoughtfully. "I think I know," he said. "As I was flying hither from Egypt, I met many ships with tall masts and they smelt of fir. You may feel proud of them, so majestic did they look."

"If I were only old enough to fly across the ocean!" sighed the Tree. "How does the ocean look? What is it like?"

"That would take a long time to explain," said the Stork, and off he flew.

"Rejoice in thy youth!" said the Sunbeams. "Rejoice in thy growth!" And the Wind kissed the Tree, and the Dew wept tears over him; but the Fir did not understand.

When Christmas came, many young trees were cut down. Some of them were neither so large nor so old as the Fir Tree, but they were always the finest looking. Their branches were left on them when they were laid carefully on the carts, and the horses drew them out of the woods.

"They are no taller than I," complained the Fir Tree. "Indeed one of them was much shorter. Why are they allowed to keep all their branches? Where are they going?"

"We know! We know!" twittered the Sparrows. "We have peeped in at the windows in the town below! We saw the trees planted in the middle of the warm rooms and ornamented with the most splendid things—with gilded apples, with gingerbread, with toys and hundreds of lights!"

A tremor ran through the Fir Tree. "And then? What happens after that?"

"We did not see anything more, but it was very beautiful."

"Ah, perhaps I shall know the same brightness some day," the Tree rejoiced. "That would be better than to cross the ocean. If Christmas would only come! I am as tall as the trees that were carried off last year. My branches spread as far. Oh, if I were only on the cart now! If I were only in the warm room with all the splendor and magnificence! Something better, something still grander, is sure to follow—but what? How I long; how I suffer! I wonder what is the matter with me!"

"Rejoice in us!" said the Air and the Sunlight. "Rejoice in thy own youth!"

But the Tree did not rejoice. He grew and grew. He was green both winter and summer. "What a fine tree!" people said, and toward Christmas he was one of the first to be cut down. The ax struck deep, and the Tree fell to earth with a sigh. He was not happy; he could only think how sad it was to be taken away from the place where he had sprung up. He knew that never again would he see his dear old comrades, the little bushes and flowers around him; perhaps he would never even see the birds again. And he didn't like it at all.

The Tree was laid on a cart with several others and taken away. When he came to himself again he was being unloaded in a big yard, and two servants in handsome livery carried him into a large and beautiful drawing room. Here there were portraits hanging on the walls and, near the white porcelain stove, two big Chinese vases with lions on the covers. There were big easy chairs, silken cushions and tables filled with picture books and toys. The Fir Tree was stuck upright in a tub filled with sand; but it did not look like a tub, for green cloth was hung all around it and it stood on a large, bright carpet.

A tremor ran through the Tree. What was going to happen? Several young ladies decorated it, aided by the servants. On one branch they hung little nets made of colored paper and filled with sugarplums. On the other boughs they hung gilded apples and walnuts, which looked as though they had grown there. Then little blue and white and red candles were fastened to the branches. In the foliage there were dolls that looked like people—the Tree had never seen anything like them before—and at the very top there was a large star of gold tinsel. It was really splendid—too splendid for any words to describe.

"Just wait till evening!" everybody said. "How the Tree will shine this evening!"

"Oh, if evening would only come!" thought the Tree. "If the candles were only lighted! What will happen then, I wonder. Will the other trees from the forest come to look at me? Will the Sparrows beat against the windowpanes? Perhaps I shall take root and stand here winter and summer covered with ornaments!" He grew so impatient that he got a pain in his bark, and this with trees is the same as a headache with us.

When at last the candles were lighted, there was such brightness, such splendor, that the Tree trembled in every bough. One of the candles set fire to the foliage, and it blazed up splendidly.

"Help! Help!" cried the young ladies and rushed to put out the fire.

After that the Tree did not dare tremble. He was quite bewildered by the glare and the brightness. Suddenly both the folding doors opened, and in rushed the children, with the older persons following more quietly. The little ones stood quite still, but only for a moment. Then they shouted for joy, and the room echoed with their shouts. They began dancing around the Tree, pulling off one present after another.

"What are they doing?" thought the Tree. "What is to happen now?"

The candles burned down to the very branches, and as they burned down they were put out, one after another. Then the children were given permission to plunder the Tree, and they rushed upon it so violently that all its branches cracked. Then the children went on playing with their beautiful toys. No one even looked at the Tree, except the old nurse, who peeped in among the branches to see if there was a fig or an apple that had been overlooked.

"A story! A story!" the children cried, dragging a little fat man over toward the Tree. He sat down under it and said, "Now the Tree can listen, too. I shall tell you only one story, so which will you have: the one about Ivedy-Avedy, or the one about Klumpy-Dumpy who fell downstairs and yet married the princess and came to the throne after all?"

"Ivedy-Avedy!" cried some. "Klumpy-Dumpy!" cried others. There was a great deal of squealing, and finally the man told about Klumpy-Dumpy and the children clapped their hands and cried, "Go on! Go on!" The Fir Tree stood quite still, thinking: "Who knows? Perhaps I shall fall downstairs, too, and marry a princess!" And he looked forward to the next day, when he hoped to be decked out again with lights and toys and bright tinsel.

"I won't tremble tomorrow," he thought. "Tomorrow I shall hear again the story of Klumpy-Dumpy and perhaps that of Ivedy-Avedy, too." And all night long the Tree stood quite still, thinking.

The next morning in came the servants.

"Ah, now the splendor will begin again!" thought the Fir.

But no. The servants dragged him out of the room, up the stairs into the attic and there, in a dark corner, they left him. "What can this mean?" wondered the Tree, and he leaned against the wall lost in thought. And he had plenty of time for thinking. Days and nights passed and nobody came near him. When at last somebody did come up to the attic, it was only to leave some trunks. There stood the Tree quite hidden. There stood the Tree quite forgotten.

"It is winter out-of-doors!" he thought. "The earth is hard and covered with snow. I could not be planted now. These people are really very kind. They have put me up here under shelter until spring comes! If only it were not so dark and lonely here! Not even a hare! I liked it out in the woods when the snow was on the ground and the hare leaped by; yes, even when he jumped over me. Ah, but I did not like it then."

"Squeak, squeak!" said a little Mouse, peeping out of his hole. Then another little Mouse came and they sniffed at the Fir Tree and ran in and out among the branches.

"It is dreadfully cold," said the Mouse. "Except for that, it would be nice here, wouldn't it, old Fir?"

"I am not old," said the Fir Tree. "There is many a tree much older than I."

"Where do you come from?" asked the Mice. "Tell us about the most beautiful place in the world. Have you ever been there? Have you ever been in the larder where there are cheeses lying on the shelves and hams hanging from the ceiling, where one may dance on tallow candles; a place where one goes in lean and comes out fat?"

"I know of no such place," said the Tree. "But I know the woods where the sun shines and the birds sing." Then he told of the time when he was young, and the little Mice had never heard the like before.

"How much you have seen!" they said. "How happy you must have been!"

"I?" said the Fir Tree, thinking it over. "Yes, those really were happy times." Then he told about Christmas Eve, when he had been decked out with beautiful ornaments and candles.

"Oh," said the little Mice. "How lucky you have been, old Fir Tree."

"I am not old," said he. "I came from the woods only this winter."

"But what wonderful stories you know!" said the Mice, and the next night they came with four other little Mice who wanted to hear the stories also. The more the Fir Tree talked about his youth, the more plainly he remembered it himself, and he realized that those times had really been very happy times. "But they may come again. Klumpy-Dumpy fell downstairs and yet he married a princess," said the Fir Tree. And at that moment he remembered a little birch tree growing out in the woods. To the Fir she seemed like a princess.

"Who is Klumpy-Dumpy?" asked the Mice. So the Fir Tree told the story, and the little Mice were so pleased they jumped to the very top of the Tree. The next night two more Mice came, and on Sunday two Rats. But they said the stories were not interesting. This worried the little Mice. They began to think the stories not very interesting either.

"Is that the only story you know?" asked the Rats.

"Only that one," said the Tree. "I heard it on the happiest night of my life; only then I did not know how happy I was."

"It's a silly story. Don't you know one about bacon and tallow candles? Can't you tell any larder stories?"

"No," said the Tree.

"Then good-by," said the Rats and went home.

At last the little Mice stopped coming, and the Tree sighed. "After all I liked having the sleek little Mice listen to my stories, but that is over now. When I am brought out again I am going to enjoy myself."

But when was that to be? Why, one morning a number of people came up to the attic. Trunks were moved and the Tree was pulled out and thrown down on the floor. Then a man drew him toward the stairs, where the sun shone.

"Now life begins again," thought the Tree. He felt the fresh air, the first sunbeam—and then he was out in the yard. Everything happened so quickly he quite forgot to look to himself. The yard was right next to a garden where fragrant roses hung over the fence and lindens were in bloom. The Swallows flew by and said, "Quirre-vit! My husband is come!" But it was not the Fir Tree that they meant.

"Now I shall enjoy life," said he joyfully, and spread out his branches. But alas, they were all withered and yellow. He lay in a corner among weeds and nettles. The golden tinsel star was still on the Tree, and it glittered in the sunlight.

In the yard some children were playing—the same children who had danced around the Fir Tree at Christmas time. They were glad to see him again, and the youngest child ran up and tore off the golden star.

"Look, what is still on the ugly old Christmas tree!" said he. And he trampled on the branches, so that they cracked beneath his feet.

The Tree looked at the beautiful garden and then at himself. He wished he had stayed in his dark corner in the loft. He thought of his youth in the woods, of the merry Christmas Eve, and of the little Mice who had listened so eagerly to the story of Klumpy-Dumpy.

" 'Tis over," said the poor Tree. "Had I but been happy when I had reason to be! But 'tis all over now."

Then the gardener's boy chopped the Tree into small pieces, and the wood flamed up splendidly under a brown kettle.

The children went on playing in the yard. On his chest the youngest wore the gold star which the Tree had worn on the happiest evening of his life. But that was over now—the Tree gone, the story finished. Every tale must come to an end at last.

Don Pedro's Christmas

ERIC P. KELLY

Madre Marta had said at dinner that Don Pedro simply couldn't go to the midnight Christmas Eve service with Lolla.

"But Don Pedro is good," declared Lolla. "He works all the time and I don't know what I'd do without him. I would just tie him outside near the door. I know he would be quiet."

"Well," said her mother finally, "take him along if you must."

Lolla's face was radiant. To be sure, remaining outside the church wasn't so good as being inside, but Don Pedro would be able to hear the music and the sermon and the bells.

She ran out from the square little adobe dwelling and hurried to find her pet, who was calmly eating dried grass.

"My good little burro," she exclaimed, throwing her arms around the shaggy neck, "I just couldn't go to church without you."

Don Pedro said nothing, but continued to eat. His tail, however, flicked merrily and his eyes twinkled, at least so it seemed to Lolla. Certainly, his ears twitched.

On both sides of the little New Mexican valley, the land rose sharply to high mesas, red in places, in others gray, slopes packed with gravel and small stones. Through its midst ran the tiny river, at the moment nearly dry in an unusually warm December, but with a bed that was many times the width of the stream. For there were times when cloudburst or sudden melting of ice in the hills above La Madeira spread its bosom and raised the sluggish current to torrential force. Off in the distance the mountains of the Sangre de Cristo

Range cut the sky, while up and down stream small adobe houses like their own, adorned with strings of brilliant chili peppers, stood out against the now bare cottonwoods and the brown fields where crops had been.

For four of Lolla's nine years, Don Pedro, the prince of little burros, had been her friend, companion, brother almost, for on those nights when a light layer of snow whirled down from the peaks she had led him inside the house, and he had folded up his legs and lain on the floor beside her cot. In the day she often went with him up on the mesas when her father gathered wood and bound it on the faithful creature's back in a neat round bundle. Sometimes she sat astride him and galloped across the mesas or climbed laboriously foot by foot up the incline leading away from the river. She was more fortunate than he, because she could express her love to him in words, while he had only ears to twitch in fond signs.

And now it was the day before Christmas, and the hot afternoon was wearing on. "If the heat goes on," her father had said that very morning, "snow will melt in the hills, and then look out for the river. And I'm not too sure about our bridge if the water rises. Part of the foundation was washed out last summer, and it's leaning badly."

By night the heat had not abated. They sat down to supper in the little room where they ate, lived, and slept, attired in light clothes, just as in summer. The father had on his best clothes, a yellow coat and blue trousers. The mother had a print dress from Santa Fe. Lolla wore her gown that a friend had sent her from a store—white, with pictures upon it of burros and men with large hats and women with veils and shawls over their heads.

All at once night was upon them. They had eaten early and lightly in preparation for the midnight service, but night comes swiftly in a New Mexican winter, the day leaping away over the mountain tops with the red, sinking sun, and darkness coming up from valleys and canyons to engulf the world. Now the evening star blazed in the sky, and Lolla, running to the door, exclaimed, "The Star! The Star. It's Christmas!"

Then suddenly she looked about perplexed. "I don't see Don Pedro." The light through the open door showed only the end of his rope.

"He didn't come back today. It's so warm. He's eating dried

grass," said the mother. "But there isn't time to look for him. We'll have to get started soon."

"I'm going to look for him," said Lolla determinedly.

"You can if you want to. Your father and I are getting started." Those pre-service minutes were very valuable to Madre Marta, for in them she met her neighbors and talked over everything of interest that had gone on during the week.

It wasn't very far from the house to the church, just down the road and over the bridge and about half a mile up to the small, steepled building that had stood there since 1590. As Lolla had been over this route a hundred times or more in the dark, her mother had no fear for her.

So in a few minutes the older members of the family set out. They went on foot, not owning a horse or automobile. Many of the Spanish families in the valleys had cars, most of them old, but all serviceable.

As the parents reached the bridge they saw the headlights of more than a dozen of these bobbing their way toward it, and as they crossed they had to be careful to keep well to one side to give the cars the right of way.

The bridge was not of the best construction, even when it had been new; it was narrow and rough, and the recent floods had loosened the underpinnings on one side so that it slanted badly.

At one point, the father looked down at the dark stream. "It's getting higher," he said as the reflection from a passing car lit up the icy water. "We'll have to be careful of this bridge. It'll go down sometime. Then we shall have to use the rougher road to the other bridge downstream."

In the meantime Lolla had roamed up and down the valley looking for the burro.

"Don Pedro. Don Pedro," she called. With every call echoes came back to her from the slanting mesa sides, but there was no sound of scampering feet, no burro voice raised in a deafening bray.

She had searched for more than an hour when she decided to give up hunting and go to the church. It would be such a pity to waste time while the Padre was there—dear old Padre Jose, the priest from Espanola, so kind, so gentle, with such a nice voice and nice hands. She loved him, she thought, almost as much as she did Don

Pedro, and that was a whole lot. Her mother had left a lantern for her beside the door. She took this up and started on her way.

As she was on the bridge, it seemed to her that it swayed more than usual. Turning to one side, she lowered the lantern a little over the rail and then sprang back in fright. The water was very high. How black it was, how swift, how silent!

Usually when the river rose there was a roar that filled the valley; the whole flood came at once. That was usually after a cloudburst. But now the stream came rushing on with mighty force and yet making little noise. It had, as a matter of fact, risen slowly. The melting ice up above had added gradually to its torrent. The river was still rising!

She hurried on, anxious now to get to the other side. But just as she was on the last little span she stopped suddenly, and her heart began to beat swiftly. Something was moving at the river's edge, and it was not ice.

At the end of the structure, where it slanted down to the road, she sat down and swung her lantern out. What a curious noise. For a moment she could see nothing. She called out. The noise ceased.

All was silent again except the rushing of the river and the crackle of small particles of ice on its surface. Deep silence lay all about the hills and the village. There was nothing to be seen, either, except for the small circle of light from her lantern.

"Who are you?" she called again.

Then without warning came the explosive, raucous accents of a burro.

"Don Pedro," she stopped in her tracks. "He's under the bridge. What shall I do to help him?"

The impulse to action gripped her. Running down the slope she turned to the right and descended the bank to the water's edge. Raising the lantern, she held it out as far as she could, and there not five feet away were a little brown tail and a pair of sturdy legs.

"He's stuck in the mud. Don Pedro!"

It came to her immediately to run for help. But then she realized that all the houses along the road were deserted. Everybody was up in the church.

So, acting on impulse, she waded out into the rising river. It was not very deep here, and the bed was all hard gravel and large stones. Her mind was so set on extricating her burro that she did not notice that the water was icy cold. Don Pedro was in the river, and some way she must get him out.

"Don Pedro, Don Pedro, I'm coming," she cried, and at the sound of her voice the brown tail began to flip.

It was impossible to get much farther. The gravel was slanting off into soft clay. To reach his head and try to urge him to back up was out of the question. She hung her lantern where its feeble gleams threw a pale light on the scene.

Then, deeper in the water, she seized her pet's tail in both hands and tugged with all her might. "Don Pedro! Kick," she commanded. "Kick as hard as you can, Don Pedro."

There was a violent effort, and one leg came clear. "That's it!" she said. "That's it. Try again." She threw her whole weight into the force of the pull.

Splash. His front feet were out of the mire. "Now——" He reared up as burros will rear and swung in a half circle. Another splash. Then suddenly by her side in the dim light the little burro went plunging up the bank.

As Lolla turned to wade toward the shore, the feeble light disclosed something that made her gasp. She had not noticed it before, for she had been so intent upon Pedro. Grasping the lantern, she turned and hurried back to the shore.

"Don Pedro. Don Pedro," she called, and he came up. Leaving the lantern on the bridge in the hope that its feeble rays might serve as a temporary warning to travelers, she flung herself upon his back. "Go, Don Pedro. Go. Quick as you can."

They were off over the rutty road, with all the speed the little burro possessed. Surefootedly he kept to the even places.

In the old church good Padre Jose had just completed a talk to the inhabitants of the villages who had come in for the midnight service. He had told them in his kind, firm voice, full of the philosophy of experience and knowledge, what the joys of Christmas Day meant to the world. Of the Child born in the manger in Bethlehem and the Wise Men and shepherds, people like themselves, who had followed the Star.

The place was crowded. Suddenly, in the back of the church, there was the sound of voices, exclamations. The rear door swung wide open, and Padre Jose looked down the narrow aisle and gasped in astonishment.

For through the door and up the aisle, scattering the men in the rear of the church and the children clustering about against the walls, came, of all things, a little burro. He was soggy and wet, his hair was dripping, and the mud was thick about his forelegs.

"What is this?" Padre Jose was indignant. "Such disturbance in a church!"

But as the burro came up the aisle, almost to the steps leading to the altar rail, he saw that riding on his back was a small girl. She was as disheveled as the burro. But her eyes were shining with purpose.

"Padre Jose," she cried. "The upper bridge is all washed out at the bottom. If anybody goes over it in an automobile, it will fall. People will be killed. Don't let them, Padre Jose."

The priest's expression changed. He instantly caught the force of the child's purpose. "You have just come from there?" he asked.

"Yes, Padre Jose."

The whole congregation had now risen to its feet in alarm. All thoughts were on the girl's words.

Still sitting on Don Pedro's back she blurted out the whole story—how the burro had wandered into the river, how she had gone to get him out, how she had seen one foundation of the bridge so badly washed that it was likely to topple at any moment. As she finished, Padre Jose came down from the steps and touched the little animal with tender hands.

"God works in ways that we know not of," he said. "Go, Juan and Mario. Take lanterns and guard the old bridge. And we who remain here, let us join in a prayer of thanksgiving that perhaps lives have been saved through this little burro." He smiled down at Lolla. "Welcome, my child. Your lateness was in a good cause."

Lolla had slipped from Don Pedro's back and knelt in the aisle. As if sensing the place, and being, moreover, tired, Don Pedro lay down at full length. As the service went on and Lolla's heart quieted, she glanced at the animal lying beside her. Lovingly, she scratched the fuzzy little head. She remembered another little burro in a story that she loved.

He has a right to be here on Christmas Eve, she thought happily.

Christmas in the Street of Memories

ELIZABETH RHODES JACKSON

The Prince and Princess live with Mr. Lifsky on the street floor, and we live on the next floor, and old Mrs. Lavendar lives on the top floor.

We first got acquainted with Mrs. Lavendar by accident. The accident happened to Beany.

There are three of us. Jack is my older brother and Beany is my younger brother. I am Dee, and I am eleven.

We live on one of the oldest streets in Boston, at the foot of Beacon Hill. The houses have alleys at the back or through their cellars, and we play tag in them. The alleys all run into each other and make a sort of maze. You run up an alley and climb over a couple of fences and down another alley and through a gate and there you are in another street. We were all playing one day after school, and Beany went to climb a fence and fell, right on his face. Beany would, you know. He's always the one of us that has the falls. He bruised his forehead and skinned his nose. He was very brave about it and didn't cry, although the tears were in his eyes.

We took him home, Jack and I, but when we took Beany upstairs to our landing, the door was locked and Mother was out. Beany had been brave so long that he couldn't wait any longer, and while I was fumbling in the regular place for the key, he burst out into a long, sad wail. Then a lady on the floor above, who was a stranger to us, leaned over the banister and said, "Bring him up to me."

Her apartment was very lovely with beautiful old furniture and soft, thick rugs on the floor and huge silver candlesticks on the mantel. But there was no fire in the fireplace, though the day was cold, and she had on a beautiful white silk shawl with an embroidered border. She took Beany on her lap and washed the dirt off his face very gently. Then she held him in her arms and we sat on the rug, and she told us about her son when he was a little boy.

That was how we got acquainted with Mrs. Lavendar. And that was the way we came to find the Prince and the Princess.

Mother calls the street we live on the Street of Memories for two reasons. One is that memories of the past are still living there. Two blocks from our house, at the corner of Boston Common, is the spot where the British soldiers embarked the night that Paul Revere got ahead of them on his famous ride. Two blocks the other way Oliver Wendell Holmes used to live. And Miss Alcott walked on our street many and many a time. I love to walk up the hill to see the little brick dwelling where she and her sister kept house—Jo and Amy—in their struggling days, and on the way home I pass the stately mansion (Dr. Holmes said that in "The Chambered Nautilus"), where she lived when she was successful and famous.

The other reason Mother calls it the Street of Memories is because of the antique shops all up and down the street. Some of them are very artistic, with nothing but two colonial chairs and a table in the window. But we like best the ones that have the windows crowded full of new and interesting things. Mr. Lifsky's is like that, on the street floor of our house. His show window is just jammed with three ship models and some colored bottles, and a battered old lantern, and andirons and silhouettes in tiny frames and an inlaid snuffbox and a pair of china dogs and a luster tea set, and hanging up are old engravings and faded samplers.

We were all three looking into Mr. Lifsky's window one day when Mrs. Lavendar came out and saw us there. We knew her very well by that time.

"Mrs. Lavendar, do see this ship's model," said Jack.

"It looks like all sorts of adventures," she said, and then she caught her breath a little.

"How long have those been here?" she said. "I haven't seen them before."

She was pointing to a pair of china figures, a lady and gentleman in elaborate old-fashioned dress. The lady had wide skirts and high, powdered hair and flowers on her breast, and the gentleman had a ruffled shirt and knee breeches and buckled shoes. They were tiny but very perfect and delicate, and the faces were exquisitely beautiful.

"I'm sure those are mine," said Mrs. Lavendar very low. Then she walked into Mr. Lifsky's shop.

"She's going in to buy them," we said, but presently she came out without them.

We told Mother about it. "Why do you think she didn't buy them?" asked Jack.

"Probably Mr. Lifsky's price was too high," said Mother.

"Oh, but Mrs. Lavendar is rich," said Beany. "You ought to see her beautiful apartment."

"I'm afraid not," said Mother. "She used to have a great deal of money, but now she is old and poor and alone. Her son gave up his life in the war, you know."

"I wonder if that is why she hasn't a fire in the fireplace," I said, for we often went up to see her now, and her apartment was usually cold. Of course, the house is supposed to be heated from the cellar, but we always have two log fires going in winter to help out. Our house is a beautiful old residence that has been made over into apartments, so the plumbing and heating are old-fashioned and often cause us trouble.

A week later we had cold weather. Cold weather in Boston is *very* cold. I don't believe even the North Pole is any colder than the Street of Memories in winter!

"I was going to suggest your going up to see Mrs. Lavendar," said Mother, when we came home from school, "but it is so cold, perhaps you'd better take a fire with you."

I followed her up the stairs and heard her saying, "Mrs. Lavendar, would it bother you if the children made a little call?"

"I'd love to have them," said Mrs. Lavendar, "only I'm afraid the room is rather cold. I can't seem to get enough heat."

"It's a frightful heating system, isn't it?" said Mother. "We've had to have a hearthfire today. Jack will bring up some wood, if you don't mind the litter."

So, soon we were on the way up, Jack with a basket of logs and

Beany carrying the paper bag of kindling and I with the hearth brush. Beany, poor child, tripped over the rug and dropped the bag, which split open, but Mrs. Lavendar was very nice about it, and I swept up the debris and it was all right. Jack made a glorious fire and we were very cozy. Knowing Mother, I suspect she planned the whole thing just to get Mrs. Lavendar warm.

While we were all sitting there as happy as could be, Beany suddenly spoke up. Beany too frequently says things he shouldn't, and what he said this time was, "Mrs. Lavendar, how did your china figures come to be in Mr. Lifsky's antique shop?"

We tried to hush him, but Mrs. Lavendar said, "I sold all the furnishings of my house some years ago, except what I have here, and the little Prince and Princess went with the rest."

"Are they a Prince and Princess?" I asked.

"That was the name my boy had for them when he was little." And somehow, from the way she said it, I knew that she missed the little china figures.

Then Beany piped up again. "Why did you have to sell your furniture, Mrs. Lavendar, when you have so much money?"

We couldn't hush him at all, but Mrs. Lavendar understood and she only smiled and said, "I haven't much money, dear. I had some, but it was taken from me. So I had to sell the furniture to get money to live on."

"How was it taken?" said Beany, all interest.

"It isn't a very pleasant story," said Mrs. Lavendar. "My investments were in a business that could not go on until the war was over."

Beany nodded, though he didn't understand. We did partly.

"My son's salary was enough for us till he went to war. Then we planned to sell our house and invest the money to take care of me till he came back."

"I see," said Beany.

"My son came in with the money from the sale one afternoon. He wouldn't take a check because sometimes checks can't be collected. He went to the bank with the man who bought the house, and the man drew the money in bills and gave it to him—forty thousand dollars. It was too late to take the money to my bank for deposit that day, so he brought it home to me, and it was taken that same day."

"Who took it?" we said together.

"I never knew," said Mrs. Lavendar. "Not the servants. They had been with me for years. Someone must have come in—but I don't know how. It has always been a mystery."

"Where was it?" we asked.

"In the Governor Winthrop desk," said old Mrs. Lavendar. "That very desk there against the wall. My son said, 'I'll put it in here, Mother.' I saw him with his hand on the open leaf of the desk. I said, 'Yes, that's a perfectly safe place.' I went out to see my son off then, and I was so confused and troubled over parting with him, that I forgot to lock it. And when I went to get the money the next day to take it to the bank, it was not there."

"This very desk!" said Jack. We were all very much excited, for we knew that some of those old desks have secret drawers and false backs to the pigeonholes. It seemed perfectly clear to us that there was forty thousand dollars somewhere inside that solid square old piece of mahogany, and if we could find it, Mrs. Lavendar would be rich again. We told her so excitedly, but she shook her head.

"I've known this desk all my life, dear," she said. "It was my great-grandfather's. I know every nook and corner of it. It has no secrets."

"May we look through it?" we said. "We might be able to find *something*."

Of course, Mrs. Lavendar let us, and we took out all the papers and the drawers, and measured and tapped and pushed to find secret springs. But we had to give it up at last. If the money was still there, hidden in some secret place, it was too successfully hidden for us to find.

I noticed that the beautiful silver candlesticks were not on the mantel, and Mrs. Lavendar was wearing a little black sweater instead of the embroidered shawl. I was afraid Beany would notice and ask if she had to sell them, too, but he was too interested in the desk to ask questions about anything else.

For several days we talked about the money and then we forgot all about it for a while, because of Christmas. We were busy as could be, writing our Christmas wants and making things and counting our savings and going shopping for presents after school. We all painted cards for Mrs. Lavendar, of course, and it was while we were doing this one snowy day, that I said, "Oh dear, I wish we could buy the

Prince and Princess and give them to Mrs. Lavendar for Christmas!"

"That's just like you, Dee," said Jack. "One of those brilliant ideas that there's no way of carrying out!"

I knew he didn't mean that to sound unpleasant. It was just that he wanted so much to do it and didn't see how we could.

"Let's ask Mr. Lifsky how much they are, anyway!" said Beany.

Beany is always so hopeful. Jack and I knew it was useless, because we had already spent all our money for Christmas. But Beany went down to ask Mr. Lifsky and came back soon to tell us.

"Seven dollars and fifty cents." He said it just as cheerfully as if we had seven dollars and fifty cents right there.

And then something very unexpected happened. We were playing tag in the back alley a few days later and by mistake we tipped over an ash barrel. When we went to pick up the junk we had spilled, we found some old bundles of letters tied with faded ribbon and photographs and some good camera films. Someone had just moved out of the house, and there was no one there but a cleaning woman. We showed her the films and asked if we could have them, and she said we could have anything we found in the back yard, but we must clean up any rubbish we spilled. There were four or five barrels in the yard and we dumped them all out, one after another, and found a number of very worthwhile articles. But the really worthwhile thing was two filled books of trading stamps, and when we saw those, we knew, after all, that there was hope of our buying the Prince and Princess.

We took the stamps home to Mother and she said they were worth two dollars for each book and that it would be all right for Jack to go and get the money for them, as otherwise they would be burned for rubbish. So while Jack hurried off across the Common to the department stores, Beany spied a row of store milk bottles, and we gathered those up and took them back to the chain store. There were twenty-one of them, and that gave us a dollar and five cents, so when Jack came back with the trading stamp money, we had five dollars and five cents altogether.

"Perhaps Mr. Lifsky would come down," said Jack. "People always do bargain for antiques, you know."

So we took the five one-dollar bills and the nickel and showed them to Mr. Lifsky. We told him that was all the money we had and asked if he would sell us the pair of china figures. We couldn't pay another cent for them.

"For fife tollars und fife cents you ask it!" said Mr. Lifsky indignantly. "Ten times ofer could I sell them little fickures for fife tollars und fife cents! Seven-fifty ist mine brice, und not one cent less than fife-fifty."

"We haven't got five-fifty," said Jack.

"Fife-fifty!" Mr. Lifsky said again, so we went out to talk it over.

"We almost have it," said Jack. "Only forty-five cents. Let's all think hard."

So we all thought hard. But it was Beany who thought of asking Mother to advance forty-five cents of our pocket money. There was a great shout of joy from us all when he came back with it. We went right in to Mr. Lifsky's and bought the Prince and Princess. They were a little bit dusty, and Jack thought we ought to put them into the bathtub and wash them. But Mother thought not, because we might chip them or wash off the color, and Mrs. Lavendar would know best how to clean them. Then we started to wrap them in Christmas paper, but we were afraid that Mrs. Lavendar might break them in opening them. Besides it would be more fun to have her see them right away, the minute she opened the door.

Jack wanted to be the one to carry the Prince and I wanted to carry the Princess, and Beany felt very bad about it.

"It's just because I'm the youngest," he said. "I have to take turns with you filling the wood-basket and going to the store, but no one ever takes turns with me being the youngest. I thought how to get the last forty-five cents, anyway. And Mrs. Lavendar was my friend first."

So we told him he could be the one to say, "Merry Christmas, Mrs. Lavendar; we've brought you a present." So it was settled.

Christmas Eve is very beautiful on Beacon Hill. All the houses are lighted with candles in every window, and the curtains are drawn back so that everyone can see the inside. The houses are all very beautiful to see, too, because most of them were built in early days and have winding staircases and paneled walls, and many of them have beautiful tapestries and paintings. A great crowd comes from all over Boston, so that you can hardly move through the streets, but everyone is quiet and reverent. It is almost like church outdoors, especially after the carols begin. Mother always takes us out for a little while, after we have lighted the candles in our own windows.

This Christmas Eve we asked Mrs. Lavendar to go out with us, but she thought she might get too tired. So when we came back, we three sang carols just for her—"Silent Night, Holy Night" and "The First Noël"—looking up at the candles in her windows.

It is such an exciting feeling to wake on Christmas morning and see the stockings all humpy. But this Christmas I had a specially joyous feeling, and I remembered we were going to take the Prince and Princess to Mrs. Lavendar.

Right after breakfast we went upstairs, Jack carrying the Prince and I carrying the Princess, just as we had planned. But halfway upstairs I caught a glimpse of Beany's face. He had a mark across his chin where the grocer's cat had scratched him when he tried to pet her, and he had such a sad look that I was sorry for him. It must be hard to be the youngest. So I said, "Here, Beany, you take her," and gave him the Princess.

We got to the top of the stairs and Jack looked around and saw how it was, and he said, "Oh, well," and he put the Prince into my hands. So after all it was Jack who lifted the brass knocker and said, "Merry Christmas, Mrs. Lavendar; we've brought you a present."

But when she saw the Prince and Princess, she said, "Oh, you dear children!" very softly.

Then she said, "Their home is on the desk, dears, one on each side of my son's picture." I walked across the room and put the Prince on the desk very carefully, and Beany came next.

But then Beany slipped and down he came—crash!—on the floor. Beany *would!*

Mrs. Lavendar stooped over the pieces.

"I am sure we can mend the Princess," she was saying, and then she gasped and picked up something from under the pieces.

It was a roll of bills that had been inside the hollow Princess.

"The money was not taken," she said slowly. "It was there all the time."

She sat down and her hands were trembling.

"I begin to understand," she said. "My son was standing by the desk. I never thought of the Princess. But of course he would put it there. From the time he was a baby he used to stow all sorts of little treasures through that hole in the base. He thought that I saw him putting it there and that no one else would know."

We had a great rejoicing after that, and since then Mrs. Lavendar hasn't gone out to do sewing any more. The silver candlesticks are back on the mantel and she wears the white silk shawl and has a fire, too, on cold days. And she has mended the Princess with china cement so you can't see the cracks at all unless you get up very close.

The Christmas Spider
A Polish Folk Tale

Retold by
MARGUERITE DE ANGELI

The gray spider worked very hard every day making long strands of silk that he wove into a web in which he caught troublesome flies. But he noticed that everyone turned away from him because, they said, he was so unpleasant to look at with his long, crooked legs and furry body. Of course the gray spider didn't believe that, because he had only the kindliest feelings for everybody. One day when he was crossing the stream he looked into the water. There he saw himself as he really was.

"Oh," he thought, "I am very unpleasant to look at. I shall keep out of people's way." He was very sad and hid himself in the darkest corner of the stable. There he again began to work as he always had, weaving long strands of silk into webs and catching flies. The donkey and the ox and the sheep who lived in the stable thanked him for his kindness, because now they were no longer bothered with the buzzing flies. That made the spider happy.

One night, exactly at midnight, the spider was awakened by a brilliant light. He looked about and saw that the light came from the manger where a tiny Child lay on the hay. The stable was filled with glory, and over the Child bent a beautiful mother. Behind her stood a man with a staff in his hand, and the ox and the donkey and all the white sheep were down on their knees.

Suddenly a gust of cold wind swept through the stable and the Baby began to weep from the cold. The mother bent over Him but could not cover Him enough to keep Him warm. The little spider took his silken web and laid it at Mary's feet (for it was Mary) and Mary took up the web and covered the Baby with it. It was soft as thistledown and as warm as wool. The Child stopped his crying and smiled at the little gray spider.

Then Mary said, "Little gray spider, for this great gift to the Babe you may have anything you wish."

"Most of all," said the spider, "I wish to be beautiful."

"That I cannot give you," Mary answered. "You must stay as you are for as long as you live. But this I grant you: Whenever any one sees a spider at evening, he will count it a good omen, and it shall bring him good fortune."

This made the spider very happy, and to this day, on Christmas Eve, we cover the Christmas Tree with "angel's hair" in memory of the little gray spider and his silken web.

(This selection is taken from *Up the Hill.*)

The First Christmas

from the Gospel
according to St. Luke and St. Matthew
King James Version

And it came to pass in those days, that there went out a decree from Caesar Augustus, that all the world should be taxed.

And all went to be taxed, every one into his own city.

And Joseph also went up from Galilee, out of the city of Nazareth, into Judaea, unto the city of David, which is called Bethlehem; (because he was of the house and lineage of David:)

To be taxed with Mary his espoused wife, being great with child.

And so it was that, while they were there, the days were accomplished that she should be delivered.

And she brought forth her firstborn son, and wrapped him in swaddling clothes, and laid him in a manger; because there was no room for them in the inn.

And there were in the same country shepherds abiding in the field, keeping watch over their flock by night.

And, lo, the angel of the Lord came upon them, and the glory of the Lord shone round about them: and they were sore afraid.

And the angel said unto them, Fear not: for, behold, I bring you good tidings of great joy, which shall be to all people.

For unto you is born this day in the city of David a Saviour, which is Christ the Lord.

And this shall be a sign unto you; Ye shall find the babe wrapped in swaddling clothes, lying in a manger.

And suddenly there was with the angel a multitude of the heavenly host praising God, and saying,

Glory to God in the highest, and on earth peace, good will toward men.

And it came to pass, as the angels were gone away from them into heaven, the shepherds said one to another, Let us now go even unto Bethlehem, and see this thing which is come to pass, which the Lord hath made known unto us.

And they came with haste, and found Mary, and Joseph, and the babe lying in a manger.

And when they had seen it, they made known abroad the saying which was told them concerning this child.

And all they that heard it wondered at those things which were told them by the shepherds.

But Mary kept all these things, and pondered them in her heart.

And the shepherds returned, glorifying and praising God for all the things that they had heard and seen, as it was told unto them.

Now when Jesus was born in Bethlehem of Judaea in the days of Herod the king, behold, there came wise men from the east to Jerusalem, saying, Where is he that is born King of the Jews? for we have seen his star in the east, and are come to worship him.

When Herod the king had heard these things, he was troubled, and all Jerusalem with him.

And when he had gathered all the chief priests and scribes of the people together, he demanded of them where Christ should be born.

And they said unto him, In Bethlehem of Judaea: for thus it is written by the prophet,

And thou Bethlehem, in the land of Juda, art not the least among the princes of Juda: for out of thee shall come a Governor, that shall rule my people Israel.

Then Herod, when he had privily called the wise men, enquired of them diligently what time the star appeared.

And he sent them to Bethlehem, and said, Go and search diligently for the young child; and when ye have found him, bring me word again, that I may come and worship him also.

When they had heard the king, they departed; and, lo, the star, which they saw in the east, went before them, till it came and stood over where the young child was.

When they saw the star, they rejoiced with exceeding great joy.

And when they were come into the house, they saw the young child with Mary his mother, and fell down, and worshipped him: and when they had opened their treasures, they presented unto him gifts; gold, and frankincense, and myrrh.

And being warned of God in a dream that they should not return to Herod, they departed into their own country another way.

Index

329

The Authors

FRANCES CAVANAH is best known for her books for young people in the fields of history and biography. A native Hoosier, she was graduated from DePauw University and then joined the staff of the old *Child Life*. One of her duties as associate editor was to read thousands of letters that poured in from youthful subscribers, and the insight she gained into their thinking proved invaluable. Later, she was biography editor of a young people's encyclopedia, and then director of "Real People," a series of biographies widely used in schools. She has combined her talents as an editor and as a writer in several anthologies. Miss Cavanah is the author of WE CAME TO AMERICA, THE BUSTERS, and (in collaboration with Elizabeth L. Crandall) MEET THE PRESIDENTS. Several of her titles have been made into talking books, and also have been transcribed into Braille and translated into other languages. Miss Cavanah, compiler and editor of this new edition of HOLIDAY ROUNDUP, lives in Washington, D. C. Lucile Pannell, collaborator in the first edition, has been a participant in the literature group of the American Association for University Women, a member of the children's book committee of the American Brotherhood of the National Conference of Christians and Jews, and a former bookseller, specializing in children's books. Because of her contribution in this field she was the recipient of the annual award of the Women's National Book Association.